PUBLIC SECTOR BANKS IN INDIA

PUBLIC SECTOR BANKS IN INDIA

Impact of Financial Sector Reforms

R.K. Raul
Jaynal Uddin Ahmed

KALPAZ

Published by

Kalpaz Publications
C-30, Satyawati Nagar,
Delhi – 110052
Ph.: 011-47034999, 9811692060
www.kalpazpublications.com
E-mail: kalpaz@hotmail.com

Distribution Network
gyanbooks.com
India, USA, Canada, UK, Australia, France

ISBN: 978-93-5722-354-6 (PB)

First Published, 2024

Printed at: Gyan Press, Delhi.

Public Sector Banks in India: Impact of Financial Sectors Reforms
Author: R. K. Raul, Jayanal Uddin Ahmed

Dedicated to
our Parents

Contents

Preface

Rapid reforms in the various segments of Indian economy are under way. The need for reforms in the financial sector was already felt and some corrective measures were undertaken before the Narasimham Committee I and II. The recommendations of Sukhamoy Chakrovorty Committee (1985) was a landmark in the sense that it stressed the need for acheiving greater competitiveness among the banks and creating an environment where they should attain greater operational freedom. Since then, several measures have been initiated to tune up the functioning and performance of financial sector but most of these measures have only addressed to the short-term perspective.

The term financial sector reform is used interchangeably with the term financial liberalisation and financial deregulation. Financial liberalization is the process of removal/reduction of financial market distortions, mainly created by government or central banks interventions. It is one of the important issues of recently pursued New Economic Policy (NEP) in India. Generally, it encompasses softening of allocation procedures, hardening of prudential regulation, catering higher quantum of credit to the industries and providing an opportunity to restructure the financial system with a view to attain competitiveness aligning with international standard.

In the new economic policy, banking and financial sector reforms assume high degree of priority in the context of globalization of economy that requires adhering to universally applicable standards and yardstick. The Indian banking industry is no longer an isolated entity. In the dynamic and highly competitive global banking environment the banks are facing several challenges, due to competition, disintermediation as well as customers' demand. They require to reduce operating costs along with designing innovative strategies to attract and retain customers as well as to react quickly to the ever-changing market forces.

The process of financial sector reform has been initiated in 1992 following the report of Narasimham Committee. The distinctive feature of recommendations of the committee is that it has re-drawn the broad contours of financial sector with a focus on how it should be organised and governed. It has emphasised the urgency of financial sectors' adherence to the internationally acceptable conventions, practices, and procedures to equip them with enough power to face the impeding competition. The components of reform involved, dismantling certain diverted credit programme, lowering cash and liquidity requirements, improving payment system, adopting international standard for capital adequacy, prudential norms, improving legal, regulating and supervisory infrastructure and reducing barriers for the new entrants in the banking sector.

The Narasimham Committee on Banking Sector Reforms (1998) recognised the need for credit risk modelling. Credit risk model offers a framework for examining risks in a timely manner and identifying the risks in the individual portfolio composition. This model-based approach would bring capital requirements into alignment with the perceived risks of underlying assets. In general, the financial liberalisation represents an insightful change in the economic rules. Against such a backdrop, the present work is an attempt to examine the impact of financial sector Reform on the working of banking sector in general and public sector banks in particular. The study covers an empirical analysis of different aspects of bank's performance in the Barak Valley, southern part of Assam in the context of national level performances of PSBs in particular during two distinct time period, pre-(1981-91) and post-(1992-2001) reform regime

The study has covered important aspects of the working of public sector banks in the context of financial sector reforms and organised in **ten chapters**. After having analyses, the need of financial sector reform in Indian context, the chapter one : **introductory**, sets forth the parameters of the study in both theoretical and problematic framework. It also highlights on the objectives and hypotheses framed, methodology adopted for collection of data and techniques used for analysis. Conceived with the framework of the study, the second chapter, **Financial Sector Reform: Need and Implications,** is devoted to examine the details of different facets of financial sector reform with special emphasis on banking sector reform. It covers the committee recommendations and their subsequent implementation. Taking the queue from the earlier chapters the third chapter, **Growth and Development of Public Sector Banks : An**

Assessment, analyses the growth and development of PSBs in the national level under the broad heads : (i) Banking scenario during post nationlisation era, (ii) performance of banks in the changing economic scenario, (iii) Comparative performances appraisal of different banks at the national level. Chapter four, **Performance of Public Sector Banks :an empirical study (Deposits, Advances and C-D Ratios),** presents an analysis of the growth and development of public sector banks in the area under study on the basis of the selected parameters viz. deposits, advances and C-D ratio. Further a comparison of growth rate has been made in two periods – pre and post reform regime. The fifth chapter, **Profitability in Public Sector Banks : An Appraisal,** deals with the nature and trend of profitability of PSBs operating in the study area in the context of their performance at national level on the basis of analysis of some standard ratios. The chapter six, **Productivity in Public Sector Banks – An Analysis,** has incorporated the productivity and efficiency analysis of Public Sector Banks with widely used indicators like labour productivity, branch productivity, cost responsiveness and return on working fund. The causes of low productivity also have been compared in two different time period as well as at national and districts level. **Non-Performing Assets : Nature and Trend – A Critical Assessment,** the contents of the chapter seven attempts to assess position of the bad loans of banks and delineates the measures adopted to contain them at the national level vis-à-vis districts level. The eighth chapter, **Asset Liability Management of Public Sector Banks : An Overview,** covers the issues relating to the asset liability management of banks with the special reference to public sector banks in the national level. The chapter nine, **Customer Services of Public Sector Banks : An Empirical Investigation,** presents an empirical study on the basis of responses in respect of suitability of bank services rendered. It has covered the analysis of the determinants as well as the level of customer's satisfaction on the basis of structured variables. It also highlighted the marketing strategies for increasing the level of customer's satisfaction. The concluding Chapter ten, **Epilogue,** gives a brief summary of main findings and some workable suggestions for further improvement of workings of the Public Sector Banks.

We have covered in this treatise all facets of ongoing banking sector reform process along with their impact on the workings of Public sector banks in the country as a whole. We earnestly hope this publication would be highly useful for students, pursuing studies in the financial sector, research scholars, policy makers, management experts and wide range of readers from various categories.

The authors are indebted to all those who extended generous help in providing relevant points gathered from all possible sources. The original sources have been indicated then and there, besides due acknowledgement. We are grateful for the comments, suggestions and assistance given by the bank professionals from time to time. It would be impossible to list them all. However, we wish to express thanks to Mr Amit Garg, Director, Publications, Gyan Books Pvt. Ltd and members of the Kalpaz Publications for the wholehearted support and cooperation to publish this book in short time and elegant manner.

Despite our best efforts of all involved, users might identify some errors in this book. We accept responsibility for these errors and welcome constructive comments from readers who have occasion to use this book.

January 23, 2005

Dr R. K. Raul
Dr Jaynal Uddin Ahmed

1

Introductory

Introduction

The financial sector plays a crucial role in mobilizing community's savings and channeling them into effective investment avenues in the country. Free flow of savings into the economic sectors generally paved the way to sustain economic growth of the country. The Government intervention in this sector is harmful for resource mobilisation and resource allocation as low interest rates discourage savings and distort the choice of investment avenues (McKinnon and Shaw, 1973)[1]. The liberalisation measures therefore, would eliminate these distortions and accelerate the pace of economic growth of the country. The economy generally gains momentum in its structural aspects from a vibrant and competitive financial system. The Indian financial system in that respect attained commendable height in promoting financial inter-mediation, particularly, in:

- accelerating the pace of growth of financial savings,
- extending credit support to vital sector; agriculture, industry of the economy and providing liquidity and payment services to the real sector of the economy,
- catering credit requirement to all sections of the economy: household, industry, weaker section of the society and so on.

Financial sector comprising financial institutions, instruments and markets acts as a conduit of transferring financial resources from savers to borrowers in the economy. Financial institutions play twin role as depository of community savings in one hand and as credit purveyor on the other. Besides, it renders various financial services to the societies like receiving deposits, granting loans and securities and so on.

Financial markets on the other hand, are the arrangements for facilitating buying and selling of financial claims and services. The corporations, financial institutions, individuals and Government involved in the trading of financial products in these markets either directly or through the middlemen/ brokers and dealers in the organised exchanges or off-exchanges (Bhole, 1999)[2].

Financial institutions (FIs) may be in form of either banking or non-banking institutions. The banking institutions have quite a few things in common with the non-banking ones. In the payment system the FIs have distinguishing characteristics unlike other institutions who participate in the payment mechanism besides the banks render transaction services related to both lending and receiving of deposits.

The deposits constitute a major part of the national money supply and they as a whole create credits. Banks, subject to legal reserve requirements, can advance credit by creating claims against themselves, while other institutions can lend only out of resources and put at their disposal by the savers. Sayers (1964)[3] has aptly has distinguished the former as 'creators' of credit while the latter is mere as 'purveyor' of credit.

Financial institutions undertake all intermediary activities in the economy. Lending money to all economic sectors through proper mobilisation of community savings constitutes major part of their activities. They remained liable to the ultimate individuals who actually save and expedite the process of forming assets in society. Non-intermediary institutions entail in the loan business but their resources are not directly acquired from the savers. All banking institutions, private or public sectors, however, undertake intermediary activities in the macro-economy of the country.

Financial markets are generally classified in two broader categories as primary (direct) and secondary (indirect) markets. The primary market deals in new financial claims or new securities and therefore they are also known as new issue markets. The secondary markets, on the other hand, constitute dealings of securities already issued, existing, or outstanding. Further, the financial markets are also classified as money markets and capital markets, although there is not much wide difference between the two as both perform the same function of transferring resources to the producers. The distinctive difference lies in form of the period of maturity of financial assets issued in these markets. The money markets deal in the short-term claims (with a period of maturity of one year or less) while capital markets do so in the long-term claims (with maturity period above one year).

Financial system deals in financial services and claims, financial assets, securities or financial instruments. These services and claims are many and in varied character. This is so because of the variety of motives behind borrowing and lending. The stages of development of the financial system can be judged from the viewpoint of multiplicity of financial instruments. The structure of financial system can be diagrammatically presented as under:

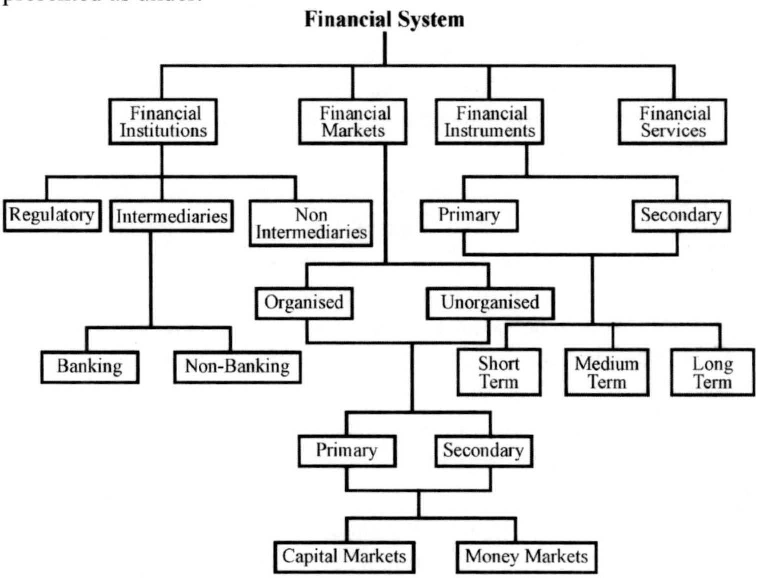

Fig. 1. The Structure of Financial System.

Globalisations, deregulation and dis-intermediation of economy ushered in new markets, new competitors, improved technologies and new products. The barriers of place and time are being removed on the one hand and strict prudential norms are introduced on the other. As a result, reforms in the financial sector have brought about a number of far reaching changes in the operational area of banking in respect of both approach and procedure that has attained satisfactory dimensions vis-à-vis global standards.

However, reform measures initiated on the basis of the recommendations of the committee on the financial system (1991, 1998; Narasimham Committee) placed the Indian banking sector on a new platform with a positive attitude. These were essential for arresting qualitative deterioration in the functioning of the banking system and making them economically viable and attaining competitive edge.

In the financial system, banking sector occupies unique position. It has played a vital role as growth facilitators and achieved commendable heights in the national economy. The banking sector has shown remarkable responsiveness to the needs of a planned economy. It has brought about a considerable progress in its efforts at deposits mobilisation and has taken a number of measures in the recent past for accelerating the pace of growth of deposits. A recourse to this, the commercial banks have opened up number of branches in urban, semi-urban and rural areas and have introduced various attractive schemes and free services for the customer to attract more deposits. It accounts about two-third of assets of formal financial sector.

Of late, by 1991, this sector has been characterised as inefficient sector in respect of profitability and average return on assets. Moreover, in the international scene, they have witnessed comparatively low *capitalisation, low ratio of capital and reserve to total assets*, poor quality of services, gradual decline in the ratio *of spread to total assets*, inadequate capital base to cover credit risk, unhealthy bottom lines, lack of transparency in balance sheet/profit and loss statements and so on. The actual picture of financial health was even worse as the indicators are based on accounting concept of profit constructed by an alternative set of accounting rule, GAAP and Accounting Standards which are not based on "income recognition and provisioning criteria". Therefore, this sector needs to be strengthened and consequently financial sector reform in India has emphasised much on reforms of the banking sector. The banks are, therefore, required to re-address their role under the market driven economy. In this respect, organizational restructuring along with need based modification of strategies for widening the pace of financial markets, accessing to modern technology, rendering customer services with innovative financial products and scheme supplement with suitable credit delivery mechanism etc are required. The financial statements are required to be more transparent particularly in respect of capital adequacy and provisioning norms as per the global standards. The private and foreign banks have taken the lead in the process in a flux with mergers, acquisition and consolidation. The onus, therefore, lies with the public sector banks (PSBs, hereafter).

Literature on Banking Operation

There exists a wide body of literature dealing with different aspects of working of public sector commercial banks and banking sector reforms. A brief review of these literature and committee's recommendations on banking sector has been made from the viewpoint of both bankers and borrowers in the following paragraphs.

Rosen (1962)[4] studied paucity of investment funds for industrial sector and concluded banks and financial institutions should be evolved to meet the financial requirements of the industry. Joshi (1965)[5] examined involvement of financial intermediaries in providing finance to large-scale industries in the private sectors. He observed that these intermediaries contributed about 17 per cent of investment of various industries and it constituted about 39 per cent of total investment of public limited companies. Jain (1971)[6] observed that financial agencies have developed a preference of investing funds in the medium and large-scale industrial units.

Varde and Singh (1981)[7], Godse and Padwal (1987)[8] studied the issues of banks' profitability and developed a simple framework to analyse the factors influencing the profitability of commercial banks. They viewed that any emphasis on the increase of the volume of business and proper management of burden would definitely result in enhancing the profitability of banks. They concluded that the key factor to the profitability of commercial banks in India is high volume of business not the control of expenses, which were popularly practised.

Sarkar (1978)[9] in his paper analysed the profits of public sector banks over a time frame and concluded that banks require more maneuverability in their operations so as to achieve the dual objective of profit and the growth.

Shah (1979)[10] examined the weaknesses of banks and suggested the remedial measures for enhancing the profitability of banks. Any such measures should address to (i) locate profit centres and cost centres in the banks (ii) identify the elements that control or determine the income and cost structure at each such centre and bank as a whole (iii) evolve measures that could widen the spread between the cost of funds; services and administration, and return on them and (iv) develop supplementary sources of income on profit.

Angadi (1983)[11] measured the efficiency in terms of responsiveness of operating cost by using important yardsticks like operating cost responsiveness, administered prices/ interest rates to the total business of banks.

Joshi (1986)[12] in his study identified banks' weakness in the fund management due to compulsory provision of SLR, CRR and priority sector lending. The study observed that the low yield rate and rising cost contributed a lot to the declining trend in profitability of banks.

Singh (1987)[13] identified many exogenous and endogenous factors causing strains and stresses in the banking system. The majority of them constitute continuous increase in the SLR, CRR by the RBI, banks' compulsion on achieving social goals, growing incidence of industrial sickness, rapid branch expansion in the under banked areas, unfavourable change of deposit mix and growing incidence of financial disintermediation.

Rangarajan (1991)[14] pointed out that improving the quality of loan assets is the true test of improving the efficiency of banking system.

Malhotra (1991)[15] examined the nature and efficacy of banking instruments and suggested the banks should diversify their product and develop instruments so as to meet the aspirations of borrowers and investors in the context of the emergence of various savings schemes of other financial institutions, post office etc.

Goiporia (1992)[16] made a general review of the profitability of banks and maintained that for adequate profit flow, the following priorities will have to be observed by the banks (a) lending operations have to be directed to areas which would maximize profitability and growth (b) non-fund based operation should be promoted and (c) charging fees for bank services should be determined after taking into consideration the cost and benefit of services offered.

Hartough (1994)[17] studied the implications of bankers action plan for profitable small business portfolio. He suggested that considering customer's payment history and market condition etc, bank should make advance to most attractive and growth potential units.

Ramala and Nagi (1994)[18] suggested proper end-use of loans supplied to the entrepreneurs that could only ensure economic development of the area and the country as a whole.

Sengupta (1995)[19] in his paper examined the impact of financial sector and economic reforms in India in the context of financial market imperfection. The study pointed out that the banks would have to move step-by-step decision to reach the goal through trial and error in the practical world.

Goldstein (1996)[20] in his study on capital norms of banking sector argued that developing countries, with few exceptions, have not set national capital standard much above the Basle minimum norms and their banks do not hold actual capital much above than the banks operating in the countries with stable environment.

Kohli (1997)[21] examined the priority sector lending. He observed the existence of significant linkages between bank credit and investment in both agriculture and industries in India. He suggested that although directed credit programme for priority sector lending is effective in India, however, positive support to small-scale units is required.

Ajit (1997)[22] examined the issue of para banking activities and suggested that banks should be allowed to undertake these activities, and use capital on the basis of experiences of other countries like USA.

Kaladhar (1997)[23] in his paper examined the micro finance and its governance and suggested separate institutions like NABARD, SIDBI to govern micro finance.

Satish and Gopalakrishna (1997)[24] suggested that systematic manner of bank operation will ensure the viability of rural banking.

Khanna (1999)[25] in his paper examined the impact of the financial reforms in the industrial sector in India and found that financial sector reform have achieved a little in its goal of making the industrial sector more efficient and globally competitive.

Patibandla and Prusty (1998)[26] analysed the financial system in the context of East Asian Crisis and suggested the need of right and effective financial institutions.

EPW Research Foundation Group examined the dynamic credit policy (1999)[27] and suggested that against the prevailing backdrop of output, price and monetary trends, the credit policy has to be decisively explanatory.

Criticizing the banking sector reform Joshi (1999)[28] in his paper viewed that banking sector reforms has been over emphasised on profits neglecting the distributive role of banks. The companies with high net worth within the organised sector are capable of raising funds at a considerable lower rate of interest while credit disbursement to small borrowers has sharply been declined over the years.

Hugar (1998)[29] analysing first phase of reforms found that with the introduction of reform packages, banks have improved their profitability, started cleaning their balance sheet, improved the NPA position, but they are yet to give more focus on rationalising cost structure.

Verma (1998)[30] viewed in the context of ongoing globalization process that Indian commercial banks are getting their shape well and becoming technologically better equipped and stronger in the capital base.

To ensure the code of best practices Gadkari (2000)[31] proposed corporate governance in the public sector banks to achieve high standard of corporate behaviour. He also suggested that the board of directors, external auditors and supervisors of PSBs strive to achieve greater degree of openness, transparency, integrity and accountability in the working of the banks.

The non-official advisory group on corporate governance (2001)[32] of RBI highlighted the importance of corporate governance for building investors confidence. In this respect, Upadhyaya (2001)[33] suggested to implement the recommendations of this group on corporate governance keeping all stakeholders' interest as the centrepiece of reform.

Roy (2001)[34] articulated that customer loyalty management programme should be an important part of the relationship marketing exercise undertaken at the bank branches.

Rao (2002)[35] observed that customer service is a dynamic, creative and interactive process where the banker and customer are actively involved in improving the process continuously. The study concluded that the bankers should aware of keeping themselves at least one step ahead of the customers.

Srivastava (2000)[36] stressed on accelerating the pace of the process of computerisation of bank branches to enhance the profitability, operating efficiency, service quality, and to diversify the earning base.

Taori (2000)[37] dealt with the NPA management in PSBs and stated that surest way of containing NPAs is to prevent their occurrences. He suggested proper risk management; strong and effective credit monitoring, co-operative working relationship between banks and borrowers etc should be the tenets of NPA management policy. Bhattacharya (2002)[38] echoed also similar opinion.

Ramaiah and Ghosh (2002)[39] hold that directed credit requirements, structure of banking industry and banks' attitude towards the risk are main caveats of banks' spread.

Banmali (2001)[40] suggested a dispassionate and unprejudiced approach to weed out NPAs. A broad based and multi-pronged attack to the problem is necessary involving all staff members right from the grass root level to the controlling points.

Das (2002)[41] analysed the level of risk and productivity of public sector banks and observed interrelationship of the fact that the productivity, capital base and risk taking attitude to be jointly determined and reinforced.

Shenoy (2001)[42] dealt issues relating to the Indian banking and has stressed on proper asset liability management and credit monitoring system.

The banking sector in India poised to meet the changing global environment observed by Kamesam (2001)[43]. In this context, he viewed the future of banks will largely depend on excellent customer service by keeping pace with changing technology and transparent operations.

In an increasingly integrated global economy, Singh and Das (2002)[44] studied the implications reforms measures in the banking sector. They found fragile banking system disrupts macro economic stability and suggested human resource development, technology, industrial relations and customer services are the main pillars of attaining banks' efficiency.

Ravi (2002)[45] emphasised on branch rationalisation policy of banks for bringing down loss making branches. He also suggested continuous emphasis should be given on reducing deposit costs and burden, manpower re-deployment of loss making branches.

Bhukta (2002)[46] articulated that the banking reform is against the long run objective of reducing fiscal deficit of the government. In this situation he argued that the reform should not be halted rather proceeded following trial and error method.

Naidu and Nair (2002)[47] attempted empirically the technical efficiency of scheduled commercial banks and found that the technical efficiency level among bank groups has declined during the post reform era which has indicated a severe competition among the bank groups.

However, not much work on banks' performance in the study area has so far been undertaken. Choudhury (1984)[48] dealt with the reasons and consequences of growth of commercial banks in the undivided Cachar district in the post nationalization phase. The study sheds little light on bank's performance. Another noteworthy study, Raul (1997)[49] examined nature and problems of financing of industries and assessed the efficacy of various financing schemes adopted by the banks specially to cater to the financial requirements of industries pertaining to the districts of erstwhile Cachar and Karimganj district of Barak valley. Thus, the impact of the significant changes owing to the onset of economic liberalization programme, occurred in banking practices in the country as a whole have remained un-researched in the area under study.

Committee Recommendations

The Dahejia Committee (1969)[50] examined the credit needs of industry and trade and observed that there was a tendency on the part of the industry to avail itself of short term credit from banks in excess of the amount based on growth in production for inventories in value terms. It recommended that the banking system should turn to the financing of industry on the basis of a total study of the borrower's operations than on security consideration alone. Further, cash credit account should be distinguished from 'hard core' and in short-term component. The study group suggested that hard-core part of the working capital in case of companies with strong financial position should be segregated and put on a formal term loan basis subject to a repayment schedule.

Despite these, the enigma of expansion in bank credit incommensurate with the level of the production and inventory continued to persist. As a result, RBI appointed a study group, widely known as Tandon Committee (1975)[51] under the chairmanship of P.L. Tandon in August 1975. It framed guidelines for rational allocation, optimum use and for proper follow up of bank credit. The study group identified the drawback of easy availability of bank finance, i.e., borrowers were able to borrow more than his current assets requirements. The committee suggested Maximum Permissible Bank Finance (MPBF) with reference to the working capital requirements and bank should have Quarterly Information System (QIS). The group also recommended norms for inventory and receivables, which represents level for holding inventory and receivables in each industry, level of the borrower's resources to enable the banker to carry on acceptable level of current assets, and the style of bank credit.

Reserve Bank of India (1967)[52] made a directional intervention in the sectoral credit flow advising commercial banks for channelizing 80 per cent of the seasonal credit expansion to the industrial sector including manufacturing industry, mining, plantation etc.

Chore Committee (1979) reviewed the working of the operation of cash credit system and suggested that bank should appraise and fix separate limit for 'normal non-peak level' as also for the 'peak level' credit requirements indicating also the period during which the separate limits would be utilised by the borrowers.

Reserve Bank of India in consultation with Indian Bank Association (IBA) constituted a committee on penal rates and service charges in 1979. The committee recommended that the penal rate, which is a justifiable part of the banks' interest, rate policy, should not be regarded as revenue raising measure but as an instrument to enforce discipline among the borrowers. As far as service charges are concerned, the committee suggested there could be no objection to bank recovery with a legal charge.

Committee on operational efficiency and profitability known as ***Productivity, Efficiency and Profitability Committee*** (PEP Committee, 1977)[53] identified practical and realistic criteria for the evaluation of bank's performance. The committee proposed a system of assessment on the four broad aspects viz, (i) productivity (ii) social objectives (Spatial) (iii) social objectives (sectoral) and (iv) profitability. The indicators of efficiency and profitability suggested by PEP committee that include ratios like, *business per employee, proportion of rural and semi-urban branches, deposits to total assets, ratio of agricultural advances to total advances and ratio of net income to establishment expenses.*

In the context of global level for greater transparency of financial intermediaries, A. Ghosh Committee (1982) was set up to prescribe the bank balance sheet format. The committee revised and enlarged the format of presentation of balance sheet and profit and loss account and suggested guidelines for compiling final accounts.

Marathe Committee (1982)[54] reviewed the credit authorisation scheme (CAS) and recommended that the banks would be allowed to deploy credit under CAS provided that projected current ratio should not low and the borrowers maintain quarterly operating statements and submit annual accounts to the banks.

Vaghul Committee (1986)[55] allowed banks issuing commercial paper to the 'A' rated companies having a net worth of Rs. 5 crore that has a considerable impact on banks working capital financing requirements.

Chakraborty Committee (1986)[56] studied the operational efficiency of commercial banks and suggested that RBI would determine spread between bank rate and bank deposit rate, goverment borrowing rate and the prime-lending rate.

Talwar Committee (1975)[57] examined the nature of the customer services rendered by the banks. The committee viewed customer service as dynamic concept and recommended that the bank should assess and reassess on a continuous basis the customers' perception about bank services and formulate strategies to appraise and improve the customer services.

Goiporia Committee (1991)[58] recommended amicable banker-customer relationship. Tiwari Committee had recommended setting up a special tribunal for recovering outstanding credit.

Narasimham Committee (1991)[59] identified weakness of banking sector and recommended provision for capital adequacy; liberalisation of interest rate; reduction in SLR, rehabilitation of PSBs by the government; introduction of prudential norms relating to income recognition, asset classification and provisioning and easy norms for entry of foreign banks. The committee also suggested for directed credit programme to ensure the credit requirement of the priority sector.

To improve further soundness of Indian banking system Narasimham Committee (1998)[60] submitted its report in April 1998. In compliance with the committee recommendations, RBI announced a package of measures in October 1998. The report emphasised on:

- Increase in the minimum capital adequacy ratio from 8 per cent to 9 per cent by March 31, 2000;
- Recognition of the market risks and prescribing the degree of risk weight for government approved securities by March 31, 2000;
- Making a provision of 100 per cent risk weight for foreign exchange and gold open limits from the year ended March 31, 1999;

- Implementation of tighter asset classification; income recognition and provisioning norms;
- Introduction of formal Asset Liability Management system with effect from April 1, 1999; and
- Transparency in accounting and disclosure practices in the line of international standard.

To evolve an efficient and competitive financial system, RBI constituted a working group under the chairmanship of S. H. Khan (1997)[61]. The Khan working group recommended a general provision on standard assets of a minimum of 0.25 per cent from the year ending March 31, 2000. Besides, it recommended the setting up an Asset Liability Management (ALM) system along with internal ALM at the top management level to oversee its implementation.

In 1998, the apex bank constituted Debt Recovery Tribunals (DRTs) working group to review the functioning of DRTs. The working group recommended certain legislative measures regarding the recovery of debts due to the banks and financial institutions and also suggested measures to improve the functioning of DRTs.

Basle Committee (1997)[63] on banking supervision released a set of 25 principles for effective banking practices. The growing apprehension of attaining of international competitiveness and capital adequacy ratio led to the formation of Basle Accord (1998)[64] which would help to arrest the erosion of banks capital ratios in the changed environment. In the light of the comments from various corners, the committee revised the capital adequacy framework by March 2000. The current Accord is based on (i) minimum capital requirement (ii) supervisory review process (iii) effective use of market discipline.

Verma Committee (1999)[65] identified three banks, viz. Indian Banks, United Commercial Banks and United Bank of India, as weak on the basis of :

(i) Extent of accumulated losses and volume of non-performing assets (NPAs)

(ii) Status of operating profit less income from recapitalisation for three consecutive years.

The committee viewed that in the long run privatization is good option for restructuring weak banks. It recommended the measures to clean the balance sheet saddled with large NPAs by creating Asset Reconstruction Fund (ARF), and suggested to introduce Voluntary Retirement Fund (VRF) enabling banks to reduce excess manpower as well as to establish Financial Restructuring Authority.

The standing committee on international financial standard and codes (1999)[66] urged RBI a nation wide debate while establishing mechanisms for continuous updating and reviewing structural aspects.

The committee while reveiwing the system of administered interest rates (2001)[67] observed that most of the small saving funds are to be managed with larger and diversified investment portfolios.

Theoretical Underpinning of the Study

Statement of the Problem

Indian banking has undergone momentous changes and radical transformation in its structure and operation in respect of priority sector lending; advances to weaker section, and implementation of various government-sponsored schemes. Further, Banks' initiative in reviving the sick industries through a number of rehabilitation packages, inclusion of factoring and venture capital activities in the banking network (Banking Regulation Act amendment, July 1990), providing cash clearing and settlement services to stock exchanges (Ahmedabad, Calcutta stock exchange, NSE and OTCEI) and so on became the new area of operations in the competitive environment.

The banks since nationalization have diverted their attention from "class banking" to "mass banking" (Pandey, 1997)[68] with little emphasis on profit element. But many problems cropped up such as inter-region inequality in bank's operations, non-recovery of loans, willful default, political interference, deterioration of customer services, redtapism, neglect in the supervision of end use of credit, declining efficiency and profitability.

The macro economic crisis in 1991 paved the way of extensive financial sector reform. (Bhagawati and Srinivasan, 1999)[69]. Despite, impressive widening of the banking system, there was a general consensus that it had not actually become sound and vibrant, as it needed to be. As a result, 90's experienced a volatile banking business (Patel, 1997)[70]. There was serious concern about the poor performance of public sector banks (PSBs), most of them became unprofitable, undercapitalized and burdened with unsustainable level of non-performing assets (NPA) in their books.

In view of the extreme volatility and as a part of the financial sector reforms, Government of India appointed Narasimham committee to address the problems and suggest remedial measures. Following the recommendations of the committee (1991)[71] important initiatives with regard to the reforms in banking system viz, introduction of new accounting and prudential norms relating to income recognition, provisioning and capital adequacy, reduction in Statutory Liquidity Ratio (SLR), a cut in Cash Reserve Ratio (CRR) and its subsequent withdrawal on the Foreign Currency Non-Resident Account (Bank) [FCNR (B)] to improve the liquidity position of financial sector, liberalization of interest rates and easy norms for entry of foreign banks, have already been undertaken to face global competition in conformity with '**Washington Consensus**'. The financial sector reforms policy by Narasimham Committee aims to make Indian financial sector more efficient as well put an end to the so called "*financial repression*" that had held back the growth of financial savings and their efficient channelisation in the industrial activity (Khanna, 1999)[72]. The financial sector reform currently underwent in India must also be seen as a component on the overall scheme of structural reforms. Apart from this, reforms are called for making the sector capable of serving the emerging needs of the growing real sector (Dhanasekran; 2002)[73].

India's experience with financial sector reforms perhaps far from happy. Some of the practices of banking sector were archaic. Many PSB had large NPA. During the first phase of the reforms (1991-93), the surge of the higher profits encouraged by many PSB to divert their funds to the booming stock market which further added to the losses of these banks. More over, bank loan as a proportion of total domestic financing to the commercial sector declined from 60 per cent of total finance in 1988-89 to 37 per cent in 1993-94 (IMF : 1995)[74]. The rate of deposit mobilization has reduced. The compulsory capture of bank deposit by the government through CRR and SLR has been reduced. The accumulation of NPAs continues to serious strain on the profitability of banks. The Second Narasimham Committee, in view of the poor performance of financial sector (banking sector in particular) recommended a package of measures in October, 1998 such as increase of minimum capital adequacy ratio, recognition of market risks, tighter assets classification, income recognition and provisioning norms, introduction of formal Asset Liability Management system and for further enhancing transparency in accounting and disclosure practices etc. The aggregate deposit of commercial banks increased from Rs. 884 crores in 1950-51 to Rs. 5025 crores in 1969-70 and further to 60,5410 crores in March 1998, then to Rs. 13,21,185 crores on April 2003. This accelerated rate of mobilisation of savings by banks has met the growing needs of economic sectors of the country. The deposits of scheduled commercial banks as a percentage to national income increased from 9.3 per cent in 1950-51 to 15.5 per cent in 1969 and further to 22.4 per cent in 1975 and 49.7 per cent in March 1999.

However, the operating profits of PSB declined by 3.0 per cent from Rs. 10274 crores in 1997-98 to Rs. 10578 crores in 1998-99, the net profit of commercial banks declined sharply by 28.3 per cent from Rs. 6502 crores in 1997-98 to Rs. 4660 crores in 1998-99. The ratio of net profit to total assets declined from 0.8 per cent in 1997-98 to 0.4 per cent in 1998-99. The gross NPA as per cent of total advances increased from 14.4 per cent in 1997-98 to 14.6 per cent in 1998-99. The capital adequacy ratio of PSBs has declined marginally from 11.5 per cent in 1997-98 to 11.2 per cent in 1998-99. The spread (i.e., net interest income minus interest expanded) increased from 2.78 per cent in 1997-98 to 2.79 per cent in 1998-99. The quantum of net NPA as a percentage of net advances increased from 7.3 per cent in 1997-98 to 7.5 per cent in 1998-99.

As a result, reform packages have resulted in increasing the cost of banks in one hand and less availability of credit to private sector on the other. Thus banking sectors have therefore landed in a peculiar situation due to reform packages. Apart from these, the role of banking sector against the backdrop of East Asian currency crisis (Joshi, 1999)[75] cannot be overlooked (Patibandla and Prusty, 1998)[76]. A number of measures have already been taken following this crisis in November, 1997 and January 1998 include, CRR cuts in monetary and credit policy, deregulation of interest rate, surcharge on bank credit for imports, minimum interest rate charge, raising of bank rate, liquidity support to primary dealer (RBI Bulletin, June 1999)[77].

It is evident, from the above discussion that bank came under severe pressure to improve their bottom line and also faced global competition with a view to attain competitiveness through judicious blending with their efficiency and profitability. A study in respect of impact of financial sector reform on PSBs is, therefore likely to be extremely relevant and interesting particularly in a backward area.

TABLE – 1
BANKING INFRASTRUCTURE IN BARAK VALLEY AS ON 31–12–2000

	Types of banks	*No. of Branches*			
		Cachar	*Karimganj*	*Hailakandi*	*Total*
1.	Public Sector Banks (PSBs)	50	32	12	94
	(a) State Bank group (SBs)				
	State Bank of India (SBI)	10	6	3	19
	(b) Nationalised Banks (NBs)	40	26	9	75
	(i) United Bank of India	17	16	4	37
	(ii) Allahabad Bank	3	2	Nil	5
	(iii) Punjab National Bank	3	2	1	6
	(iv) Central Bank of India	7	2	1	10
	(v) Indian Bank	1	Nil	Nil	1
	(vi) Union Bank of India	1	1	2	4
	(vii) Punjab & Sind Bank	2	1	Nil	3
	(viii) Bank of Baroda	2	1	Nil	3
	(ix) United Commercial Bank	2	1	1	4
	(x) Canara Bank	1	Nil	Nil	1
	(xi) Vijaya Bank	1	Nil	Nil	Nil
2.	Regional Rural Bank (RRBs)				
	Cachar Gramin Bank (CGBs)	19	17	8	44
3.	Private Sector Banks				
	Federal Bank	1	Nil	Nil	1
	Co-operative Banks	1	3	2	6
	Total	**71**	**52**	**22**	**145**

Source : Lead Bank Office, United Bank of India, Cachar, Karimganj and Hailakandi district

The Study Area

We selected our study area in the Barak Valley, southern part of Assam comprising of three districts (viz., Cachar, Karimganj and Hailakandi) with a population of 30.19 lakhs (Government of Assam 2000). Choudhury (1984) studied the reasons and consequences of growth of commercial banks in the undivided Cachar district during the post nationalization phase. The study sheds little light on bank's performance. Another noteworthy study, Raul (1997) examined nature and problems of financing of industries and assessed the efficacy of various financing schemes adopted by the banks specially to cater to the financial requirements of industries pertaining to the districts of erstwhile Cachar and Karimganj district of Barak valley.

The incidence of poverty as well as unemployment is significantly high. The infrastructure hazards, industrial backwardness and agrarian biased population added the dimensions of economic backwardness of this valley. The districts of the valley are industrially backward and have been declared by the government as "A" category districts.

The table exhibited that there are 94 number of branches of PSBs operating in the valley. The district Cachar is bestowed with 50 branches (10 from SBI and 40 from other nationalised banks) while the district Karimganj got 32 branches (6 from SBI and 26 from nationalised bank) and 12 branches (3 from SBI and 9 from nationalised groups) in the Hailakandi district are catering to the banking requirements. It is also revealed that the branches of PSBs constitute 64.3 per cent of total existing commercial bank branches in the districts under study. However, the valley is economically and industrially backward. The socio-economic backwardness of the valley is discerned by the symptoms like under utilization of resources, agrarian bias of population, low level of industrialisation, fragility of prevailing infrastructure and high incident of unemployment. Thus, development of infrastructure like transport, communication, power, education and banking network etc is urgently needed for overall development of socio-economic life of the people in the districts under study.

However, the impact of banking sector reform on the performance of PSBs has remained largely un-researched so far in this part of the country. It is expected therefore that this study will provide intellectual stimulus for many more studies on various aspects of banking sector reform and also serve as basis for bank executives to frame guidelines for better performance of the banks in other areas similar to this.

References

1. McKinnon R.I. 1973. *Money and Capital in Economic Development, Brooking Institutions.* (Washington D.C.) in Shaw, E.S., 1973. *Financial Deepening in Economics*, Oxford University Press. New York.
2. Bhole, L. M. 1999. *Financial Institutions and Markets : Structure, Growth and Innovations.* Tata McGraw-Hill Publishing Company Ltd. New Delhi. pp 4, 5.

3. Sayers, R. S. 1964. *Modern Banking.* Oxford University Press. Oxford.
4. Rosen, G. 1962. *Some Aspects of Industrial Finance*, Asia Publishing House, Bombay.
5. Joshi, M.S. 1965. *Financial Intermediaries In India*, Makhanlal and Sons Pvt. Ltd. Bombay.
6. Jain, S.C.1971. *Institutional Finance of Small Scale Industries in U.P since 1956 with Particular Reference to Meerut*, Agra University, Agra.
7. Varde, V.S.and Singh, S.P., 1981. *Profitability : The Inter-Banks Comparison*, Prajnan, (April-June) X. (2).
8. Godse, V.T. and Padwal, S.M. 1987. *Profit Planning, Budgeting and Control.* Seminar on Bank Profitability (Ed.) Kangasabathy. K. Bankers Training College. RBI, Bombay.
9. Sarkar, H.C. 1978. *Profitability of Commercial Banks*, Commerce. (August). 137 (3507).
10. Shah, S.G. 1979. *Bank Profitability : The Real Issues.* The Journal of the Indian Institute of Bankers, (July-Sept.).50 (3).
11. Angadi, V.B. 1983. *Measurement of Efficiency in Banking Industry.* RBI Occasional Paper.(June) 4. (1).
12. Joshi, P.N. 1986, *Profitability and Profit Planning in Banks.* The journal of Indian Institute of Bankers (April-June) 57 (2).
13. Singh, S. 1987, *Profitability of Commercial Banks in India.* Punjab National Bank Monthly Review. (October) II (II).
14. Rangarajan, C.1991. *Banking Development Since 1947;Achievement and Challenges. Financial System in India. Vol. II.*
15. Malhotra, R.N. 1991. *Banking in the 90's.* Financial System of India.1:1-4.
16. Goiporia, M.N. 1992. *Bank's Profitability-Some Issues.* Pigmy Economic Review, (April). 37 (9).
17. Ramala, K.S. and Negi, K.S. 1994. *Sickness in Small Scale Industries; Problems and Prospect*, New trends in Indian Industries. Chugh Publications, Allahabad. Vol. 2.

18. Hartough K.J., 1994. *Entrepreneurial Banker; The Bankers' Personal Action Plan For Building a Profitable Small Business Portfolio*, Probus Publishing, Chicago.
19. Sengupta, A., 1995. *Financial Sector and Economic Reforms in India*. Economic and Political Weekly, (January 7). pp. 39, 43.
20. Goldstein, M. 1996. *The Case for an International Banking Standard*. Washington, D.C. Institute for International Economics.
21. Kohli, R. 1997. *Directed Credit and Financial Reforms*. Economic and Political Weekly, (Oct. 18).
22. Ajit, D. 1997. *Para Banking in India, Some Issue*. Economic and Political Weekly, (October 18) XXXII, (42).
23. Kaladhar, K. 1997. *Micro Finance in India : Design, Structure and Governance*. Economic and Political Weekly, (Oct.18). pp. 2687-2705.
24. Satish P. and Gopalakrishna, C. K. 1997. *Viability of Rural Banking*. Economic and Political Weekly, (Oct.,18). pp. 2711-2716.
25. Khanna, S. 1999. *Financial Reforms and Industrial Sector in India*. Economic and Political Weekly, (November 6). p. 3239.
26. Patibandla, M. and Prusty, R. 1998. *East Asian Crisis as a Result of Institutional Failure, Lessons for India*. Economic and Political Weekly, (February 28).
27. EPW Research Foundation, 1999. *High Cost of Funds Forces Industrial Slowdown*. Economic and Political Weekly, (August 10).
28. Joshi, P.N. 1999. *Banking Sector Reforms; The Other Side of Coin*. Economic and Political Weekly, (April 3) : XXXIV (14); 797-798.
29. Hugar, R.S. 1998. *Challenges to the Banking Industry*. The Indian Institute of Bankers, (Oct-Dec). pp. 157, 158.
30. Verma, M.S. 1998. *Commercial Banking in The Next Millennium*. The Journal of the Indian Institute of Bankers, (October-December). pp. 152-155.

31. Gadkari. 2000. *Corporate Governance; An Agenda for Public Sector Banks*. Banking Finance. (January). pp. 18-21.
32. RBI's Standing Committee on International Financial Standards and Codes constituted *Non-Official Advisory Group on Corporate Governance* in March 2001.
33. Upadhyaya, G. 2001. *Corporate Governance in the Financial System.* Banking Finance. (December). pp. 24-25.
34. Roy, D. C. 2001. *Customer Loyalty Management; Branch level Perspective.* Vinimaya, XXI. (2) ; 54-57.
35. Rao, C.S. 2001. *The Dynamic of Customer Service.* IBA Bulletins (March). p. 116.
36. Srivastava, R. 2000. *Computerisation in Indian Banks.* Banking Finance. (February).
37. Taori, K. J. 2000. *Management of NPAs in Public Sector Banks.* Banking Finance, (August). pp. 98-11.
38. Bhattacharya K.M. 2001. *Management of Non Performing Advances in Banks.* Journal of Accounting and Finance, (October 2001- March 2002). pp. 58-69.
39. Ramaiah and Ghosh. 2002. *Understanding the Determinants of Bank Spreads in India. An Empirical Analysis.* Prajnan. (July). XXXI (1); 18.
40. Banmali, O. P. 2001. *Lifeline of Banking; New RBI formula for NPA Recovery.* IBA Bulletin (January) pp. 23-25.
41. Das, A. 2002. *Risk & Productivity change of Public Sector Banks*, Economic & Political Weekly, (February 2). pp. 437-447.
42. Shenoy, B. S. 2001. *Indian Banking Emerging Challenges, Some Key issues.* IBA Bulletins, (March) pp. 59-62.
43. Kamesam, V. 2001. *Developments in the Indian Banking Industry and the Emerging Challenges.* IBA Bulletin, (March). pp. 24-27.
44. Singh, N. T. and Das N. C. 2002. *Reforms in the Banking Sector; An overview.* Banking Finance, (July). pp. 3-4.
45. Ravi, K. 2002. *Rationalising Bank Branches; Some Issues*, IBA Bulletin, (March). pp. 66-72.

46. Bhukta, A. 2002. *Banking Sector Reform in India.* A study ; Yojana, (July) pp. 5-7.

47. Naidu, V. N. and Nair M.S. 2002. *Technical Efficiency of Scheduled Commercial Bank Groups.* Productivity, (July – September) 43 (2) ; 297-298.

48. Choudhury, S. 1984. Growth of Commercial Banking in Cachar and Its Impact of the District with Special Reference to Nationalised Banks. Ph.D. dissertation, Guwahati University.

49. Raul, R.K. 1997. *Industrial Finance in India*, Anmol Publications Pvt. Ltd. New Delhi.

50. Dehejia Committee Report. 1969. *On the Extent to which Credit needs of Industry and trade are likely to be inflated and how such trend could be eluded*, RBI Bombay.

51. The Report of the Study Group to frame the guidelines for follow-up of Bank Credit. Tandon Committee Report (1975), RBI, Bombay.

52. Chore Committee Report (1979), Report of the Working Group of review the system of cash credit, RBI, Bombay.

53. Report of the Committee of Productivity, Efficiency and Profitability of Banks, RBI, Bombay, 1977.

54. Marathe Committee Report (1983), Report of the Committee to review the working of credit authorisation scheme, RBI, Bombay.

55. Vaghul Committee Report (1987), Report of the Working Group on Many Market, RBI, Bombay.

56. Report of Committee to Review the Working of Monetary System (Chairman : Prof. Sukhmay Chakrabortty) RBI, Bombay, 1985.

57. Report of the Talwar Committee (1975).

58. Goiporia Committee (1991). Report on Customer Service, December.

59. Government of India (1991) Report of the Committee on Financial System, Ministry of Finance, (December).

60. Government of India (1998), Report on Banking Sector Reforms (Narasimham Committee – II) Ministry of Finance, (April).

61. Report of Working Group to examine the harmonising the role and Operations of DFIs and Banks (Chairman ; S.H. Khan), RBI, April 1998.

62. Report of the Working Group to review the Functioning of DRTs (Chairman; N.B. Desh Pande). August 1998.

63. Basel Committee on Banking Supervision (1997) ; Risk Disclosure and Related matters, Bank for International Settlements. BIS, Basel.

64. Bank for International Settlements. BIS, Basel. (1999) Basle Accord.

65. RBI. (1999). Report on the Working Group on Restructuring of Weak Public Sector Banks. (Chairman ; M.S. Verma) [Verma Committee].

66. RBI. (1999). Report of the Standing Committee on International Financial Standard and codes (Website ; www.rbi.org.in. (December).

67. RBI : (2001). Expert Committee to Review the System of Administered interest Rates and other related Issues (Chairman: Dr. Y. V. Reddy). September.

68. Pandey, R.K. 1997. *A Study on Priority Sector Financing by Commercial Bank in India*, Ph.D. dissertation, Banaras Hindu University, Varanasi.

69. Bhagawati, J.N. and Srinivasan T.N. 1999. *Indias Economic Reforms*, New Delhi.

70. Patel, U.R., 1997. *Emerging Reforms in India Banking; International Perspectives*. Economic and Political Weekly, (Oct. 18). XXXII (42); 2655-2658.

71. Government of India (1991a). *Report of the Committee on Financial System* (Narasimham Committee), Ministry of Finance.

72. Khanna, S. 1999. *Financial Reforms and Industrial Sector in India*. Economic and Political Weekly, (November 6), pp. 3231.

73. Dhanasekran, K.B. 2002. *Banking Sector Reforms in India: An Assessment*. In Banerjee A. and Singh, S.K. (ed.). Banking and Financial Sector Reform in India, Deep and Deep Publications Pvt. Ltd., p. 97.

74. IMF. 1995. *India : Economic Reforms and Growth.* Occasional Paper, Washington, No. 134.
75. Joshi, P.N. 1999. *Banking Sector Reforms : The Other Side of Coin.* Economic and Political Weekly, (April 3) : XXXIV (14); 797-798.
76. Patibandha, M. and Prusty, R. 1998. *East Asian Crisis as a Result of Institutional Failure, Lessons for India.* Economic and Political Weekly, (February 28). pp. 467-471.
77. Reserve Bank of India, RBI Bulletin, June 1999.

2

Financial Sector Reform : Need and Implications

The Background

The financial world has been witnessing tremendous changes during the last couple of decades, to be specific, since the days of Bretton Woods. Rapid strides have been made in respect to many indicators explaining better dimensions and gaps. Technological change and cut-throat competition have virtually forced the financial world to adopt better techniques to attract customers. For, some leaps have been bigger than the others, and for the others, it was a necessity to survive among thousands.

Till 70s, the product range or the range of services available from the banking industry had been limited. Now, they have a wider range of services like securitization, leasing and hire purchase, custodial service, depositories, factoring etc. Until 1991, there has been over regulations like administered interest rates, government control and lopsided development. Since then, there had been rapid and radical changes consequent upon the implementation of Narasimham committee recommendations. Likewise, liberalisation and globalisation of Indian banks have resulted in providing financial dis-intermediation, emergence of new financial services, greater professionalism, as well as technological innovation. Side by side, with capital adequacy norms, income recognition and assets classification provision were introduced in the ambit of banking activities and banks were compelled to cope up with the process of globalisation, deregulation, competition and assets-liability management at the micro-level.

The Need of Financial Sector Reform

After gaining independence in 1947, India followed the Soviet model of planned economic development with emphasis on heavy industries and self-sufficiency. More over, in 1954 it adopted the goal of socialistic pattern of society that necessitated curbing concentration of economic power in a few hands. Coupled with pessimism on exports, the whole development strategy in India centered on direct intervention of the state in terms of providing direction, controls, regulation and even direct participation in economic activities. The restrictive interventionist policies meant the existence of a complex structure of permissions, licenses, quotas, rationing and absolute bans in many spheres including industrial production, infrastructural facilities, raw materials, credit, foreign exchange and trade. In short, government policy interventions have distorted the price and quality signals in all markets. Dholakia and Kapur, 2001). The wave of economic reform in India started in 1985 with internal liberalisation in respect of selective price decontrol deregulation of industries, increase exchange rate adjustment, monetary policy reforms and so on.

The major objectives of these reforms were particularly to attain the productivity with the help of modern technology. The basic thrust of the new reforms was to assign greater role to the private sector. To provide a level playing field to the private sector, a number of changes in policy were introduced with regard to the industrial licensing, export import policy, foreign direct investment (FDI), rationalisation and simplification of the system of fiscal and administrative regulation.

The aforesaid economic reform policy measures had not produced with desired result rather the country faced a serious balance of payment crisis in the later period. The country earned high percentage of current account deficit. The foreign exchange reserves had plummeted to US $ 1.2 billion, barley sufficient to pay for two weeks of imports. The fiscal deficit of the country for 1991 accounted 8.5 per cent of GDP. Industrial production was falling and inflation was rising which touched all time high to an uncomfortable level of 17 per cent by mid 1991. The current account deficit constituted 3.5 per cent of GDP in 1990-91. The country was on the verge of defaulting on its external debts. To overcome from the situation particularly to maintain external liquidity, the government transferred abroad a part of country's gold stocks.

This macro-economic imbalance led the Government of India to conceive the idea of pursuing economic reforms. In mid 1991, India was forced to seek assistance from the International Monetary Fund and World Bank to provide a huge loan of about $7 billion to bail India out of the crisis. The World Bank and IMF while agreeing to provide assistance to India, insisted that it must put its economy back on rail (Hajela and Goswami, 1999).

On June 21, 1991 Government of India (GoI) initiated new economic reforms, precisely different from the earlier because they have recognised the need for a systematic change, larger role of private sector, greater integration with world economy and liberalisation of government control. Though the outline of the economic reform was not much different from the reform policies undertaken by many developing countries, but the pace of implementation of such policies was relatively sluggish (Ahluwalia, 1999).

The economic reforms 1991, adopted a number of stabilisation measures that were designed to restore internal and external confidence. Monetary policy was tightened through increase in interest rates; consequently, the exchange rate of the rupee was adjusted. Further, fiscal policy rationalisation along with procedural simplification and liberalisation in the trade policy were announced. The new reform policies, therefore, were essential to import a new element of dynamism to the growth process of the economy. The major thrust areas of economic reform 1991 were,

- Fiscal Policy reform.
- Monetary Policy reform.
- Pricing Policy reform.
- External Policy reform.
- Industrial Policy reform.
- Foreign Investment Policy reform.
- Trade Policy reform and
- Public Sector Policy reform

The reform measures pursued over the years are presented in brief as under –

External Sector

1991-92

- Rupee devalued by 18 per cent.
- Administered import licensing replaced in many cases by tradable import entitlements (eximscrips) based on export earnings.
- Advance license for exporters simplified to improve access to duty-free inputs.
- Actual user conditions on capital goods, raw material and intermediates under OGI, scrapped.
- Many import curbs lifted. Exporters allowed keeping forex accounts and raising overseas credit to finance trade transactions.
- FDI limit rose from 40 to 51 per cent in priority sectors.
- FIPB set up to handle 51 per cent plus FDI proposals in other sectors.

1992-93

- Many import curbs lifted.
- Liberalised Exchange Rate Mechanism (LERM), under which 40 per cent of all export earnings were convertible under an official (overvalued) exchange rate and 60 per cent under the market rate, introduced in the Budget. LERM scrapped within the year.
- Import licensing of capital goods, raw materials, intermediaries and components diluted.
- FERA provisions made less stringent.
- Customs duties cut.
- Peak tariffs cut to 110 per cent.
- Baggage rules relaxed.

1993-94

- Dual exchange rates unified and made partially convertible on the current account.

1994-95

- Two categories of NRI deposit scheme, FCNRA and FCONR, terminated.

1996-97

- FIPB issues first guidelines for approving FDI not under the automatic approval list.
- 48 industries become eligible for 51 per cent foreign equity under automatic approval.
- FIIs allowed investing in utilised companies. ECB guidelines relaxed.

1997-98

- Number of industries that qualify for FDI under automatic approval from the RBI expanded.
- NRIs allowed investing 100 per cent in priority sectors and ECB guidelines eased.
- A committee, headed by S S Tarapore, recommends that India should gradually open up its capital account from 1997-98 to 1999-00. The fiscal, financial and banking systems should be strengthened for convertibility to materialise.

1998-99

- 340 items moved from licensed to OGL category.
- QRs on 2,300 imports from SAARC removed from August, 1998.
- India-Sri Lanka free trade agreement: zero tariffs on most things by 2007.
- Private software technology parks permitted.
- EOU/EPZs get 10-year tax break.
- 100 per cent automatic FDI for power generation, T&D, roads, bridges, and ports allowed.
- End-use of restrictions on GDR/ADRs go except for stock and real estate investors.
- FIIs allowed to trade government securities and treasury bills.
- FIIs permitted to take forward cover on incremental investments.

- 100 per cent FII debt funds allowed buying unlisted corporate debt.
- Greater flexibility in deploying and raising external commercial borrowings (ECBs).
- Prepayment of ECBs allowed if met out of foreign equity inflows.

1999-00

- FEMA 1999 enacted, replacing FERA.
- Quantitative restrictions (QRs) removed on 1,300 items.
- Apart from sectors under negative list, FDI in other sectors go under RBI's automatic system. Sectoral caps, however, continue. NRIs/OCBs are allowed to invest in most sectors.
- Indian corporate allowed to access to ADR/GDR markets automatically, subject to sector caps.

2000-01

- Indian loses trade dispute with US, agrees to remove QRs on the remaining 1,429 items by April '01. In April 2000 QRs on 714 items are removed.
- The arrival of cheap Chinese imports sparks panic in local industry. Government imposes pre-emptive duties pending results of anti-dumping investigations; non-tariff barriers like compulsory MRP stickers slapped on imports.

Banking and Finance

1992-93

- Narasimham Committee on bank reforms submits report.
- SLR, CRR cut to reduce state pre-emption of loanable funds.
- Number of lending rates cut from six to four.
- Capital adequacy norms were laid down for the first time.
- 364-day treasuries bill introduced with market related rates.
- 'Other securities' rates raised to bring them close to market rates. Guidelines for entry of new private banks issued.
- Deposit rates freed subject to ceiling.

1993-94

- SBI Act amended to allow the bank to access to equity market.
- The number of interest rates cut from 4 to 3. Floor lending and deposit rates brought down.
- Budget provides Rs 5,700 crores to capitalise banks to meet new provisioning norms.
- Prudential norms laying down maximum NPAs introduced.
- Debt recovery tribunals set up.
- Malhotra committee report recommends private sector entry into the insurance sector.

1994-95

- Banks free to determine primary lending rates (PLRs).
- No minimum lending rate for loans above Rs 2 lakh.
- Ad hoc treasury bills limited by agreement between government and the RBI, to limit monetisation of government debt.

1995-96

- IDBI Act amended. IDBI raises Rs 1,200 crores through its initial public offering.
- SBI becomes first Indian bank to be listed overseas, following a GDR issue.
- RBI allows setting up of primary dealership firms to deal in government securities.
- Six primary dealership firms, promoted by banks and financial institutions, granted licence to operate.

1996-97

- CRR cut from 13 per cent to 10 per cent.
- PLRs cut. Government decides to allow setting up of private sector Local Area Banks, which will operate in three contiguous non-metro districts.

1997-98

- Interest on foreign currency deposits deregulated to 'not more than LIBOR'.

- Fixed interest rate regime relaxed.
- Banks freed to assess working capital needs of borrowers.
- RBI Act amended after CRB Scam.
- RBI gets sweeping powers to register and regulate NBFCs.

1998-99

- Banks get tougher provisioning norms for government securities, state guaranteed loans.
- Risk weights assigned to government securities, state government guaranteed loans, forex open positions.
- NBFC regulations tightened.
- Insurance Regulation and Development (IRD) Bill introduced in Parliament.

1999-00

- IRDA Act passed in Parliament, allows private equity in insurance, caps foreign equity at 26 per cent of total, sets up Insurance Regulation Development Authority (IRDA).
- Banks allowed to operate different PLRs for different maturities.
- Times Bank merged with HDFC Bank.
- ICICI and ICICI Bank get listed in NYSE after their respective ADR issues.

2000-01

- Amendments of Banking Ccompanies Acquisition and Transfer of Undertakings Act allow banks to enter into insurance.
- Government says it will cut its stake in public sector banks to 33 per cent, but will retain the 'public sector character' of these banks.
- State owned banks announce voluntary retirement schemes (VRS) to shed staff. About 10 to 15 per cent of bank staff apply.
- RBI allows NBFCs to convert themselves into banks. However big industrial groups such, as the Tatas, Birlas and Reliance

not allowed starting banks. Large industrial houses not allowed holding more than 10 per cent.

- IRDA issues licenses to private insurers-initially, 11 joint ventures get licenses.
- Bank of Madura merged with ICICI Bank.
- Global Trust Bank merged with UTI Bank.
- RBI announces cut in bank rate to combat slowdown and announce cut in CRR.
- IDBI Act amended to make film financing an eligible activity for financial institution.

Capital Market

1991-92

- FIs free to decide on debt-equity swaps. Harshad Mehta led boom begins.

1992-93

- SEBI announces guidelines on equity market disclosure and transparency.
- FIIs allowed to hold up to 24 per cent of local companies. Individual FIIs can hold maximum five per cent of total equity in a single company. Sensex record 4,367, the highest-ever level at that time. Harshad Mehta led boom run comes to an end in April '92.

1993-94

- Comptroller of Capital Issues (CCI) abolished, issue pricing to be market determined.
- Securities and Exchanges Board of India (SEBI) empowered as market regulator.
- Indian firms allowed to access European markets via Euro equities. Private mutual funds allowed. OTCEI set up.
- Screen based NSE in the process of being set up.

1994-95

- SEBI (Substantial Acquisition of Shares and Takeovers) Regulations, 1994 – India's takeover code, passed.

- State owned mutual fund, Unit Trust of India (UTI), brought under SEBI jurisdiction.

1996-97

- IPO norms tightened to boost quality of issues.
- IPO issuers need to have three-year dividend paying record.
- Public sector banks allowed to access markets and price issues at premium.
- Stock exchanges asked to set up clearing houses.
- Stock lending scheme announced.
- A committee, headed by P. N. Bhagwati, modifies the takeover code to make management changes less difficult.

1997-98

- Entry barriers for unlisted companies lowered.
- SEBI rules changed to create walls between issuer and registrars of issues.
- Disclosure norms made more stringent.
- Multiple categories of merchant bankers merged into one category.
- Merchant bankers banned from non-capital market transactions.

1998-99

- Rolling settlements for dematerialised shares.
- Infrastructure companies get easier public issue norms.
- IPOs to go through depositories.

1999-00

- Securities Laws Amendment Bill, 199, passed in Parliament, incorporating derivatives and units of investment schemes as securities; as defined by the securities Contract and Regulation Act, 1956.
- Rolling settlement allowed in 10 Scrips.
- Companies free to determine par value of new issues. Sensex crosses 6,000 on the back of the dotcom boom.

- Rediff and Satyam infoway come out with ADR issues. Software companies like infosys start overtaking the likes of Hindustan Lever and Reliance in market capitalisation.

2000-01

- Dematerialised trading made compulsory.
- Rolling settlements introduced.
- Internet trading permitted. Volumes start to pick up.
- Dotcom boom turns to bust on US bourses as doubts like Amazon. The depressed sentiments spread to the Indian market resulting in Indian software scrips being hammered even though the Indian bourses have no listed dotcoms.
- Hughes Tele. com first telecom operator to come out with an IPO, which however desolves.
- First hostile bids start to take place.
- Hostile bid by Abhishek Dalmia for Great Eastern Shipping fails. However, Dalmia makes a lot of money.
- Damani Brothers make hostile bid for FIs return to the Indian market in force. Pour in record amounts in January and February '2001.
- Old economy stocks regain their charm.
- PSU scrips such as VSNL and oil sector PSUs start moving up in anticipation of privatisation.

Services and Industry

1991-92

- Prime Minister Narasimha Rao abolishes licensing for almost 80 per cent of all sectors. Only 18 industries remain licensed.
- Monopolies and Restrictive Trade Practices Act (MRTP) amended to allow industries to grow without government approval.
- Phased Manufacturing Programme (PMP) discontinued.
- Sectors reserved for the public sector cut from 12 to 8
- Industry location, except in major cities, does not need government clearance.

- SICA amended to bring PSUs under its ambit.
- PSU amended to bring PSUs under its ambit.
- PSU disinvestment programme starts.
- Disinvestment target Rs. 2,500 crores; achievement Rs. 3,038 crores.

1992-93

- National Renewal Fund (NRF) to fund lay off costs.
- PSUs allowed to access capital markets. IPCL the first to do so.
- ONGC corporatised. Disinvestment target Rs. 2,500 crores, achievement Rs. 1,913 crores. Government reduces stake in Maruti from 60 to 50 per cent making Suzuki an equal shareholder.

1993-94

- Car and white goods manufacturing de-licensed.
- Large-scale readymade garments making opened up for foreign equity. Subject to export obligations.
- 13 minerals, formerly reserved for the public sector, opened up for private investments.
- Disinvestments target Rs. 3,5000 crores; achievement zero.

1994-95

- Almost all bulk drugs delicensed.
- Automatic 51 per cent foreign equity allowed in bulk drug making.
- Disinvestments target Rs. 4,000 crores, achievement, Rs. 362 crores. Daewoo starts manufacturing the Cielo in July 1995- the foreign first car manufacturer to do so.

1996-97

- Delicensing brings the number of licensed industries down to 14. Consumer electronics is the latest sector to be delicensed.
- Investment ceilings for SISIs raised from Rs. 75 lakh to Rs. 3 crores.

- Disinvestment target Rs. 5,000 crores; achievement Rs. 380 crores.
- FIPB revamped to make FDI policy 'more transparent'.

1997-98

- Number of industries under compulsory licensing cut from 14 to 9. Eleven profitable public sector companies are named 'Navaratnas' (nine jewels). This gives them more freedom to invest, set up JVs, raise overseas funds as well as greater managerial autonomy.
- Disinvestment Commission recommends 50 PSUs for sell offs.
- Disinvestment target Rs. 4,800 crores; achievement Rs. 902 crores. Software export boom starts.

1998-99

- Coal, lignite, Sugar, mineral oils, bulk drugs delicensed. Petroleum (not crude, though) also delicensed.
- Corporates allowed to buy back up to 25 per cent of their total net worth.
- Patent Bill approach in Parliament and promulgated by ordinance.

SSI list shortened by removing tools and farm implements.

- Disinvestment target Rs. 5,000 crores; achievement Rs. 5,371 crores, including Rs. 3,500 crores worth of share swaps among state owned energy companies.
- Hyundai launches the Santro in October 1998 and becomes the first small car to challenge Maruti. Tata Indica launched. Wipro, Infosys emerge as major Indian corporate success stories.

1999-00

- IT Bill introduced in Parliament.
- Tax provisions for housing liberalised.
- Disinvestments target Rs. 10,000 crores; achievement Rs. 1,584 crores. Modern Foods privatized for Rs. 105 crores.

2000-2001

- Bank reforms allow banks to enter insurance sector with partners.
- IRDA finalizes entry norms for private insurers. Eleven insurance joint ventures enter the market.
- Maruti Udyog (MUL) added to the list of companies for privatisation. Telco runs up huge losses because of Indica.
- Disinvestment target Rs. 10,000 crores; achievement zero.

It is evident from the foregoing discussions that as a part of the economic reforms a number of measures have been introduced, since 1991, in the financial sector. The reforms programme follows the well known path of deregulating capital markets and banks, interest rates, withdrawing directed credit and subsidies and encouraging stricter income recognitions norms and integrating the domestic financial market with global financial flows (IMF: 1995).

The objective of financial sector reforms was to make the financial sector more efficient as well as to put an end to the so called 'financial repression' that had held back the growth of financial savings and their efficient channelisation in to industrial activity (Khanna, 1999).

With this backdrop, an attempt has been made in the following paragraph to delineate the implications of reform measures on financial sector with a special emphasis on banking sector.

Indian Banking System

Indian banking system (IBS) in promoting economic development has undergone a sea change. It however, appears that IBS has grown haphazardly. The "free for all" sort of banking ambience prevalent in the early forties invited strict control measures through the enactment of Banking Companies Act of 1949. Despite regulatory measures, when a few banks failed in the sixties, the compulsory merger of banks was imposed on weaker banks. Social controls were introduced in 1968 and before giving them a fair trial, the major banks were nationalised. From 1969 to 1992, various control measures were introduced before a beginning in liberalisation measures were initiated.

The numbers of banks operating in India have undergone rapid changes as a result of the controlled expansion. There were 648 banks operating in India in 1947. A large number of them were very small non-scheduled banks with high mortality rates and poor capital base. Introduction of minimum capital base for the banks under banking companies Act 1949 was succeeded largely in eliminating the weaker banks. It aimed at to strengthen the financial base of trimming their number. At the time of nationalisation of banks, there were only 85 banks. The establishment of regional rural banks (RRBs) in 1995 reversed the trend of slimming the banking structure. Since then, 196 RRBs have joined the banking system, fattening it beyond recognition. Moreover, in the latter period the number of banks, both the private sector banks set up by the term lending institutions and foreign banks have joined the bandwagon of Indian banking.

Chart A

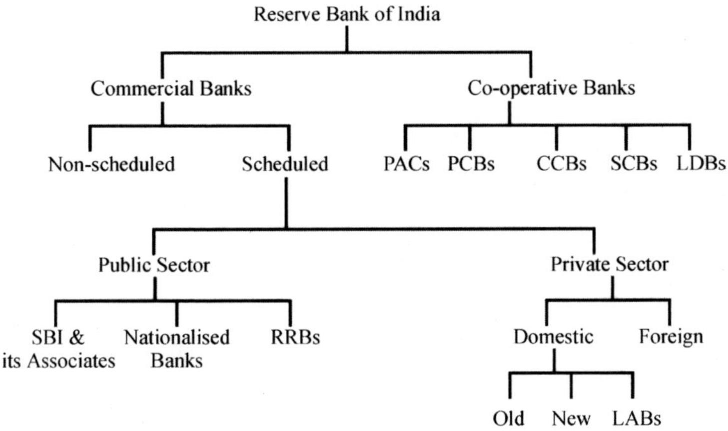

Notes : PACs ; Primary Agricultural Credit Societies
PCBs ; Primary Co-op. Banks.
CCBs ; Central Co-op. Banks.
SCBs ; State Co-op. Banks.
LDBs ; Land Development Banks.
LABs ; Local area Banks.

Source : Hanson, J.A., & Kathuria S., et-al *"India ; A financial sector for the 21st century"*, Oxford University press, The world Bank, 1999©.

The present institutional set-up of Indian commercial banking is demonstrated in chart-A. The banking sector is dominated by scheduled commercial Banks – (SCBs) which accounted about 95 per cent of banking operation. In includes, Public Sector Banks (PSBs) namely State Bank of India and its seven subsidiaries, 19 nationalised Banks (NBs) and 196 Regional Rural Banks accounts 90 per cent of the total banking operation.

Pre-Reform Banking Scenario : A performance appraisal

Prior to 1969, all banks except State Bank of India and its seven associate banks were privately owned. However, there was a perception among policy makers that under the private ownership the rural and most part of semi-urban areas remained unserved by banks. Further, as India increasingly became planned economy, they felt that it would be difficult to undertake credit planning for the industries without nationalisation of banks (Tandon: 1989). These considerations sparked off the drive for 'social control of banks by the Government of India (GOI) and under the nationalisation Act of 1969. As a result, fourteen privately owned commercial banks were nationalised. In 1980, Government of India acquired the ownership of other six more banks, bringing the total number of nationalised banks to twenty. The privately owned banks, on the other hand, were allowed to function side by side with nationalised banks. However, the foreign banks were allowed to continue their operation under the strict regulation. The progress of commercial banks since 1969 is exhibited in the following table. The table delineated a significant expansion of the banking sector between 1969 to 1991 on the basis of major development indicators such as number of branches, deposit mobilisation, credit disbursed, per capita deposits and credit.

The tremendous expansion of the bank branches especially in the rural areas coupled with a drastic reduction in population served per bank branch, and an increase in deposits and credit per office demonstrated that since nationalization the banks are playing a catalytic role in the development of every nook and corner of the country.

The Table – 2 shows the population group-wise position of banking operation in India. It is evident from the table that the percentage of rural branches to total branches has gone up significantly from 22.2 per cent in June 1969 to 58.5 per cent in March 1991. The semi-urban and rural coverage when taken together accounted for 76.9 per cent in March 1991 against 62.6 per cent in June 1969. In the spheres of the communities' financial savings, the commercial banks have emerged as one of the major financial intermediaries in the country. Since nationalisation there has been a spectacular rise in the volume of deposits that was Rs.4666 crore in June 1969 rose to Rs. 219539 crores in March 1991 accounting 42, fold increase. The deposits in the rural areas increased both in absolute and percentage term from 3.1 per cent (Rs. 145 crores) in June 1969 to 15.1 per cent (Rs. 33166 crores) in March 1991. The credit deployment of commercial banks have also been increased in absolute term since nationalisation but there has been a significant change in the direction of flow of credit. The share of rural areas credit has increased from a meagre share of 1.5 per cent (Rs. 54 crores) in June 1969 to 14.8 per cent (Rs. 10026 crores) in June 1987 and fell marginally to 14.7 per cent (Rs 19688 crore) in March 1991.

TABLE – 1
PROGRESS OF COMMERCIAL BANKING 1969-1991

Indicators	*June 1969*	*March 1980*	*June 1985*	*March 1987*	*March 1991*	*Per-centage change of 1991 over 1969*
A. No. of Commercial Banks:	71	153	267	276	272	283.0
1. SBI and its associates	8	8	8	8	8	0.0
2. Nationalised Banks (NBs)	14	20	20	20	20	42.8
3. Private Sector Banks	36	104	31	33	25	-30.5
4. Foreign Banks (FB)	13	16	20	21	23	76.9
5. Regional Rural Banks (RRBs)	NA	5	188	194	196	NA
B. No. of Bank Offices in India :	8832	32419	53165	53565	60646	586.7
1. SBI and its associates	2602	8351	10742	10833	12461	378.9
2. Nationalised Banks (NBs)	4617	20511	25145	25485	29812	545.7
3. Private Sector Banks	1483	2719	4540	4202	3703	149.6
4. Foreign Banks	130	136	136	136	139	6.9
5. Regional Rural Bank, (RRBs)	NA	NA	12602	12909	14531	-
C. Quantitative Expansion :						
i) Population per office (,000) Nos.	64	20	15	14	14	– 7.8
ii) Deposit per office (Rs. bn)	16.6	13.2	12.0	15.1	18.3	1.2
iii) Credit Per office (Rs. bn)	13.0	10.1	7.9	8.3	11.0	– 15.3
iv) Per capita deposit (Rs.)	261.1	440.1	818.2	1374.2	1296.1	1531.2
v) Per capita credit (Rs.)	201.7	316.2	540.7	618.6	784.9	289.2
vi) Share of rural branches to total in (per cent.)	22.2	46.9	58.7	56.2	58.5	NA
vii) Bank deposit as per cent of GDP at current prices.	13.7	32.6	39.4	40.1	42.4	NA
viii) No. of banks employee (000)	220	582	723	826	926	320.7

NA–Not available

Source: RBI, Banking Statistics and RBI, Annual Report, various issues.

TABLE – 2 POPULATION GROUPWISE BANK OFFICES, DEPOSITS AND ADVANCES

Population group	*June 1969*	*June 1980*	*Sept. 1985*	*June 1987*	*March 1991*
A. Bank Offices; (in number)					
Rural	1833 (22.2)	14817 (45.7)	30664 (57.9)	30201 (56.1)	35216 (58.1)
Semi-urban	3342 (40.4)	8331 (25.7)	9845 (18.9)	10629 (19.7)	11379 (18.8)
Urban	1584 (19.2)	5243 (16.2)	6230 (12.0)	7215 (13.4)	8233 (13.6)
Metropolitan	1503 (18.2)	4021 (12.4)	5275 (10.1)	5795 (10.5)	5769 (9.5)
Total	**8262 (100)**	**32412 (100)**	**52014 (100)**	**53840 (100)**	**60597 (100)**
B. Bank deposits; (Rs. in crores)					
Rural	145 (3.1)	3966 (11.9)	14375 (14.0)	15632 (14.4)	33166 (15.1)
Semi-urban	1025 (22.0)	7712 (23.1)	21404 (20.8)	23146 (21.4)	43938 (20.0)
Urban	1209 (25.9)	8368 (25.2)	26660 (26.0)	28179 (26.0)	51412 (23.4)
Metropolitan	2287 (49.0)	13275 (39.8)	40186 (39.2)	41397 (38.2)	91026 (41.5)
Total	**4666 (100)**	**33321 (100)**	**102625 (100)**	**108354 (100)**	**219539 (100)**
C. Bank Credits; (Rs. in Crores)					
Rural	54 (1.5)	2161 (9.6)	7489 (14.1)	10026 (14.8)	19688 (14.7)
Semi-urban	407 (11.3)	3641 (16.3)	9089 (17.1)	11614 (17.2)	20624 (15.4)
Urban	722 (20.0)	5026 (22.5)	11854 (22.3)	15539 (23.0)	28476 (21.3)
Metropolitan	2426 (67.2)	11552 (51.6)	24730 (46.5)	30476 (45.0)	64958 (48.6)
Total	**3609 (100)**	**22380 (100)**	**53162 (100)**	**67655 (100)**	**133745 (100)**

Note : Figures indicate the aggregate of SBI and its associates, nationalised, Pvt. and foreign sector banks.

Source : (I) RBI Banking statistics

(II) Quarterly Hand Out : Statistical Tables Relating to Banks in India.

Table-3 shows the credit deposit (C/D) ratios of commercial banks. Since nationalisation, C/D ratio dwindled from 71.9 per cent in December 1969 to 60.7 per cent in March 1991. The rate of decline rate in the backward region is more significant than that from advanced region of the country. The level of C/D ratio has declined to 47.6 per cent and 49.8 per cent in northern region and central region respectively in March 1990. The population groupwise C/D ratio shows that rural and semi-urban areas accounted with a very low ratio (around 40 per cent) while metropolitan areas had high ratio (around 80 per cent) throughout the period 1969 to 1990. This indicates bank's insignificant performance in lending activities in the rural areas. Moreover, low C/D ratio in the backward areas clearly signifies siphoning of loanable funds to the developed region of the country.

TABLE – 3
POPULATION GROUPWISE REGIONWISE CREDIT DEPOSIT RATIO

(In percentage)

Region/Population group	*Dec. 1969*	*Dec. 1980*	*Dec. 1985*	*March 1990*
A. Regionwise				
1. Northern	65.1	69.1	47.4	47.6
2. North Eastern	67.2	63.0	43.0	70.0
3. Eastern	52.8	55.0	48.2	52.6
4. Central	50.1	49.4	48.7	49.8
5. Western	73.2	70.1	69.3	63.7
6. Southern	78.5	80.9	76.7	83.2
All India Total	71.9	66.9	60.5	60.7
B. Population groupwise				
1. Rural	37.6	56.9	63.9	60.7
2. Semi-urban	43.0	49.2	50.0	48.7
3. Urban	59.1	59.7	53.4	58.7
4. Metropolitan	98.2	85.2	73.1	82.0
All India Total	71.9	66.9	61.8	60.7

Source : RBI, Banking statistics; Quarterly Handout; Statistical tables relating to Banks in India.

Table – 4 shows the sectoral deployment of bank credit during 1969 to 1991. The sectorwise allocation of advances by commercial banks has undergone a sea change during post nationalisation. The commercial banks have diverted an increasing proportion of their credit to sectors like agriculture, small-scale industries.

TABLE – 4
BANK CREDIT TO VARIOUS SECTORS (1969 – 1991)

(In percentage)

Sector	*1969*	*1976*	*1982*	*1988*	*1991*
1. Food Procurements	6.5	18.8	7.3	3.1	3.3
2. Large Scale Industry	60.9@	43.4	38.3	36.3	39.4
3. Small Scale industries	7.9	10.5	13.4	15.5	13.8
4. Agriculture	5.3	9.4	15.8	17.1	14.0
5. Wholesale Trade	10.0	7.0	7.6	4.9	4.8
6. Others	9.4	10.9	17.6	23.1	24.8
Total	**100**	**100**	**100**	**100**	**100**

@ include medium industries.

Source : RBI, Banking statistics; Basic statistical Return, various issues.

The Major Constraints of Banks

The banks played a positive role since nationalisation in institutionalizing the community savings. They emerged as the purveyor of credit requirement of the small borrowers. An excessive focus has been laid on quantitative achievement and social obligations at the expense of achieving profitability and efficiency. On the other hand, the reason of expansion of bank branches may be attributed to –

- develop a strong banking base to serve the economy efficiently.
- meet the banking needs of various segments of the economy by developing specialized banks.

As a result, to achieve the first aforesaid objectives there is a need for consolidating the widespread banking that led to high percentage of NPAs, preponderance of less remunerative populist lending programmes 'excess staff' and over extended branch network and low propensity for adopting modern technology. These factors impaired the efficiency of banks in general, though there are a few exceptions.

The private banks were introduced to provide banking facilities in certain specialised fields that were not well addressed. They brought about an element of competition for PSBs by extending customer friendly mode of services particularly in providing working capital along with long term funds requirements of business units. Thus they grabbed the cream of remunerative business of older banks, and further weakening their profit earning capacity.

However, the external environment of the banks may be summarized as under :

- There exists extraordinary high level of pre-emption of bank resources through statutory liquidity ratio (SLR) and cash reserve ratio (CRR). The CRR requires banks to hold a part of their deposits in the form of cash balance with RBI. The SLR stipulates certain percentage of NDTL should be compulsorily deposited in government papers that constitute about 38.5 per cent. Moreover, the compulsory lending to priority sector has further deteriorated the situation as only 25-30 per cent deposits received are left with the hands of banks for commercial lending. The following table delineates the facts:

TABLE – 5
YEARWISE CASH RESERVE RATIO (CRR) AND STATUTORY LIQUIDITY RATIO (SLR) (1981-1992)

Year	*CRR (as per cent of NDTL)*	*SLR (as per cent of NDTL)*	*Bank rate*	*Minimum rate (% p.a.)*
August 1981	7.0	34.5	10.0	13.5
December 1981	7.5	35.0	-	-
July 1985	-	37.0	-	16.0
October 1985	9.0	-	-	16.0
September 1990	9.0	38.5	11.0	15.0
1991-92	15.0	38.5	-	-

NDTL = Net demand and time liabilities
Source : RBI, Annual Report, various issues.

- Insufficient attention to prudential accounting norms and capital adequacy. As a result the capital adequacy level was very low in banks in general even in some cases it became negative indicating thereby complete erosion of capital base.
- Excessive recourse to subsidised credit channeled through unduly complex system of administered interest rates. Banks were required to direct a sizeable part of their lending to certain priority sector like agriculture, small farmer and weaker section at concessional rate of interest.

- Lax in regulation and supervision of banking operation due to absence of clear, internationally comparable accounting norms for banks.
- Inadequate internal control and rigidities in personnel policies and management structure.
- Credit market was subject to political interference.
- Inconvenience and non-uniform system of loan recovery of banks.
- Non-availability of incentive that would encourage the bankers to face competitive environment.
- Regulated interest rate as well as stringent credit allocation mechanism eliminated the scope of price competition among banks and destroyed their incentive to allocate resources according to highest value use.

As a result, banking system was virtually bankrupt and ill suited to the task of allocating credit and performing ordinary banking business. (Joshi and Little, 1999). Thus stronger doses of reform measures are required to improve their health. The GOI consequently employed a committee under the chairmanship of M. Narasimham, Ex-Governor of Reserve Bank of India to address the problems and suggest remedial measures (Committee on Financial System : 1991).

The Committee : Terms of Reference and Major Recommendations

Terms of Reference

The following were the major terms of reference before the "Committee on financial system" constituted under the chairmanship of M. Narasimham.

- Examine the existing structure of financial system and make recommendations for improving the efficiency and effectiveness of the system with particular reference to 'economy of operations, accountability and profitability'.
- Make recommendations for improving and modernising the organisational systems and procedure as well as managerial policies.

- Make recommendations for enforcing greater competitiveness into the system.
- Examine the cost composition and adequacy of capital structure.
- Review the existing supervisory arrangements and make recommendations for ensuring appropriate and effective supervision.
- To review the existing legislative framework and suggest necessary changes.

The committee had identified the following as the major issues confronting the operation of Indian banks –

- Constant erosion of profitability of banks.
- Social Banking provisions depressed the potential income of banks.
- Directed investments also affected profitability of the banks adversely.
- The phenomenal expansion of branches is unremunerative.
- Accounting practices are not uniform and the true position of banks is not transparent.
- Excessive administrative and political interference.

The Major Recommendations of First Narasimham Committee

The committee submitted its reports on November 1991. It recommended gradual deregulation of banking sector and financial sector in general. The recommendations included –

- A reduction of statutory liquidity Ratio (SLR) to 25 per cent over the next five years with a reduction in current year itself.
- Reduction in the CRR to 10 per cent, payment of interest on the CRR and use of CRR as an instrument of monetary policy.
- Gradual phasing out of the directed credit programmes by redefining the priority sector. The stipulation that 40 per cent of all credit should go to the priority sector. Priority sector is redefined as "small & marginal farmer, tiny sector of industry, small business and transport operations, village and cottage

industry, rural artisans and other weaker section". The total flow of credit to the priority sector should be fixed at 10 per cent of aggregate bank credit.

- Deregulation of interest rates in a phased manner and bringing interest rates on government borrowing in the line with market determined rates.
- Attaining Basle norms (BIS) of capital adequacy in a phased manner, 4 per cent by March 1993 and full 8 per cent by March 1996.
- Tightening the prudential norms. It is necessary for banks to follow a uniform practice of income recognition, valuation of assets and provisioning against doubtful debt.
- Bringing more transparency in the banks balance sheet.
- Accelerating the pace of loan recoveries and tackling doubtful debts through establishment of assets reconstruction fund (ARF) and debt recovery tribunals (DRTs).
- Entry of private banks and easing of foreign banks.
- Sale of bank equity to public.
- Phase out the development finance Institutions (DFIs) to access to fund.
- Increased competitions in lending between DFI, and a switch from consortium lending to syndicated lending.
- Easing of regulations on capital markets, combined with entry of Foreign Institutional Investors (FIIs) and better supervision.

The Level of Implementation of Narasimham Committee Recommendations

1. **Reduction in Reserve Ratios** : CRR obligates a bank to hold a certain fraction of its net demand and time liabilities (NDTL) as reserves with the central bank in order to ensure liquidity of the banking system. The SLR requires banks to invest a pre-determined proportion of its NDTL in government and other approved securities. These requirements serve as instruments of monetary control, pre-empt lendable resources of banks and distort portfolio choice, The CRR which was 15 per cent in 1991-92, has been gradually reduced over the years

(as shown in Table-6). It became 10.5 per cent on January 1998 and further reduced to 5.5 per cent in December 2001. The SLR that stood at 38.5 per cent in 1991-92 has also been reduced to a uniform level of 25 per cent throughout the years ending on December 2001. However, the system of multiple prescriptions for the SLR has been withdrawn. Finally since October 1997, all cash balances maintained by banks with the RBI on account of the CRR have earned at a uniform interest of 4 per cent as against earning an effective interest rate of 3.5 per cent earlier.

TABLE – 6

TREND OF CASH-RESERVE RATIO (CRR) AND STATUTORY LIQUIDITY RATIO (SLR) 1991-92 TO 2000-01

Year	*CRR (as % of NDTL*)*	*Base SLR (as % of NDTL*)*
1991 – 92	15	38.5
1992 – 93	15	37.75
1993 – 94	14	34.75
1994 – 95	15	33.75
1995 – 96	14	31.5
April '96	13	31.5
July '96	12	31.5
October '96	11.5	31.5
January '97	10	31.5
October '97	9.75	25.0
January '98	10.5	25.0
April '98	10	25.0
March '99	10.5	25.0
April '2000	10.5	25.0
December '01	5.5	-

*Note : * Net demand and time liabilities*

Source : RBI, Annual Report, various issues, and RBI, Credit Policy, October 1997 and April 1998.

2. **Interest rates deregulation** : The RBI stipulated maximum deposits rates on both savings and time deposits of all maturity as well as minimum lending rates on loans of all maturity and sizes. These have guaranteed the banks a minimum interest rate spread and a measure of protection against increasing cost of operation.

The first step in deregulating lending rates was taken in October 1994, when rates were deregulated for advances more than Rs. 2,00,000. However, banks were advised to announce and maintain a specified rate over the prime-lending rate (PLR) to keep the range of lending rates across different type of risks within reasonable limit. Lending rates for loans less than Rs. 2,00,000 have also been partially deregulated since April 1998 in order to remove the disincentive to the flow of credit towards small borrowers. The process of deregulating deposit rates in phases began in April 1992 and has gathered momentum in recent years. Deregulation of term deposits rates first took the form of the RBI switching of term deposit to announcing ceiling rate deposit rates. Since July 1996, RBI has been abolishing the ceiling for deposit of different maturity, starting from those with the highest maturity and by April 1998, interest rates on deposits beyond fifteen days have been freed. The phased reduction in interest rates since the reforms is shown in Table – 7.

3. **Prudential regulations** : The RBI introduced internationally accepted prudential norms relating to income recognition, asset classification, and provisioning and capital adequacy. Capital adequacy norms require commercial bank to maintain capital to risky asset ratio (CRAR) of not less than 8 per cent, as recommended by the Banks for International Settlement (BIS). Further at least 4 per cent of risk-weighted assets were to be in the form of pure capital (Tier – I), that is equity capital and free reserves. Such norms are expected to minimise the problem of inadequacy of capital compared to risk exposure that has persistently been plagued the public sector banks (Sankar; 1999). New norms of income recognition, asset classification and provisioning were introduced to reflect quality of loan portfolios and to obtain a true picture of the financial situation of each bank. The Ministry of Finance, 1993, estimated a reduction about 28 per cent of profit of 28 PSBs due to implementation of the new accounting norms. Prudential regulations have been strengthened especially with respect to classification of assets into four categories; standard, sub-standard, doubtful and loss assets. Standard assets are

defined as credit facilities with respect to sum of which interest or principal or both are paid by due date and for others, where the amount due is paid within 30 days of the due date. An asset is treated as NPAs if it remains 'past due' for a period of two quarters while pre-reform period banks were not classify accounts with outstanding below Rs. 25000 into four categories but were required to make provisions at a flat rate. Details in subsequent chapter.

4. **Deregulation :** Entry of private banks has been allowed in the deregulated environment since January 1993. As a result, 19 new private sector banks; 9 domestic and 10 foreign banks have commenced their operation during 1993 - 97. The RBI has sought to ensure the new entrants are professionally managed, financially viable, and technically strong, and there would be no adverse consequences such as concentration of credit.

5. **Supervisory strategy and transparency:** The RBI supervisory strategy comprises both off-site surveillance and on-site inspection. A detailed off-site surveillance system is based on a prudential supervisory reporting framework on a quarterly basis covering capital adequacy, asset quality, loan concentration, operational results, and connected lending which has been made operational. An on-site inspection is conducted annually since July 1997. It involves an evaluation of the total operations and performance of banks under CAMELS (capital adequacy, asset quality, management, earning, liquidity and system) followed in many countries including US. The role of external auditors has also been made compulsory.

The RBI has also taken a number of measures to improve transparency and disclosure norms in the published accounts of banks. From 1996-97 disclosure under the head 'provisions and contingencies' in the profit and loss account has been emphasised. The banks are now required to list the bad and doubtful debts, provision for erosion in the value of investments, and provisions for taxes. Banks are also required to disclose the capital adequacy ratio, as well as percentage of net NPA to net advances that were not required earlier.

TABLE – 7
STRUCTURE OF INTEREST RATES 1994-97

Rates	1994 18 Oct.	1 Nov.	1995 10 Feb.	18 Apr.	1 Oct.	1996 2 July	20 Aug.	20 Oct.	1997 16 April	26 June	21 Oct
Lending rates											
Size of credit limit											
i. Up to and Rs. 25,000	12.0	12.0	12.0	12.0	12.0	12.0	12.0	12.0	12.0	12.0	12.0
ii. Above Rs. 25,000 – 200.000	13.5	13.5	13.5	13.5	13.5	13.5	13.5	13.5	13.5	13.5	13.5
iii. Over Rs. 200.00	Free (14)	Free (14)	Free (15)	Free (15.5)	Free (15.5)	Free (16.5)	Free (16-16.5)	Free (14.5-15[a])	Free(14-14.5)	Free (13.5-14)	Free (13-13.5)[b]
Deposit rates											
i. Current	0	0	0	0	0	0	0	0	0	0	0
ii Savings	5.0	4.5	4.5	4.5	4.5	4.5	4.5	4.5	4.5	4.5	4.5
iii. Term											
a. 46 days to 3 yrs & over	Max 10	Max 10	Max 10	Max 10	-	-	-	-	-	-	-
b. 46 days to 2 yrs	-	-	-		Max. 12	-	-	-	-	-	-
c. Above 2 yrs	-	-	-	-	Free	-	-	-	-	-	-
d. 30 days to 1 yr.	-	-	-	-	-	Max 11	Max 11	Max 10	Not>bank rate minus 2%	Not>bank rate minus 2%	Free
e. Above 1 yr.	-	-	-	-	-	Free	Free	Free	Free	Free	Free
Inflation Rate [a]	8.9	9.7	11.7	10.0	8.4	5.7	6.6	6.5	6.3	4.7	3.5
Bank rate	12	12	12	12	12	12	12	12	11	10	9

Notes : 'Free' means banks are free to charge interest rates decided by them; :- Not applicable; Figures in brackets denote the Prime Lending Rate (PLR) of five major scheduled commercial banks. A : Annualized monthly rate. B : PLR of three major scheduled commercial banks as of end October 1997.

Sources : RBI, Annual Report, several issues, RBI, Busy Credit Policy, October 1997, Centre for Monitoring Indian Economy. Monthly Review. Several issues.

TABLE – 8
PERFORMANCE OF REFORM DURING FIRST PHASE (1991-98)

Sl. No.	*Performance Indicators*	*1991-92*	*1992-93*	*1993-94*	*1994-95*	*1995-96*	*1996-97*	*1997-98*
1.	Population per Bank Offices (000,)	14	13	14	14	15	15	15
2.	Percentage share of rural bank offices	58.5	57.6	57.2	56.2	52.4	50.2	51.2
3.	Per capita deposit (Rs)	1296.1	–	–	4242	4643.8	5323.3	6270
4.	Per capita credit (Rs)	618.6	–	–	2719	2908.1	3356	3759
5.	Bank deposit as per cent of GDP at current prices	42.4	41.2	42.8	39.8	43.3	42.6	–
6.	Credit/Deposit ratio's	61.0	60.5	56.6	59.2	61.9	57.3	55.5
7.	No. of banks attaining capital adequacy ratio	–	–	8	13	19	25	26
8.	Percentage of NPAs to total advances	Nil	23.2	24.8	19.5	18.0	17.8	16.0
9.	No. of banks with gross NPAs more than 20 per cent	Nil		16	10	10	–	–
10.	Percentage of net NPA to total assets	Nil	Nil	Nil	4.0	3.6	3.6	3.3
11.	No. of banks with net NPA more than 20 per cent	–	–	–	10	2	1	1
12.	Recapitalisation of banks (bn)	–	Nil	Nil	52.9	8.5	15.1	–
13.	No. of banks capitalised	–	–	57.0	13	6	6	6
14.	Gross Profit as per cent of total assets	1.84	0.94	19	1.41	1.49	1.60	1.58
15.	Net profit as per cent of total assets	0.28	- 0.99	0.99	0.25	- 0.07	0.57	0.77
16.	Intermediation cost as per cent of total assets	2.61	2.63	2.65	2.83	2.99	2.88	2.66
17.	Provisions & contingencies as per cent of total assets	1.57	1.92	2.14	1.16	1.56	1.03	0.81

Source : Computed from Indian Banks' Association, Performance Highlight of Banks, various issues and Report on trend & Progress of Indian Banking, various issues.

6. **Debt recovery and financial supervision :** In order to supervise financial institutions more effectively, the board of financial supervision became operational in November 1994 and its supervisory scope was gradually extended. To facilitate the recovery of loans, debt recovery tribunal (DRTs) are set up in the major cites due to the Banks and Financial Institutions Bill 1993. The details will be discussed in a separate chapter.
7. **Directed credit :** The priority sector target of 40 per cent of net bank credit will continue under some modification of the definition and target norms of priority sector as advised by RBI.
8. **Customer Service :** An independent evaluation of customers satisfaction by an independent out side agency is to be arranged by the end March 1994 with signing the memorandum of understanding (MOU) by individual banks with RBI. A separate chapter has been devoted in this respect. The banking "*Ombudsman*" scheme was instituted in 1995 for expeditious and inexpensive resolution of customers' complaint about deficiencies in banking services.

Response of First Phase of Banking Sector Reforms

The different aspects of bank's performance during first phase of reforms have been exhibited in the Table – 8. These are summarised under the following heads:

1. **Quantitative expansion:** The populations per bank office have been increased from 14,000 in 1991-92 to 15,000 in 1997-98. The total number of bank offices in absolute term has been increasing while the share of rural branches has declined from 58.5 per cent in 1991-92 to 51.2 per cent in 1997-98.
2. **Deposit mobilisation :** The deposit mobilization of banks during the post reform era was significant, however, bank deposit as percentage of gross domestic product (GDP) at current prices remained constant (around 42 per cent) during the period under consideration. The credit deposit ratios declined from 61 per cent in 1991-92 to 55.5 per cent in 1997-98. However, the reform era experienced a slow growth of deposit, 6.8 per cent during 1990-91 to 1995-96 while the

same was 9.8 per cent during 1980-81 to 1989-90 (base1981-82 = 100)

3. **Portfolio choice:** In spite of deregulation of interest rates and reduction in Cash Reserve Ratio (CRR) and Statuary Liquidity Ratio (SLR) requirements the trend in credit deployment and investment shows that asset portfolio of banks was not in favour of loans. The rate of growth of real credit has significantly declined to 4.2 per cent during 1990-96 compared to the average growth rate of 8.7 per cent during 1980-90. However, there was a fluctuation in the rate of growth of credit in 1994-95 and 1995-96 particularly experienced a negative growth. The decline in the rate of growth of credit has occurred concurrently with an increase in the rate of growth of investment in government securities and an increase in the proportion of government investment in major earning assets.

It is important to note that increase in investment in the post reform period took place in the context of declining SLR requirements. This has resulted in excess holding of government securities above the SLR requirements by the commercial banks. The study however, showed that the industry and trade suffered from lack of availability of credit. (Caprio et. al., 1997).

4. **Profitability :** The trends in profitability during post reform era demonstrate a significant variation in all banks except private banks measured in terms of return to working fund. The gross profit increased from 0.94 per cent in 1992-93 to 1.58 per cent in 1997-98, and net profit from a negative figure of (–) 0.99 per cent to 0.77 per cent during the same period. The number of loss making banks reduced from 8 in 1993-94 to 3 in 1996-97. The details discussion has been made in the Chapter – 5.

5. **Capital adequacy :** The target set by RBI, for attaining BIS norms of an 8 per cent of risk weighted capital to assets ratio had nearly been achieved. As on 1996-97, 25 out of 27 PSBs have attained BIS a norm that indicates an improvement in the soundness of Indian banking sector. This improvement may be due to compromise on their lending activities. (Sen and Vaidya, 1999).

6. **Non - performing assets :** The average percentage of NPAs to total advances for 27 PSBs declined from 23.2 per cent in

1992-93 to 16.0 per cent in 1997-98 . The number of banks above 20 per cent gross NPA has also reduced from 16 in 1993-94 to 10 in 1995-96. According to RBI estimates, priority sector NPAs to total NPAs reduced from 50.0 per cent in 1994-95 to 46.4 per cent in 1997-98. This drastic reduction of NPAs may be due to liberal definitions in India compared to international standards as India recognises NPAs only after 180 days of default, while the international norms is 90 days to 45 days. (Details in Chapter-7).

The foregoing discussion revealed a positive impact of the first phase of reform on the performance and the soundness of Indian banking. Banks have been recapitalised and became healthier than pre-reform era. It has been discerned that the rate of deposit mobilisation has reduced over the years. The compulsory capture of bank deposits by the government through CRR and SLR has also been reduced. There has been a significant deregulation of interest rate. Indian banking system attempted to improve the quality of services through technology up-gradation. In spite of expansion of private and foreign banks, the oligopolistic dominance of PSBs still continues (Tarapure, 1999) and non-performing assets continue to drug down banks profitability. The indicators measuring profitability and efficiency of PSBs do not conclusively suggest an improvement in their performance. There exists a significant difference in profitability between public sector banks, private sector banks and foreign banks. Further, there had not been much progress in expediting the debt recovery. Similarly, further reform measures are required on directed credit that has been imposed over the year on financial institutions' lending to agriculture and small sector as well as concessional credit, i.e., at the reduced rate of interest, to specified sector. Concessional credit is not a cost-effective method of poverty alleviation. There had been signs of portfolio shift of banks from credit to risk-less government Securities.

The banks had attained BIS norms of capital adequacy which is neutralised by the existence of high volume of NPAs, periodic injection of capital by the Government. It is in this context argued that a proactive policy will only ensure the corrective measures of the problem. In this respect Narasimham committee recommended a package of measures in October 1998 (GOI). Major emphasis is on increase in minimum capital adequacy ratio, recognition of market risks; tighter asset classification, income recognition and provisioning norms; introduction of Asset Liability Management system and for further enhancing the transparency and disclosure practices etc.

The Recommendation of Narasimham Committee (1998) and the Level of Implementation by RBI

The implementation of the recommendations of Narasimham Committee (1998) has been summarized in the following tabular form:

Recommendations	*Decisions Announced*
(i) 5 per cent weight for market risk for Government approved securities.	To be implemented in phase: 2.5 per cent risk weight by the year ending March 31, 2000. Balance of 2.5 per cent will be announced later. An additional risk weight (of 20 per cent) is proposed for securities of government undertakings that do not form part of the approved market-borrowing programme with effect from the financial year 2000-2001. This will be implemented in the case of outstanding stock of such securities as on March 31, 2000, in two phases at the rate of 10 per cent each in 2001-2002 and 2002-2003.
(ii) The risk weight for Government guaranteed advances to be the same as for other advances.	Risk weights will be assigned for government guaranteed advances sanctioned from April 1,1999 as under: Against the guarantee of the: (a) Central Government : 0 per cent (b) State Governments : 0 per cent (c) State Governments who have remained in default as on March 31, 2000 in case where the guarantee has been involved : 20 per cent

(Contd. Table)

Recommendations	*Decisions Announced*
	(d) State Governments who continued to be in default after March 31, 2001 in respect of such invoked guarantees : 100 per cent
(iii) Foreign exchange open position limit to carry 100 per cent risk weight.	To be implemented from the current financial year ending March 31, 1999.
(iv) A minimum target of 9 per cent CAR to be achieved in the year 2000 and 10 per cent by 2002	Banks should achieve a minimum CAR of 9 per cent on March 31, 2000. Decision about further enhancement of CRAR will be announced later.
(v) An asset is classified as doubtful if it is in the sub-standard category for 18 months in the first instance and eventually for 12 months and loss if it has been so identified but not written off.	An asset will be treated as doubtful. If it has remained in sub-standard category for 18 months instead of 24 months, by March 31, 2001. Banks may make provisions therefore, in two phases as under : As on March 31, 2001 : Provisioning of not less than 50 per cent on the assets which have become doubtful on account of the new norms, i.e., reduction of the period from 24 months to 18 months. As on March 31, 2002 : Balance 50 per cent of the provisions should be made in addition to the provisions needed as on March 31, 2002. The proposal to introduce the norm of 12 months will be announced later.

(Contd.)

(Contd. Table)

Recommendations	*Decisions Announced*
vi) a) The Government guaranteed advances which have turned sticky to be classified as NPAs.	The state Government guaranteed advances in respect of which guarantee has been invoked and the concerned Government has remained in default for more than two quarters are to be classified as NPAs with effect from April 1, 2000.
(b) Income recognition, asset classification and provisioning norms should apply to Government guaranteed advances in the same manner as for any other advances.	Provisions on these advances should be made over a period of 4 years as detailed below : Provisions against existing/old state Government guaranteed advances where guarantee has been invoked and the concerned State Government has remained in default for more than two quarters are to be made during the next four years from the year ending March 31, 2000 to March 31, 2003 with a minimum of 25 per cent, each year.
(vii) A general provision of 1 per cent on standard assets be introduced.	To start with, banks should make a general provision of a minimum of 0.25 per cent for the year ending March 31, 2000. The decision to raise further the provisioning requirement on standard assets would be announced in due course.

(Contd.)

(Contd. Table)

	Recommendations	Decisions Announced
(viii)	Banks and financial institutions should avoid the practice of 'ever greening'.	The Reserve Bank reiterates that banks and financial Institutions should adhere to the prudential norms on assets classification, provisioning, etc., and avoid the practice of "ever greening".
(ix)	Any effort at financial restructuring must go hand in hand with operational restructuring. With the cleaning up of the balance sheet, simultaneously steps to be taken to prevent/limit re-emergence of new NPAs.	The banks are advised to take effective steps for reduction of NPAs and also put in place risk management systems and practices to prevent re emergence of fresh NPAs.
(x)	To enable banks in difficulties to issue bonds for Tier II capital. Government will need to guarantee these instruments, which would then make them eligible for SLR investment.	Public Sector Banks are encouraged to raise their Tier II Capital. Government guarantee to these instruments does not seem appropriate.
(xi)	To enable banks in difficulties to issue bonds for Tier II capital. Government will need to guarantee these instruments, which would then make them eligible for SLR investment.	Banks have already been advised to put in place a formal Asset-Liability Management (ALM) system with effect from April 1, 1999. Instructions on further disclosures will be issued in due course.
(xii)	There is a need for disclosure in a phased manner of the maturity pattern of assets and liabilities, movements in provision account and NPAs.	Banks are advised to strictly comply with instructions which are already in place.
(xiii)	Concentration ratios need to be indicated in respect of bank's	Arrangement should be put in place for regular

(Contd. Table)

	Recommendations	*Decisions Announced*
	estate. These exposure norms need to be carefully monitored.	
(xiv)	Banks should bring out revised operational manuals and update them regularly.	Banks should ensure a loan review mechanism for larger advances soon after its sanction and continuously monitor the weaknesses developing in the accounts for initiating corrective measures in time.
(xv)	There is need to institute an independent loan review mechanism especially for large borrower accounts and to identify potential NPAs.	Banks should ensure a loan mechanism for larger advances after its sanction and continuously monitor the weaknesses developing in the accounts for initiating corrective measures in time.

Impact of Second Phase of Reforms

Table 9 summarises the Performances of banks during the second phase of the reform. The share of rural bank office declined to 49.4 per cent in 2000-01. The credit deposit ratio witnessed slight improvement from 55.5 per cent in 1998-99 to 58.5 per cent in 2000-01. The target of attaining BIS norms for capital adequacy of 9 per cent attained by 22 banks. The per cent of NPAs to total advances declined to 12.4 in 2000-01 from 15.9 per cent in 1998-99.

TABLE - 9
PERFORMANCE OF BANKS DURING SECOND PHASE OF REFORMS (1998- 2001)

Sl. No.	*Performance indicators*	*1998-99*	*1999-2000*	*2000-2001*
1	Population per bank office (000)	15	15	15
2	Percentage share of rural bank offices	50.5	49.9	49.4
3	Bank deposit as per cent of GDP at current prices	43.7	50.3	53.5
4	Credit Deposit ratios (percentage)	55.5	57.1	58.5
5	No. of banks attaining capital adequacy ratio	–	22	22
6	Percentage of NPAs to total advances	15.9	14.0	12.4
7	No. of banks with gross NPA more than 20 per cent	–	Nil	Nil
8	Percentage of net NPA to total assets	3.1	2.9	2.6
9	No. of banks with net NPA more than 20 per cent.	1	Nil	Nil
10	Gross Profit as per cent of total assets	1.37	1.46	1.34
11	Operating profit/staff express	0.42	0.57	0.66
12	Intermediation Cost as per cent of total asset	2.66	2.53	2.72
13	Provisions & contingencies as per cent total assets	2.66	2.52	2.49
14	Percentage variation of bank credit over previous yrs.	13.0	16.5	15.3
15	Percentage variation of deposit over previous year	16.3	13.9	14.9

Source : Computed from Indian Banks' Association, Performance Highlight of Banks, various issues and Report on Trend & Progress of Indian Banking, various issues.

It has been felt further the need of broad-based measures for accelerating the momentum of progress of banking sector. As a result, Verma Committee 1999 (third committee in the banking reform trilogy) was appointed, under the chairmanship of M.S. Verma. The committee identified three, viz. Indian Banks, United Commercial Banks and Union Banks of India out of 27 PSBs are weak on the basis of :

(1) Accumulated losses and net NPAs exceed the net worth of banks.

(2) Negative operating profits for three consecutive years.

3

Public Sector Banks (PSBs) : Growth and Development

Introduction

On the eve of independence, commercial banks were mostly concentrated in major cities and provincial headquarters (Thingalaya, 1987). The uniform operation of banks started only when planning era was ushered in the fifties. Following the nationalisation of many European Central Bank after the Second World War, the RBI was formed as bankers bank under the Banking Companies Act in 1949 (Chandrasekhar, 1989)[2]. It is a landmark in the history of banking legislation in India, which provided the RBI with a number of controlling, powers for regulating the banking business in the country.

The All India Rural Credit Survey Committee (1954)[3] recommended the creation of one strong integrated state sponsored and state partnered commercial banking institution with an effective machinery of branches spread across the country. In pursuance of its recommendations, the Imperial Bank of India, was nationalised and renamed as State Bank of India (SBI) from July 1, 1955. The nationalisation of Imperial Bank of India paved the way of the entry of PSBs into commercial banks (Rangaswamy, 1985)[4]. Further, for strengthening the Public Sector Banking structure, eight small associated banks were taken over by the State Bank of India as its subsidiaries under of the SBI Act 1959 (Chandrasekhar, 1987)[5]. After independence, some serious gap existed in the development of banks, although it made considerable progress both in the functional and geographical coverage. In order to bring about a far reaching changes in concept and working of banks in the country, the scheme of social control over banks was introduced with a view to ensure equitable and purposeful distribution of credit within the economic sectors. The government felt that the social control experiment failed to achieve the social goals and objectives (Chandrasekar; 1987)[6].

On July 19,1969 the Indira Gandhi Government nationalised 14 major banks each with a deposit of Rs. 50 crore and above. One of the main objectives of bank nationalisation was to extend credit facilities to all segments of the economy and also mitigate regional imbalance through proper supply credit requirements. The banks in collaborations with central and state government were authorised to sponsor Regional Rural Banks (RRBs) in different parts of the country. The Government of India promoted regional banks through the RRBs Act 1976.[7] Their equity is held by the central government, concerned state bank and sponsor bank in the proportion of 50:15:35. There were 196 RRBs with over 14000 branches by 2003. (Their deposits rose from Rs. 4035 crore in 1990-91 to Rs. 48,346 crore in 2003, while their credit disbursal went up only half as rapidly, from Rs. 3,378 crore to Rs. 21,773 crore in the same period. Despite their strong rural branch structure, accounting for 30 per cent of all rural branches of SCBs, their share in the total agriculture credit at national level has remained at 8 to 9 per cent right from their inception). However, on 15 April 1980, another 6 commercial banks each with a deposit of Rs 200 crores and above were nationalised. Thus, from 1980 onwards, the government came to own 27 PSBs consisting of 19 nationalised Banks and SBI along with seven subsidiaries (Chadha, 1994)[8].

TABLE – 1
BRANCH EXPANSION OF PUBLIC SECTOR BANKS VIS-A-VIS OTHER BANKS DURING PRE AND POST REFORM PERIOD

(Figures in number)

Year	Public Sector Banks			Private Banks			Foreign Banks	Total
	SBI groups	NBs	Total	Old	New	Total		
1969	2462	4134	7015	900	–	900	130	8045
	(30.60)	(51.39)	(87.19)	(11.18)		(11.18)	(1.61)	(100)
1980-81	17308	25309	30583	4723	–	4723	136	35442
	(84.83)	(71.41)	(86.29)	(13.32)	–	(13.32)	(0.38)	(100)
1985-86	10512	24434	34946	4614	–	4614	136	19696
	(26.55)	(61.55)	(77.95)	(11.62)	–	(11.62)	(0.34)	(100)
1986-87	10815	25248	36063	4298	–	4298	136	40497
	(26.70)	(62.35)	(89.05)	(10.61)	–	(10.61)	(0.34)	(100)
1987-88	10836	25618	36454	4185	–	4185	136	40775
	(26.58)	(62.82)	(89.40)	(10.26)	–	(10.26)	(0.33)	(100)
1988-89	11058	26404	37592	4175	–	4175	136	41803
	(26.45)	(63.16)	(89.68)	(9.98)	–	(9.98)	(0.33)	(100)
1989-90	11559	27574	39133	4254	–	4254	136	43523
	(26.56)	(63.35)	(89.91)	(9.77)	–	(9.77)	(0.31)	(100)
1990-91	11887	29046	40933	3825	–	3825	138	44869
	(26.48)	(64.70)	(91.17)	(8.52)	–	(8.52)	(0.30)	(100)

(Contd.)

(Contd. Table 1)

Year	Public Sector Banks			Private Banks			Foreign Banks	Total
	SBI groups	NBs	Total	Old	New	Total		
1991-92	12400	29955	42355	3803	–	3803	140	46299
	(26.8)	(64.7)	(91.5)	(8.2)	–	(8.2)	(0.3)	(100)
1992-93	12586	3031	42901	3867	–	3867	140	46909
	(26.8)	(64.6)	(91.5)	(8.2)	–	(8.2)	(0.3)	(100)
1993-94	12789	30472	43338	3993	–	3993	144	47477
	(26.9)	(64.2)	(9193)	(8.4)	–	(8.4)	(0.3)	(100)
1994-95	12875	30880	43755	4087	–	4087	151	47994
	(26.8)	(64.3)	(91.2)	(8.5)	–	(8.5)	(0.3)	(100)
1995-96	12992	31342	44334	4233	82	4316	160	48810
	(26.6)	(64.2)	(90.8)	(8.7)	(0.2)	(8.8)	(0.3)	(100)
1996-97	13112	31644	44756	4334	128	4462	176	49394
	(26.5)	(64.1)	(90.6)	(8.8)	(0.3)	(9.0)	(0.4)	(100)
1997-98	13109	31904	45013	4436	227	4793	182	49909
	(26.3)	(63.9)	(90.2)	(8.8)	(0.5)	(9.4)	(0.3)	(100)
1998-99	13359	32503	45860	4463	329	4792	172	50824
	(26.3)	(63.8)	(90.2)	(8.8)	(0.6)	(9.4)	(0.3)	(100)
1999-00	13482	32803	46285	4342	460	4802	181	51268
	(26.3)	(64.0)	(90.3)	(8.5)	(0.9)	(9.4)	(0.4)	(100)
2000-01	13561	32757	46318	4424	809	5233	190	51741
	(26.5)	(63.3)	(89.5)	(8.6)	(1.6)	(10.1)	(0.4)	(100)

- *NBs—Nationalised Banks.*

Note : Figures in the parenthesis indicate percentage of branches to total branches of Commercial banks

Source: IBA Bulletins, Indian Banks Associations, Performance Highlight of Banks, various issues. *CIER's Industrial Data Book, 1998, Centre for Industrial and Economic Research. pp. 819, Table – 122, 40.*

Banking Scenario During Post Nationalisation Era

During post nationalisation era there has been a significant progress in the expansion of branch network across the country. With a view to assess the pace of growth of PSBs particularly, we have used different parameters discussed here under. The growth rate has been compared during pre and post reform period pertaining to 10 years duration of each.

1. **Branch Expansion:** The country witnessed branch expansion both in PSBs and private banks in absolute term during pre reform, i.e., 1980-91. The percentage share of PSBs to total branches had been increased from 86.3 per cent in 1980-81 to 91.2 per cent in 1990-91. While, the same in private banks has slipped from 71.4 per cent to 64.7 per cent and for foreign banks from 0.38 per cent to 0.30 per cent during the period under consideration. However, post reform period witnessed a reverse scenario in terms of percentage share of each bank group to total branches of all categories of banks. The percentage share of PSBs to total branches of SCBs has reduced from 91.5 per cent in 1991-92 to 89.5 per cent in 2000-2001 while the private and foreign banks have captured such lost ground of PSBs during the period under consideration. The branch expansion during pre and post reform periods is presented in table – 1.

The bank group wise growth has been demonstrated in the following table :

GROWTH OF BANK OFFICES (1980 – 2001)

Period	*Rates*	*SBI group*	*Nationalised Banks*	*PSB as a whole*	*Private Sector Banks*	*Foreign Banks*	*All Banks*
Pre	b	535.23	912.69	982.746	-79.797	0.108	903.14
Reform	Cgr.	4.578	6.272	2.71	-0.186	0.0797	2.241
Post	b	122.116	251.892	456.053	153.736	146.616	614.10
Reform	Cgr.	0.938	0.872	1.025	3.519	2.117	1.25

$$\text{Compound growth rate (cgr)} = \frac{b}{\text{Harmonic Mean (H.M.) of y}} \times 100$$

$$= \frac{b}{N/\Sigma^{1}/_{y}} \times 100$$

Source : Self calculated on the basis table –1.

A comparison of growth of bank branches between pre and post reform era can be made by linear growth rate (b) as well as compound growth rate (cgr)*. For this we have assumed the linear regression line, y = a + bt (where y = total no. of branches, t = year, a = constant, b =(dy/dt)= linear growth rate) (origin at 1980-81 and 1991-92 in the pre and post reform era respectively).

It is revealed that during post reform period PSBs experienced a lower growth of branch expansion than that of pre-reform period. However, there has been a spectacular jump in the growth of private sector bank branches, which attained positive growth rate surpassing the negative growth rate during pre-reform era. The nationalised banks, on the other hand, witnessed a higher growth rate (b = 912.69, Cgr = 6.27 and b = 456.05, Cgr = 1.02 in pre & post reform era respectively). SBI group, however, has lost their credibility in branch expansion during the post reform period. Thus, the analyses revealed that, banks of new generation; private banks, and foreign banks in particular are gradually entering into the business dominated by PSBs earlier.

Population groupwise branch expansion

The population group-wise number of bank offices show that the percentage share of rural branches during the reform era have significantly been declined from 58 per cent in 1991 to 49.4 per cent in 2001 while semi-urban, urban and metropolitan areas have witnessed an increasing trend during the same period under consideration. Table-2 presents the Population groupwise number of offices. This can further be verified by the analysis of co-efficient of variation (cv*) during pre and post reform period. The results of CV summarised as under –

ANALYSIS OF CO-EFFICIENT OF VARIATION (CV)

Period	*Rural*	*Semi-urban*	*Urban*	*Metropolitan*	*All total*
Pre-reform 1981-90	1.75	8.37	13.04	8.73	13.91
Post-reform 1991-01	3.51	9.45	7.59	15.45	2.91

Source : Self calculated on the basis of data presented on Table – 3.

* $cv = \sigma/\mu \times 100$

where, σ = standard deviation, μ = mean.

TABLE – 2
POPULATION GROUP WISE GROWTH OF NUMBER OF BANK OFFICES SINCE NATIONALISATION

Year	Number of Offices				
	Rural	*Semi-urban*	*Urban*	*Metropolitan*	*Total*
Dec. 1969	1443 (17.6)	3337 (40.8)	1911(23.3)	1496(18.3)	8187
Dec. 1972	5274 (36.0)	4607 (31.4)	2637(18.0)	2132(14.6)	14650
Dec. 1973	6024 (36.5)	5012 (30.4)	2983(18.1)	2484(15.1)	16503
Dec. 1974	6447 (35.9)	5462 (30.5)	3332(18.6)	2696(15.0)	17937
Dec. 1975	7112 (35.5)	6156 (30.7)	3779(18.8)	3002(15.0)	20049
Dec. 1976	8588 (36.6)	7133 (30.4)	4413(18.8)	3351(143)	2348 5
Dec. 1977	10856 (40.3)	7702 (28.6)	4769(17.7)	3631(13.5)	26958
Dec. 1978	12534 (42.5)	8019 (27.2)	5037(17.1)	3886(13.2)	229476
Dec. 1979	14171 (44.0)	8295 (25.7)	5494(17.1)	4259(13.2)	322119
Dec. 1980	16111 (46.9)	8678 (25.2)	5462(15.9)	4134(12.0)	34385
Dec. 1981	19453 (51.2)	8718 (22.9)	5622(14.5)	4225(11.1)	38018
Dec. 1982	21626 (53.0)	8921 (21.9)	5511(13.5)	4735(11.6)	40793
Dec. 1983	23782 (52.4)	10115 (22.3)	6649(14.7)	4839(10.7)	45385
Dec. 1984	25541 (52.9)	10331 (21.4)	7347(15.2)	5101(10.6)	48320
Dec. 1985	29408 (54.6)	10745 (19.9)	8117(15.1)	5629(10.4)	53899
Dec. 1986	29700 (55.7)	10658 (20.0)	7649(14.3)	5357(10.0)	53364
Dec. 1987	30585 (56.2)	10731 (19.7)	7722(14.2)	5393(9.9)	54431
Dec. 1988	31641 (56.2)	11179 (19.9)	7929(14.1)	5533(9.8)	56282
Dec. 1989	33572 (57.3)	11263 (19.2)	8082(13.8)	5651(9.6)	58685
Dec. 1990	34867 (58.1)	11309 (18.9)	8062(13.5)	5656(9.4)	59897

(Contd. Table 2)

Year	*Number of Offices*				
	Rural	*Semi-urban*	*Urban*	*Metropolitan*	*Total*
Dec. 1991	35216 (58.0)	11379(18.6)	8233(13.6)	5769(9.5)	60597
Dec. 1992	35218 (58.0)	11397 (18.6)	8285(13.7)	5790(9.5)	60690
Dec. 1993	35301 (57.0)	11417 (18.6)	8628(14.1)	5889(9.6)	61235
Dec. 1994	35379 (57.2)	11720 (18.9)	8824(14.3)	5929(9.6)	61852
Dec. 1995	35008 (56.2)	12270 (19.7)	8982(14.4)	6004(9.6)	62264
Dec. 1996	33092 (52.7)	13399 (21.3)	9025(14.4)	7333(11.7)	62949
Dec. 1997	33008 (52.0)	13641 (21.5)	9298(14.6)	7587(11.9)	63534
Dec. 1998	32890 (51.2)	13876 (21.6)	9637(15.0)	7864(12.2)	64267
Dec. 1999	32856 (50.5)	14140 (21.7)	9971 (15.3)	8151(12.5)	65118
Dec. 2000	32719 (49.9)	14301 (21.8)	10176 (15.5)	8385(12.7)	655.21
Dec. 2001	32533 (49.4)	14508 (22.0)	10354 (15.7)	8513(12.9)	65908

Figures in the parentheses indicate percentage to total offices.

TABLE – 3
STAFFS IN PUBLIC SECTOR BANKS VIS-À-VIS OTHER BANKS

(In number)

Sl. No.	Category of banks	1991-92	1992-93	1993-94	1994-95	1995-96	1996-97	1997-98	1998-99	1999-00	2000-01
1	Public Sector Banks	876339	884265	891785	894791	894889	888415	887403	883189	873569	797811
	(26 banks)	(93.0)	(93.0)	(93.0)	(92.9)	(92.5)	(92.2)	(92.0)	(91.9)	(91.9)	(90.5)
(a)	SBI group	302804	304811	309106	313003	314252	318307	321162	319874	315548	291199
	(7 banks)	(32.1)	(32.0)	(32.2)	(32.5)	(32.5)	(33.0)	(33.3)	(33.3)	(33.2)	(33.0)
(b)	Nationalised Banks	573535	579454	582679	581788	580637	570108	566241	563315	558021	506612
	(19 banks)	(60.9)	(61.0)	(60.8)	(60.4)	(60.0)	(59.0)	(58.7)	(58.6)	(58.7)	(57.5)
2	Private Sector	52719	53714	54133	54858	58872	60921	62209	63355	63877	69073
	Banks (35 banks)	(5.6)	(5.6)	(5.6)	(5.7)	(6.1)	(6.3)	(6.4)	(6.6)	(6.7)	(7.8)
(a)	Old Private Banks	52711	53705	54124	54849	57241	58464	58504	58565	56533	56819
		(5.6)	(5.7)	(5.6)	(5.7)	(5.9)	(6.1)	(6.0)	(6.1)	(5.9)	(6.4)
(b)	New Private Banks	-	-	-	-	1620	2457	3705	4790	7344	12254
						(0.2)	(0.3)	(0.4)	(0.5)	(0.8)	(0.4)
3	Foreign Banks	13126	13435	13051	13262	13518	13915	14893	14846	13509	14205
	(29 banks)	(1.4)	(1.4)	(1.4)	(1.4)	(1.4)	(1.4)	(1.5)	(1.5)	(1.4)	(1.6)
	Total	942184	951414	958969	962911	967279	963251	964505	61390	950955	881089
		(100)	(100)	(100)	(100)	(100)	(100)	(100)	(100)	(100)	(100)

Figure in the brackets indicate percentage to total staffs of commercial banks

- not available.

Source : Indian Banks Association (IBA), Performance Highlights of Banks, various issues.

The analysis revealed that the total branch expansion during post reform period was more or less uniform and remained consistent (**cv** = 2.91) than that of pre-reform (**cv** = 13.91) period. However, interestingly the **coefficient of variation** turned higher in post-reform era than that of pre-reform period in the rural areas. The reason may be attributed to closure of unprofitable bank branches, which accounted 49.4 per cent of total branch offices in March 2001 sliding from 58 per cent in March 1991. This may be due to stringent rules imposed on banks during post-reform era consequent upon the implementation of Narasimham Committee recommendations.

Growth of Bank Employees

The number of employees of PSBs has been reduced during the post- reform era (Table-3). The total staff in absolute number and percentage term reduced from 876339 in 1991-92 to 797811 in 2000-2001 and from 93 per cent in 1991-92 to 90.5 per cent in 2000-2001 respectively. While of private banks and foreign banks have generated more employment during post- reform era. The staff recruitment policy as recommended by Narasimham Committee thus had very little impact on PSBs in particular. This may be due to computerisation of bank offices over the years during post-reform period.

Growth of Deposit Mobilisation

The resource mobilisation is an integral part of banking activity. The basic principle of branch expansion is to tap deposit and culminate savings habit among the community. Further, tapping of potential savings and marshalling them for strategic uses for productive purposes in particular is the main objective. As a result, various schemes were launched over the years. Under 20-point programme (1975) the government directed the banks to make all possible efforts to access to new deposits that can only expedite the pace of lending activities.

There has been a substantial rise of bank deposits since nationalisation. The total deposits which was Rs 4822 crores in December 1969 rose to Rs 42584 crores in 1980-81 and further increased to Rs 10,25,975 crores in 2000-2001 recording a 212 fold increase since nationalisation. Table – 4A. and 4B. delineate the bank groupwise deposit mobilisation in pre-reform period (1980-91) and post-reform (1991-2000) period respectively.

TABLE – 4A
GROWTH OF BANK DEPOSIT IN THE PRE REFORM ERA (1980-81 TO 1990-91)

(Amount Rs. in crores)

Year	Public Sector Banks (Rs. in crores) SBI group	Nationlised Banks	Total	Private Sector Banks	Foreign Banks (Crores)	Total Amount (Crores)	Increase over Previous year (percentage)	Deposit per Offices (Rs. in crore)	Per capita bank deposit (in Rs.)
1980-81	12179	28043	40222	1475	888	42584	-	1.20	452
	(28.6)	(65.6)	(94.5)	(3.5)	(2.1)	(100)			
1981-82	15021	33752	48773	1797	914	51484	20.8	1.31	560
	(29.2)	(65.6)	(94.7)	(3.5)	(1.8)	(100)			
1982-83	17607	3898	56605	2109	1073	59787	16.1	1.42	712
	(29.4)	(65.2)	(94.7)	(3.5)	(1.8)	(100)			
1983-84	21566	45713	67279	2530	1296	71099	18.9	1.47	878
	(30.3)	(64.3)	(94.6)	(3.5)	(1.9)	(100)			
1984-85	25077	54220	79297	3059	1435	83791	17.9	1.50	1026
	(29.9)	(64.7)	(94.6)	(3.6)	(1.8)	(100)			
1985-86	29796	64503	94299	3604	1781	99684	19.0	2.51	1198
	(29.9)	(64.7)	(94.6)	(3.6)	(1.8)	(100)			
1986-87	34311	77268	111579	4298	2278	118155	18.5	2.92	1374
	(29.0)	(65.4)	(94.4)	(3.6)	(2.0)	(100)			
1987-88	38382	90005	128387	10197	2598	141182	19.5	3.46	1586
	(27.2)	(63.7)	(90.9)	(7.2)	(1.8)	(100)			
1988-89	48417	108712	157129	5861	4073	167063	18.3	4.00	1821
	(29.0)	(65.0)	(94.0)	(3.5)	(2.4)	(100)			
1989-90	56825	128999	185824	6969	5667	198460	18.8	4.56	2075
	(28.6)	(65.0)	(93.6)	(3.5)	(2.9)	(100)			
1990-91	65494	145317	210811	8388	7472	226671	14.2	5.05	2360
	(28.9)	(64.1)	(93.0)	(3.7)	(3.3)	(100)			

Figures in the parentheses indicate percentage to total

Source : Indian Banks Association (IBA); IBA Bulletin, various special issues.

TABLE – 4B

BANKS GROUPWISE GROWTH OF BANK DEPOSITS IN THE POST REFORM PERIOD (1991-92 TO 2000-2001)

(Amount Rs. in crores)

Year	*Public Sector Banks (in crores)* *SBI group*	*Nationalised Banks*	*Total*	*Private Sector Banks (in crores)*	*Foreign Banks (in crores)*	*Total Amount (in crores)*	*Increase over Previous Year*	*Deposits per Office (in crores)*
1991-92	70403 (29.1)	142757 (59.0)	213160 (88.0)	12082 (5.0)	16898 (7.0)	242140 (100)	16.7	5.99
1992-93	81009 (28.8)	163895 (58.3)	244904 (87.2)	15231 (5.4)	2.875 (7.4)	281010 (100)	16.1	6.97
1993-94	95521 (28.9)	189338 (57.2)	284859 (86.1)	19984 (6.0)	25897 (7.8)	330740 (100)	17.6	6.97
1994-95	107910 (28.2)	221018 (57.7)	328928 (85.8)	26257 (6.9)	28034 (7.3)	383219 (100)	15.8	7.98
1995-96	121938 (28.0)	246410 (56.7)	368348 (84.7)	30069 (8.3)	30630 (7.0)	429047 (100)	12.0	8.79
1996-97	140861 (27.4)	285506 (55.4)	426367 (82.8)	51039 (9.9)	37394 (7.3)	514800 (100)	19.9	10.42
1997-98	166060 (26.9)	338004 (54.8)	504064 (81.7)	69516 (11.3)	43447 (7.0)	617027 (100)	19.8	12.36
1998-99	210498 (28.6)	396770 (53.8)	607268 (82.4)	83252 (11.3)	46476 (6.3)	736996 (100)	19.4	14.50
1999-00	247106 (28.4)	458938 (52.8)	706043 (81.3)	113471 (13.1)	49324 (5.7)	868838 (100)	17.9	16.94
2000-01	304185 (29.0)	526129 (51.3)	830314 (80.9)	136470 (13.3)	59190 (5.8)	1025975 (100)	18.1	19.83

Figures in the parenthesis indicate percentage to total

Source : Indian Banks Association (IBA); IBA Bulletin, various special issues.

TABLE - 5
POPULATION GROUPWISE GROWTH OF BANK DEPOSITS SINCE NATIONALISATION

(Amount Rs. in crores)

Year	*Rural*	*Semi-urban*	*Urban*	*Metropolitan*	*Total*
June 1969	145(3.1)	1024(20.0)	1209(25.9)	2287(49.0)	4665
June 1974	836(7.8)	2437(22.6)	2665(24.8)	4818(44.8)	10756
June 1979	3053(10.6)	6443(22.5)	7134(24.9)	12054 (42.0)	28684
June 1984	9243(14.4)	13342(20.7)	26693(26.0)	25038(38.9)	74316
June 1985	10411(13.4)	16578(21.5)	20416(26.3)	30187(38.8)	77772
June 1986	12809(13.9)	19512(21.1)	23892(25.7)	36219(39.3)	92432
June 1987	15522(14.3)	23032(21.3)	28208(26.0)	41582(38.4)	108344
June 1988	19215(15.1)	27632(21.6)	32684(25.6)	48062(37.7)	127593
June 1989	22046(15.0)	31432(21.4)	36841(25.0)	56713(38.6)	147032
June 1990	27608(15.4)	37979(21.1)	45416(24.6)	71956(38.9)	182959
Compound Growth rate (Cgr)	**28.56**	**18.67**	**18.63**	**17.41**	**18.71**
March 1991	33163 (15.1)	43937 (20.0)	51411 (23.4)	91026 (41.5)	219539
March 1992	35058 (15.0)	45869 (19.7)	53892 (23.1)	98266 (42.2)	233086
March 1993	40672 (14.8)	52436 (19.1)	62389 (22.8)	118569(43.3)	274068
March 1994	47776 (15.0)	61814 (19.4)	73221 (23.0)	135106(42.5)	317918
March 1995	57399 (15.3)	74223 (19.7)	88715 (23.6)	155525(41.4)	375864
March 1996	61106 (14.3)	82425 (19.3)	94673 (22.2)	187870(44.1)	426073
March 1997	72511 (14.7)	96657 (19.6)	110292 (22.4)	212766(43.2)	492227
March 1998	86484 (14.6)	114483(19.3)	133605 (22.6)	257497(43.5)	592068
March 1999	102602(14.6)	136681(19.5)	160050 (22.8)	302537(43.1)	701871
March 2000	102447(14.7)	160060(19.5)	189186 (23.0)	352440(42.9)	822133
March 2001	139427(14.7)	186733(19.6)	217862 (22.9)	406683(42.8)	950705
Compound Growth rate (Cgr)	**19.94**	**18.38**	**17.52**	**20.19**	**18.92**

Figures in the bracket indicate percentage to total deposit

Source : Reserve Bank of India, Banking statistics (BSR) various issues.

It has been observed that during 1980-81 to 1990-91, the deposits in all bank groups have increased in absolute term but the proportion of deposits of PSBs to total deposits of all bank groups have been declined. During the post-reform era however, the rate of downward trend in the share of PSBs was more significant than that of pre-reform era (Table-4A). The banks' performance in deposit per offices increased from 1.20 crores in 1980-81 to Rs. 5.99 crores in 1991-92 and further to Rs. 19.83 crores in 2000-2001.

A comparison of growth of bank deposit may be made by the analysis of linear growth rate (***b***) as well as compound growth rate (**cgr**) in the pre- and post-reform period. In this respect we have assumed the linear regression line $Y = a + bt$ where Y = total deposits corresponding to year 't' origin at 1980-81 and 1990-91 in the pre- and post-reform period respectively. The consistency of deposit mobilisation of the bank further been tested with the help of analysis of co-efficient of variation (**cv**). The bank groupwise of deposits growth rate and cv are obtained as under.

The analysis shows that the compound growth rate of deposits has considerably been declined during post reform period against the pre-reform era in case of all banks except private banks. The PSBs in this respect attained **cgr** at 17.74 post reform period against 20.621 during 1980-91. This may be due to the drastic reduction of SBI group's deposits (**cgr** 45.30 per cent in pre- to 19.49 per cent in post-reform) which contributed much in the reduction of growth rate of deposits of PSBs as a whole.

It has further been revealed that the PSBs witnessed comparatively more variation in deposits mobilisation during post-reform era ranging from 29.2 per cent to 43.5 per cent. In contrast, the foreign banks have failed to maintain the same pace of deposits mobilization during the post reform era. As a result, **cv** declined to 36.1 per cent against its peak of about 83 per cent during post-reform period. This requires further analysis to redress the causes underlying in the declined trend in the deposit mobilisation.

In order to analyse other dimensions of deposit mobilisation, we have considered parameters like population group-wise, account-wise and regionwise distribution of bank deposits described as under.

Population Groupwise Growth of Bank Deposits

The population groupwise growth of bank deposits has been analysed by compound growth rate (**cgr**). The accompanying Table-5 presents the

COEFFICIENT OF VARIATION & GROWTH RATE OF BANK DEPOSITS 1980-81 TO 2000-01

Period	*Value of*	*SBI group*	*Nationalised Banks*	*PSBs Total*	*Pvt. Banks*	*Foreign Banks*	*Total Banks*	*Deposit per office*
Pre reform	b	11710.29	10201.23	16883.80	755.29	626.17	18224.52	4.314
(1980-91)	Cgr	45.301	32.410	20.621	23.841	37.353	36.42	209.621
	CV	76.0	42.8	29.2	60.6	82.96	51.52	50.3
Post reform	b	24454.39	58022.79	6532.21	13783.38	4458.6	84775.33	1.495
(1991-2001)	Cgr	19.487	21.432	17.721	45.75	14.38	19.24	15.67
	CV	36.0	53.8	43.5	74.4	36.1	46.08	41.03

Source: Self calculated on the basis of Table 4A and Table 4B.

population groupwise growth of deposits. It is found that during June 1969-June 1990 the deposits both in absolute and percentage term was increased in rural and semi-urban. On the other hand, the deposits in the urban and metropolitan areas increased in absolute term only. While it has been reduced during the post-reform years in percentage term except in the metropolitan areas. **cgr** analysis reveals that growth of deposits in the rural areas has drastically been reduced in the post-reform era from 28.56 per cent in pre-reform to 16.94 per cent in post-reform period. The declining trend also continued both in the semi-urban and urban areas against slight improvement in **cgr** in the metropolitan areas. Hence, it could be inferred that banking reform had no significant impact on banks' attempt for capturing deposits and inculcating saving habit among the people in the rural areas in particular.

TABLE – 6
GROWTH OF BANK DEPOSIT BY ACCOUNTWISE

(Amount Rs. in crores)

Year	*Type of Deposit*			
	Current deposit	*Saving deposit*	*Term deposit*	*Total*
Dec. 1972	1770.9 (21.4)	2119.6 (25.6)	4381.7 (53.0)	8272.2
Dec. 1975	2453.2 (17.9)	3607.4 (26.3)	7650.1 (55.8)	13710.7
June 1979	4828.1 (16.8)	7840.7 (27.3)	16016.0 (55.9)	18684.8
Dec. 1980	5752.5 (15.5)	10605.7 (28.7)	20665.9 (55.9)	36997.0
June 1984	9700.2 (15.1)	19241.2 (29.9)	35374.0 (55.0)	64315.4
June 1985	12366 .0 (15.9)	22951.5 (29.5)	42449.1 (54.6)	77766.6
June 1986	13772.0 (14.9)	22176.4 (29.5)	51285.5 (55.6)	87233.9
June 1987	15534.4 (14.4)	30820.5 (28.5)	61989.1 (57.2)	81344.0
June 1988	17718.2 (13.9)	36486.1 (28.6)	73388.7 (57.5)	127593.0
June 1989	20331.7 (13.8)	41417.2 (28.8)	85282.1 (58.6)	147031.0
March 1990	26046.6 (15.2)	48497.4 (28.2)	97367.5 (56.6)	171911.4
March 1993	44538.4 (16.1)	66555.5 (24.1)	164765.6(59.7)	275850.4
March 1994	6268.3 (11.1)	6853.1 (12.1)	43552.7 (76.8)	56674.1
March 1995	62081.0 (16.4)	94573.0 (24.9)	222520.0 (58.7)	379174.0
March 1996	63656.0 (15.2)	103443.0 (24.1)	270904.0 (59.2)	438003.0
March 1997	72687.0 (14.5)	119415.0 (23.9)	308455.0 (61.6)	500556
March 1998	79770 (13.4)	142412 (23.9)	374286 (62.8)	596469
March 1999	91082 (13.0)	167019 (23.9)	440069 (63.0)	698169
March 2000	105458 (12.8)	199734 (24.3)	516228 (62.8)	821420
CV	**98.59**	**97.21**	**103.79**	**102.16**

Figures in the parentheses indicate percentage to total deposits.

Source : (I) RBI Bulletins, Surveys on compositions and ownership's of bank deposits. Various issues (II) RBI, Banking statistics, Basic Statistical Return. Various issues.

Accountwise Distribution of Deposits

The Table – 6 manifests distribution of deposits on the basis of accounts pertaining to the current account, savings account and term deposits during 1972 to 2000. The term deposit constitutes more than half of the total deposits. It has increased during post reform era and touched its peak 76.8 per cent in March 1994. However, more variation has been found in the term deposit that ensures more availability of stable funds for long-term investment financing.

Regionwise Distribution of Deposit

The Table – 7 depicts the region wise distribution of aggregate deposits. The regionwise analysis of aggregate deposit shows that western region comprising well-off states like, Gujarat, Maharashtra etc. owned lion share of deposits during December 1985 to March 2001 followed by the northern region, southern region, central, eastern and north-eastern region respectively. The northeast region, being backward, marked a very small share of aggregate deposits, which was 2.0 per cent in 1985 further reduced to 1.6 per cent in March 2001.

TABLE – 7
REGIONWISE DISTRIBUTION OF AGGREGATE DEPOSITS

(Amount Rs. in crores)

Region	*Dec. 1985*	*March 1993*	*March 1995*	*March 2001*
Northern region	10237 (23.0)	55916 (20.3)	108755 (22.1)	221464 (23.3)
North Eastern region	900 (2.0)	4169 (1.5)	8101 (1.6)	15367 (1.6)
Eastern region	7331 (16.5)	39344 (14.3)	65254 (13.3)	126205 (13.3)
Central region	7055 (15.9)	35704 (12.9)	66432 (13.5)	131063 (13.8)
Western region	9850 (22.2)	81141 (29.4)	135134 (27.5)	236184 (24.8)
Southern region	9033 (20.4)	59577 (21.6)	108552 (22.0)	220421 (23.2)
All India	**44414 (100)**	**275850 (100)**	**492227 (100)**	**950705 (100)**

Figures in the parentheses indicate the percentage share of total deposits.
Source :RBI, Banking Statistics, Basic Statistical Returns, various issues.

On the other hand a noteworthy performance among states is that, the PSBs in the well off states like Maharashtra, West Bengal, Gujarat, etc. have captured highest quantum of deposits both in the pre- and post-reform era. Further, the banks have mobilised relatively more deposits, almost double in the states like, Andhra Pradesh, Tamil Nadu, Delhi, Kerala and Punjab during March 1995-2001. The reason may be attributed to

TABLE – 8
STATEWISE DISTRIBUTION OF DEPOSITS OF COMMERCIAL BANKS

(Amount Rs. in crores)

Region/State	*June 69*	*June 79*	*Dec. 85*	*June 89*	*March 93*	*March 95*	*March 2001*
Andhra Pradesh	163 (3.5)	1451 (5.1)	2778 (6.2)	8039 (5.5)	14055 (4.8)	25850 (5.3)	54410 (9.8)
Arunachal Pradesh	-	-	41 (.03)	92 (0.1)	198 (.04)	394 (.08)	611 (0.1)
Assam	34 (0.7)	296 (1.0)	600 (1.4)	1645 (2.0)	2692 (0.5)	5084 (1.0)	9864 (1.7)
Andaman & Nicobar Islands	-	-	13 (.02)	-	80 (.01)	189 (.03)	385 (0.07)
Bihar	169 (3.6)	1177 (4.1)	2396 (5.8)	7155 (4.9)	11325 (4.5)	21222 (4.7)	26505 (4.8)
Chandigarh	-	-	361 (0.8)	-	2022 (0.6)	4061 (1.0)	7521 (1.4)
Delhi	-	-	4326 (4.7)	-	24151 (8.7)	48847 (9.9)	105382 (18.9)
Daman & Diu	-	-	-	-	81 (.01)	206 (1.1)	401 (.07)
Goa	-	-	255 (0.5)	1203 (0.8)	2030 (0.6)	3834 (1.7)	7289 (1.3)
Gujarat	40 (8.6)	2045 (7.1)	2458 (5.9)	9049 (6.1)	16421 (7.1)	29059 (5.8)	54436 (9.8)
Haryana	54 (1.2)	485 (1.7)	913 (2.0)	2934 (1.2)	5200 (1.9)	10355 (2.1)	19804 (3.6)
Himachal Pradesh	14 (0.3)	152 (0.5)	394 (0.8)	1048 (0.7)	1918 (0.4)	3676 (0.7)	7347 (1.3)
Jammu & Kashmir	29 (0.6)	262 (0.9)	525(1.3)	1386 (0.9)	2350 (0.6)	4717 (0.9)	10105 (1.8)
Karnataka	237 (5.1)	1440 (5.0)	2147 (4.5)	7101 (4.8)	13787 (4.7)	26357 (5.3)	55592 (10.8)
Kerala	152 (3.3)	1119 (3.9)	1776 (3.9)	5680 (3.9)	12083 (4.6)	22995 (4.7)	45238 (8.1)
Madhya Pradesh	111 (2.4)	861 (3.0)	1821 (4.0)	5496 (3.7)	9633 (3.9)	18127 (0.6)	29233 (5.3)
Maharashtra	1125 (24.1)	5616 (19.6)	7132 (16.0)	27189 (18.5)	62582(22.6)	101954(20.1)	173831 (31.2)
Manipur	1 (-)	19 (0.1)	24 (0.5)	82 (0.1)	113 (.03)	264 (0.9)	423 (.07)
Meghalaya	9 (0.2)	37 (0.1)	81 (0.9)	262 (0.2)	463 (1.2)	892 (2.0)	1647 (0.3)

(Contd.)

(Contd. Table-8)

Region/State	*June 69*	*June 79*	*Dec. 85*	*June 89*	*March 93*	*March 95*	*March 2001*
Mizoram	-	-	33 (0.6)	65 (.04)	115 (.03)	285 (0.5)	390 (.07)
Nagaland	1 (-)	15 (0.1)	69 (0.7)	166 (0.1)	243 (.08)	490 (0.7)	890 (0.1)
Orissa	31 (0.7)	284 (1.0)	632 (1.7)	1876 (1.3)	3608 (0.7)	7153 (1.4)	15111 (2.7)
Punjab	203 (4.3)	1430 (5.0)	2474 (5.9)	7758 (5.3)	12911 (4.6)	23043 (4.7)	43950 (7.9)
Rajasthan	85 (1.8)	613 (2.1)	1245 (2.8)	3931 (2.6)	7364 (2.6)	14055 (2.9)	27355 (4.9)
Sikkim	-	-	17 (.03)	73 (0.1)	111 (.04)	240 (0.4)	616 (0.1)
Tamil Nadu	293 (6.3)	1926 (6.7)	2274 (4.5)	9362 (6.4)	19184 (6.9)	32487 (6.6)	63488 (11.1)
Tripura	4 (0.1)	25 (0.1)	62 (0.9)	207 (0.1)	344 (1.0)	694 (1.0)	1542 (0.2)
Uttar Pradesh	365 (7.8)	2615 (9.1)	5234 (11.8)	15185 (10.3)	26071 (9.1)	48304 (9.8)	85057 (10.3)
West Bengal	644 (13.8)	3348 (11.7)	4271 (9.6)	14030 (9.5)	24221 (8.8)	36450 (7.4)	68257 (12.3)
Union territories	539 (11.6)	3468 (12.1)	-	16017 (10.9)	-	-	-
All India	4605 (100)	28684 (100)	44414 (100)	147031 (100)	275850 (100)	492227 (100)	56438 (100)

– Not available

Figures in the parentheses indicate percentage to total deposits

more economic activities have been occurred in these states during the New Economic Policy (NEP) regime. Thus it can be inferred that deposits mobilisation is directly associated with the economic activities of the states. The Table – 8 clearly discerns the relevant fact.

Factors Influencing the Deposits Mobilisation of PSBs

The foregoing discussions have been centred on the trend in growth of deposits of PSBs in the context of deposit mobilisation of commercial banks. An attempt has been made hereunder to analyse the determinants of deposit mobilization of PSBs during the period 1985-2000 on the basis of available literature relating to the determinants of deposit mobilization. We have considered the following as independent variables in this respect. (i) The variable representing the supply of deposits, i.e., Gross Domestic Product, (ii) The premium on deposits, i.e., the interest rate, (iii) Variations in prices affecting the flow of expenditure of the depositors, i.e., General Price index of all commodities in India, (iv) The collecting centres of deposits, i.e., the branch expansions.

In order to measure the interdependency as well as interrelationship between dependent variable, i.e., total deposits and independent variables, as mentioned above, we have used the following functional relationship.

$$Y_t = f(X_{1t,} X_{2t,} X_{3t,} X_{4t.})$$

where,

Y_t = Deposit of PSBs for 1985 – 2002

X_{it} = GDP_t : Gross domestic product of India at current prices.

X_{2t} = $Indw_t$: index of whole sale prices of all commodities in India

1981-82 = 100

X_{3t} = $Intd_t$: Interest rate and

X_{4t}, = Br_t : number of offices of PSBs (1985-2000)

In this respect we have assumed the following linear relationship explained by the regression equation.

$$Y_t = b_o + b_1 Gdp_t + b_2\, Indw_t + b_3 Intd_t + b_4 Br_t + U_t$$

here, b_i = regression coefficient, U_t =error term

(i = 1,2, ...4)

b_0 = constant

The regression equation based on the data displayed in the accompanying table found to be

Y (Deposit) = 20597.231 + 0.201 Gdp + 846.063 Indw. + 12228.099 Intd. + 1.475 Br

SE (171525.55) (0.100) (624.859) (5890.499) (6.599)

The other results obtained as under :

Variables	*β*	*'t' value*	*Sig.*	*F*	*R^2*	*Adjusted R^2*
β_0 Constant	-	1.20	0.907			
GDP at current prices	0.560	2.013	0.075			
Index of whole sale price	0.458	1.354	0.209	211.577	0.989	0.985
Interest rates	-0.131	-2.076	0.068	(0.000[a])		
Branch expansion	0.036	0.224	0.828	Sig		

Significant at P = .05

The aforesaid econometric analysis relating to determinants of deposit mobilisation shows that $R^2 = 0.989$. This indicates about 99 per cent of variation in the deposit mobilisation is explained by independent variables. It is further confirmed by the F ratio, which turned to be statistically significant. This implies the independent variables are perfect determinants in the variation of dependent variable. However, β value (beta) of each of the independent variable is statistically not significant indicating thereby the individual variables have no direct impact on the deposit mobilisation. In other words, independent variables along with other exogenous factors may have direct influences on deposit mobilization of PSBs.

Growth of Advances

The credit from the commercial bank is an important input in the production function of agriculture, industry, commerce and allied productive activities for the socio-economic development of the country. Apart from the quantum, the bank credits; its development, composition and direction are equally important in realising the country's various macro-economic goals. Pandey (1968)[9] suggested for the channelisation of bank credit in proper direction, as otherwise, there will be adverse affect on the economy of the country. Raj committee (1977)[10] recommended 40 per cent of lending to the priority sector. The bank had earlier adopted a purely traditional approach in lending based on "self liquidating theory". Under this approach the banks followed the "commercial loan theory" i.e., the banks granted loans only against negotiable and tangible securities offered as well as on the basis of business reputation of borrowers (Mithani, 1999)[11]. After nationalisation, banks have attempted to steer the direction of change and strive for achieving fundamental objectives of mitigation of regional disparities, dispersal of industries and reduction of concentration of economic wealth (Raul : 1997)[12]. As a result, implicit weightage given to the socially desirable sectors in the credit policy with sizable increase in the sectorwise advances. Ramala and Nagi (1994)[13] suggested proper end-use of loans to the entrepreneurs, which could ensure economic development of the area and the country as a whole. Hartough (1994)[14] studied the implications of bankers' action plan for profitable small business portfolio and suggested that Bank should make advances to most attractive and growth potential units on the basis of customers' payment track record and market condition etc. Kohli (1997)[15] found significant linkages between bank credit and investment in both agriculture and industries in India. He suggested that although directed credit programme is effective and in that respect positive support to SSI is required. This section attempted to study the development, composition, direction of bank credit in the post nationalisation phase and a comparison and contrast has been made during pre- and post-reform periods.

During the post nationalisation period the bank credit grew from Rs. 3467 crores in 1969 to Rs. 121984 crores in December 1990 and further increased to Rs. 5,56,436 crores in March 2001 recording a 160 fold increase during the period. Table – 9 depicts the population groupwise growth of bank credit.

It has been observed that a steep increase of bank credit in all areas (population group) viz., rural, semi-urban, urban and metropolitan. However, in the rural and semi-urban bank credit has declined significantly in the post reform period against the same in urban areas. Further, the percentage share of advances in the metropolitan areas has increased to 61.6 per cent in March 2001 from 48.6 per cent in March 1991.

Compound growth rate (**cgr**) of credit in each population group (with origin at 1980 and 1991) in pre and post reform era respectively would reveal efficacy of bank credit disbursed. The co-efficient of variation (**cv**) has been used to assess the variations in growth rate in bank credit. The analysis reveals that the growth of total bank credit in pre-reform era was higher (**cgr** = 21.01) than that of post reform period (**cgr** = 14.57). It is further observed that except metropolitan, **cgr** in the rural, urban, semi-urban areas has reduced during the post reform era. The analysis of **cv** revealed that except in the metropolitan areas lending activities have been thwarted during post reform era and in that respect the rural areas witnessed lesser volume of deployment of bank credit. The bank group-wise growth of advances, increase of advances over previous years and advances per office are presented in Table – 10.

TABLE - 9

DISTRIBUTION OF BANK CREDIT

(Amount Rs. in crores)

Year	*Rural*	*Semi-Urban*	*Urban*	*Metropolitan*	*Total*
Dec. 1969	115 (3.3)	453 (13.1)	756 (21.8)	2143 (61.8)	3467 (100)
Dec. 1980	2643 (10.7)	4201 (17.0)	5535 (22.4)	12382 (50.0)	24760 (100)
Dec. 1981	3600 (11.9)	5261 (17.4)	6713 (22.3)	14581 (48.4)	30155 (100)
Dec. 1982	4473 (12.5)	6114 (17.1)	7577 (21.2)	17515 (49.1)	35679 (100)
Dec. 1983	5576 (13.6)	7575 (18.5)	8716 (21.3)	19119 (46.6)	40986 (100)
Dec. 1984	6589 (13.5)	8349 (17.1)	10894 (22.3)	23100 (47.2)	48931 (100)
Dec. 1985	7489 (14.1)	9089(17.1)	11854 (22.3)	24730 (46.5)	53162 (100)
Dec. 1986	9387 (14.5)	10985 (17.0)	14631 (22.6)	29675 (45.9)	64677 (100)
Dec. 1987	1127 (15.3)	12664 (17.5)	16393 (22.6)	32366 (44.6)	72549 (100)
Dec. 1988	13452 (15.3)	15110 (17.2)	19649 (22.4)	39536 (45.1)	87746 (100)
Dec. 1989	15546 (14.8)	17094 (16.3)	22875 (21.8)	49351 (47.1)	104866 (100)
Dec. 1990	17352 (14.2)	18990 (15.6)	26655 (21.9)	58985 (48.4)	121984 (100)
Cgr	**23.27**	**17.32**	**18.90**	**16.91**	**21.01**
Cv	**64.60**	**44.81**	**48.19**	**48.43**	**48.38**
March 1991	19688 (14.7)	20624 (15.4)	28476 (21.3)	64958 (48.6)	133745 (100)
March 1992	20587 (14.5)	21779 (15.3)	29268 (20.6)	70578 (49.6)	142211 (100)
March 1993	23156 (14.0)	23590 (14.2)	33011 (19.9)	86078 (51.9)	165836 (100)
March 1994	25074 (13.9)	24650 (13.7)	36685 (20.4)	93608 (52.0)	180017 (100)
March 1995	28183 (12.7)	28665 (12.9)	45758 (20.6)	119901 (53.9)	222507 (100)
March 1996	29122 (11.1)	33444 (12.7)	48716 (18.5)	152251 (57.8)	263533 (100)
March 1997	32372 (11.5)	37478 (13.3)	51299 (18.2)	160188 (57.1)	282237 (100)
March 1998	36697 (11.2)	41680 (12.7)	57409 (17.5)	192852 (58.7)	328637 (100)
March 1999	41193 (10.6)	48230 (12.4)	67293 (17.3)	232745 (59.8)	389460 (100)
March 2000	47396 (10.1)	55022 (11.7)	76767 (16.4)	289847 (61.8)	469032 (100)
March 2001	56017 (10.1)	63857 (11.5)	93659 (16.8)	342903 (61.6)	556437 (100
Cgr	**11.44**	**12.92**	**12.97**	**17.32**	**14.57**
Cv.	**33.85**	**38.11**	**38.38**	**53.56**	**46.52**

Figures in the parentheses indicate percentage to total bank credit.

Source : RBI, Banking Statistics; *Quarterly Handout*, various issues.

TABLE – 10
GROWTH OF ADVANCES : BANK GROUPWISE

(Amount Rs. in crores)

Year	*Public Sector Banks*			*Private Sector Banks*	*Foreign Banks*	*Total*		*Advances Per Office*
	SBI group	*Nationalised Banks*	*Total*			*Amount*	*Increase over P/Y*	
1990-91	35897	69627	105524	4917	6928	117369	-	2.02
	(30.6)	(59.3)	(89.9)	(4.2)	(5.9)	(100)		
1991-92	39714	74870	114585	6239	9182	130004	10.76	2.81
	(30.5)	(57.6)	(88.1)	(4.8)	(7.1)	(100)		
1992-93	48360	82865	131225	7836	10410	149472	14.97	3.19
	(32.4)	(55.4)	(87.8)	(5.2)	(7.0)	(100)		
1993-94	46973	82695	129668	9707	11453	150828	0.91	3.18
	(31.1)	(54.8)	(86.0)	(6.4)	(7.6)	(100)		
1994-95	56740	102983	159723	13818	15327	188867	25.22	3.94
	(30.0)	(54.5)	(84.6)	(7.3)	(8.1)	(100)		
1995-96	69979	117333	187311	22224	22458	231927	22.80	4.75
	(30.2)	(50.6)	(80.7)	(7.6)	(9.7)	(100)		
1996-97	82902	137349	220251	28540	26759	275550	18.81	5.58
	(30.1)	(49.8)	(79.9)	(10.4)	(9.7)	(100)		
1997-98	97567	162336	259903	35313	29290	324506	17.77	6.50
	(30.1)	(50.0)	(80.1)	(10.9)	(9.0)	(100)		
1998-99	97123	164156	261279	41259	19300	331838	2.26	6.53
	(29.3)	(49.5)	(78.7)	(12.4)	(8.8)	(100)		
1999-00	116493	208920	325413	54034	35857	415305	25.15	8.10
	(28.1)	(50.3)	(78.4)	(13.0)	(8.6)	(100)		
2000-01	135620	245610	381230	67886	42996	492113	18.49	9.51
	(27.6)	(49.9)	(77.5)	(13.8)	(8.7)	(100)		

Figures in the Parenthesis indicate percentage to total advances.

Source : IBA, Performance Highlights of Banks, Various Issues.

It is observed that lion share of bank advances are owned by PSBs, which was 89.9 per cent in 1990-91, reduced to 77.5 per cent in 2000-2001. The share of private and foreign banks, although very small 4.2 per cent for private banks and 5.9 per cent for foreign banks in 1990-91, rose to 13.8 per cent for private and 8.7 per cent for foreign banks in 2000-2001 may be due to reform packages. The growth scenario of credit increase over previous year is around 20 per cent during 1992-93 to 2000-2001 except the year 1993-94 and 1998-99. The reform package thus made notable impact on the growth of advances per office, which reached, to the tune of Rs. 9.51 crores in 2000-2001 from very small figures of Rs 2.81 crores in 1991-92.

Linear growth rate (*b*) as well as compound growth rate (cgr) have been used to compare the growth of advances of several bank groups during the post reform period with origin at 1990-91. The consistency of growth of banking operations has been assessed by the coefficient of variation (**cv**). The results of bank group wise ***b***, **cgr** and **cv** are obtained as under.

GROWTH OF ADVANCES (1991-2001)

Value of	*SBI group*	*Nationalised Banks*	*PSBs*	*Pvt. Banks*	*Foreign Banks*	*Total*
b	10462.05	20621.89	28791.85	6783.37	4235.64	39244.86
Cgr	15.44	16.28	15.42	42.67	23.67	17.57
Cv	38.70	40.27	39.14	69.22	55.15	42.96

Source :Self-calculated on the basis of Table - 10.

It is noticed that private banks have dominated in area of the advances (**cgr** = 23.67 and **cv** = 55.15). In contrast PSBs have poorly ventured during post reform era due to stringencies envisaged in the reform packages.

Sectorwise Deployment of Bank Credit

Diversification of a large part of banks credit from the traditional sector to the priority sector is a remarkable feature of credit deployment in the post nationalisation era. Dr. K. S. Krishnaswamy the former Deputy Governor of the Reserve Bank of India observed, "the concept of priority sector lending is mainly intended to ensure that assistance from the banking system in an increasing manner to those sectors of the economy which have not received adequate support of the institutional finance in the past". Since seventies, RBI and GOI have stipulated some guidelines viz,

TABLE – 11
SECTORAL DEPLOYMENT OF GROSS BANK CREDIT

(Amount Rs. in crore)

Sectors	*June 1969*		*March 1986*		*June, 1990*		*March 1995*		*March 1997*		*March 1998*		*March 1999*		*March 2000*	
	Amount	*% to Total*	*Amount*	*% to Total*	*Amount*	*% to Total*	*Amount*	*% to Total*	*Amount*	*% to Total*	*Amount*	*% to Total*	*Amount*	*% to Total*	*Amount*	*% to Total*
1. Priority Sectors	504	14.0	21566	39.0	41030	38.9	64141	32.3	84880	32.8	99507	33.1	114611	33.5	131827	32.9
a. Agriculture	188	5.2	9058	16.4	16939	16.1	23980	12.1	31442	12.1	34869	11.6	39634	11.6	44381	11.1
b. Small Scale industry	286	7.9	7816	14.1	15672	14.9	27612	14.0	35944	13.9	43508	14.5	48483	14.2	52814	13.2
c. Other Priority Sectors	30	0.9	4692	8.5	8419	8.0	12549	6.4	17494	6.8	21130	7.0	26494	7.7	34632	8.6
2. Industry ; Large and Medium	1879	52.2	18422	33.4	38752	36.7	42327	3801	102604	39.9	117530	39.1	130576	38.2	147319	36.8
3. Whole Sale trade	385	10.0	3066	5.6	5029	4.8	9749	4.9	12340	4.8	13217	4.4	13965	4.0	16818	4.2
4. Export credit	258	7.9	2409	4.4	8496	8.1	25382	12.9	30008	11.6	33947	11.3	35891	10.5	39118	9.8
5. Public food procurement	233	6.5	5535	10.0	3917	3.7	19907	6.2	7597	3.0	12485	4.1	16816	4.9	25691	6.4
6. Other Sectors	341	9.4	6624	12.0	16769	15.9	36097	18.3	51570	19.9	57544	19.2	66104	19.3	79163	19.7
Gross Bank Credit	3599	100.0	55213	100	105497	100	197603	100	258991	100	300283	100	342012	100	400818	100

'Percentage to total' indicates the percentage to total bank credit of respective years.

Source : RBI Reports on Currency and Finance, Various Issues, RBI.

financing in the priority sector on an increasing scale 40 per cent of total bank credit, more deployment of credit backward regions, preparation and implementation of district credit plan (DCP) and measures for enhancing productivity, employment and economic growth with social justice.

Table – 11 furnishes the sector-wise deployment of bank credit during June 1969 to 2001. It is revealed that gross bank credit increased from Rs. 3599 crores in June 1969 to Rs. 105497 crores in June 1990 and further increased to Rs. 400818 crores in March 2000. The priority sector advances also increased in absolute term from Rs. 504 crores in June 1969 to the tune of Rs. 131827 crores in March 2000. It is worth mentioning that the share of priority sector to total bank credit increased from 14 per cent in June 1969 to 38.9 per cent in June 1990. It, however, decreased to 32.9 per cent in March 2000. However, since nationalisation the share of bank credit in the industry (both large and medium) and export credit have increased considerably while the whole sale trade and food procurement attracted comparatively less credit over the years.

An analysis of commercial bank credit to agriculture, village industries and small-scale sector during the period 1973-1999 is presented in Table – 12.

TABLE – 12

COMMERCIAL BANK CREDIT TO AGRICULTURE, VILLAGE INDUSTRIES AND SMALL SCALE INDUSTRIES (1973 – 1999)

(Rs. in crores at constant prices)

Years		*Agriculture*		*Village*	*Small Scale*	*All*
	Direct	*Indirect*	*Total*	*industries*	*Sector*	*sectors ***
1973	2115 (-)	2953 (-)	2953 (-)	43 (-)	3920 (-)	32714 (-)
1980	7472 (19.8)	2269 (15.3)	9741 (18.6)	186 (23.3)	7831 (10.4)	65861 (10.5)
1990	19629 (10.1)	2979 (2.8)	22608 (8.8)	1259 (21.1)	16298 (7.6)	14843 (7.9)
1999	21887 (1.2)	4480 (4.6)	26367 (1.7)	1624 (2.9)	20266 (2.5)	246,605 (6.3)

Figure in parentheses indicates the compound rate of growth per annum over the previous period (at constant prices)

** All sectors refer to total bank credit to all occupations, which include industry, personal loans, professional services, transport, trade.

Source : RBI, Banking statistics, various issues.

The analysis reveals that the compound growth rate, at constant prices of agriculture (1.7), village industries (2.9) and small sector (2.5) in the post reform era (1990-1999) was much lower than that of growth (8.8, 21.1 and 7.6 respectively) during pre reform era (1980-90).

Priority Sector Advances of PSBs

The bank group-wise distribution of priority sector advances by the banks and percentage share to total bank credit in each bank group are furnished in Table – 13. It is noticed that in the pre reform period percentage share of priority sector advances of PSBs has reduced to 32.1 in 1990-91 from 43.4 per cent in 1980-81. While the post reform era experienced an improvement of the same from 37.6 per cent in 1991-92 to 43.6 per cent in 2000-2001. Further during post reform era, PSBs lending in this sector remains higher than private and foreign banks.

Moreover, the position of PSBs in the Indian banking set up in respect growth of priority sector advances, may be exhibited by compound growth rate (**cgr**) during both pre and post reform era [with origin at 1981-82 and 1991-92 respectively]. The co-efficient of variation (**cv**) has been used to determine the variation in the quantum of advances made during both the period under consideration. The result of cgr and cv is presented as under.

GROWTH OF PRIORITY SECTOR ADVANCES

Period	*Value of*	*SBI Group*	*Nationalised Banks*	*Public Sector Banks*	*Pvt. Banks*	*Foreign Banks*
Pre reform						
(1980-81 to 1991)	Cgr	18.65	11.14	14.72	-	-
	Cv	58.43	38.03	47.76	-	-
Post reform						
(1991-92 to 2000-01)	Cgr	13.62	13.50	14.52	60.59	39.64
	Cv	39.05	38.52	38.08	167.60	59.42

Source: Self-calculated on the basis of data available in Table-13.

The econometric analysis revealed that growth of priority sector advances of PSBs was comparatively better in the pre-reform period (**cgr** = 14.72) against the post reform period (**cgr** = 14.52) The nationalised banks also achieved better growth rate during post reform era (**cgr** 13.50) than that of pre reform (**cgr** = 11.14) period. However the private and foreign banks during post reform era attained better growth rate. [(**cgr**) for private banks 60.59 per cent and foreign banks 39.64 per cent]. On the other hand, there was more variation in the quantum of advances made by the SBI groups during the post reform era. While private banks and foreign banks have emerged as comparatively good lender during post reform

TABLE – 13

PRIORITY SECTOR ADVANCES BY PUBLIC SECTOR BANKS VIS – A – VIS OTHER BANKS

(Amount Rs. in crores)

Year		*Public Sector Banks* *SBI group*	*Nationalised*	*Private Sector Banks* *Total*	*Foreign Banks*
1980-81	3093 (35.5)	9676 (46.8)	12769 (43.4)	—	—
1985-86	7094 (42.8)	20648 (42.7)	22220 (34.2)	—	—
1990-91	14833 (30.2)	27443 (33.3)	42276 (32.4)	1507 (30.5)	596 (7.0)
1991-92	14314 (36.0)	28720 (38.4)	43033 (37.6)	1794 (28.8)	712 (7.8)
1992-93	14955 (30.9)	29787 (35.9)	44741 (34.1)	2377 (30.4)	1131 (10.9)
1993-94	15514 (33.0)	30003 (36.3)	45517 (35.1)	2869 (29.6)	2292 (20.0)
1994-95	17627 (31.1)	34776 (33.8)	52403 (32.8)	3906 (28.3)	3321 (21.9)
1995-96	21393 (30.5)	40416 (34.4)	61809 (36.6)	6049 (34.3)	4439 (29.0)
1996-97	24203 (29.2)	44722 (32.6)	68925 (37.8)	6283 (34.0)	5019 (32.1)
1997-98	28111 (28.8)	52463 (32.3)	79131 (41.7)	88321 (41.2)	6139 (37.7)
1998-99	33087 (34.1)	60626 (36.9)	91319 (41.8)	11614 (40.9)	6940 (34.3)
1999-2000	37607 (32.3)	70602 (33.8)	107200 (43.5)	14155 (41.4)	8270 (37.0)
2000-2001	43713 (32.2)	83303 (33.9)	127807 (43.6)	10819 (38.7)	9699 (34.5)

Note : Figures in parentheses indicate percentage to total bank credit.

Source : *RBI, Statistical tables Relating to Banks in India. IBA Bulletins.*

TABLE – 14
ADVANCES OF PSBs TO THE PRIORITY SECTORS (CATEGORY-WISE)

(Amount Rs in crores)

Sector	*June 1960*	*June 1969*	*June 1971*	*Dec. 1985*	*June 1992*	*March 1995*	*March 1996*	*March 1998*	*March 1999*	*March 2000*
1. Agriculture	160	162	340	8850	18464	23513	26351	34305	40078	46190
	(5.2)	(5.4)	(8.3)	(16.9)	(16.1)	(13.9)	(14.3)	(15.7)	(16.3)	(15.8)
(i) Direct	40	40	NA	7550	15380	20813	22892	28303	31681	34432
	(1.3)	(1.3)		(14.4)	(13.4)	(12.3)	(12.4)	(13.0)	(12.9)	(11.8)
(ii) Indirect	120	122	NA	1300	3084	2700	3459	6002	8397	11758
	(3.9)	(4.0)		(2.4)	(2.7)	(1.6)	(1.9)	(2.8)	(3.4)	(4.0)
2. Small Scale Industries	260	257	440	6162	17689	25843	29482	38109	42674	45788
	(8.6)	(8.5)	(10.8)	(11.8)	(15.4)	(15.3)	(16.0)	(17.5)	(17.3)	(15.6)
3. Other Priority Sectors	20	22	130	3987	8842	12438	13751	18881	24448	32079
	(0.6)	(0.7)	(3.1)	(7.6)	(7.7)	(7.4)	(7.5)	(8.7)	(9.9)	(11.0)
4. Total Priority Sector	440	441	910	18999	44995	61794	69609	91319	1,07,200	127807
	(12.0)	(14.6)	(25.0)	(36.4)	(39.3)	(36.6)	(37.8)	(41.8)	(43.5)	(43.6)
5. Net Bank Credit	3020	3016	4080	52228	114492	169038	184391	21829	246203	2,92,943
	(100)	(100)	(100)	(100)	(100)	(100)	(100)	(100)	(100)	(100)

* includes small transport operators, self-employed persons and rural artisans.
Figures in the parentheses indicate per cent to net bank credit.
NA = not available.

Source : RBI, Report on Currency and Finance Vol. 1, 1975-76 and
RBI, Report on Trend & Progress of Banking in India, 1992-93, 1998-99, 1999-2000.

period. This indicates that these banks, private banks in particular, lent larger quantum to the priority sector in recent years though the volume of advances are meagre than that of PSBs.

TABLE – 17
POPULATION GROUPWISE CREDIT DEPOSIT RATIOS SINCE NATIONALISATION

(Ratios in Percentage)

Period	*Year*	*Population Groups*				
		Rural	*Semi-Urban*	*Urban*	*Metropolitan*	*Total*
	Dec. 1969	37.6	43.0	59.1	98.2	71.9
	Dec. 1975	51.9	47.6	64.5	96.4	73.5
	Dec. 1980	56.9	49.2	59.7	85.2	66.9
PRE	Dec. 1981	60.6	51.4	61.3	85.1	68.2
REFORM	Dec. 1982	60.3	51.0	58.3	88.0	68.3
PERIOD	Dec. 1983	63.2	52.8	57.1	84.2	67.0
	Dec. 1984	68.6	53.1	57.2	84.6	68.3
	Dec. 1985	619	50.0	53.4	73.1	61.8
	Dec. 1986	65.3	51.3	54.9	73.8	63.0
	Dec. 1987	63.5	50.1	53.3	71.3	64.0
	Dec. 1988	64.3	50.2	54.7	72.1	61.8
	Dec. 1989	63.8	50.0	57.4	77.6	64.7
	Dec. 1990	60.7	48.7	58.7	82.0	65.9
	Dec. 1991	59.4	46.9	57.4	71.4	60.91
	Dec. 1992	58.7	47.5	54.3	71.8	61.0
POST	Dec. 1993	56.9	45.0	52.9	72.6	60.5
REFORM	Dec. 1994	52.5	39.9	50.1	69.3	56.6
PERIOD	Dec. 1995	49.1	38.6	51.6	77.1	59.2
	Dec. 1996	47.7	40.6	51.5	81.0	61.8
	Dec. 1997	44.6	38.8	46.5	75.7	57.3
	Dec. 1998	42.4	36.4	43.0	74.9	55.5
	Dec. 1999	40.1	35.3	42.0	76.9	55.4
	Dec. 2000	39.4	34.4	40.6	82.2	57.0
	Dec. 2001	40.2	34.2	43.0	84.3	58.5

Source: RBI, Banking statistics; Quarterly Handout; various issues.

Table – 14 depicts sector-wise priority sector advances of PSBs and percentage share to net bank credit. It is found that SSIs and agriculture sectors have captured lion share of priority sector advances since nationalisation. It surged from Rs. 114492 crores in 1992 to the tune of Rs. 292942 in March 2000.

Credit Deposit Ratio

The credit deposit ratios (C/D) indicating channelisation of bank credit among the economic sectors. The population group-wise distribution of C/D ratio has been presented in the following Table – 15. The table shows that the C/D ratio from its peak of 71.9 per cent in December 1969 declined to 58.8 per cent in March 2000. The declining rate of C/D ratio in rural and semi-urban areas are more significant than that of urban and metropolitan areas.

In March 1979, the PSBs were advised by the government to attain C/D ratio of 60 per cent in rural and semi-urban branches by 1985. However, rural branches of PSBs attained 60 per cent C/D ratio in the pre-reform era but failed to maintain same tempo during post reform era except 1991-93. The reason may be attributed to banks have gradually adopted safe policy in the lending activities and emphasised on investment in the secured return like government securities. A comparison among the bank groups relating to C/D ratio has been presented in Table-16.

TABLE - 16
BANK GROUPWISE CREDIT-DEPOSIT RATIO SINCE 1980.

Year	*Public sector Banks*			*Private Sector*	*Foreign*	*All Scheduled*
	SBI group	*Nationalised*	*Total*	*Banks*	*Banks*	*Com. Banks*
1980-81	70.23	68.21	73.06	NA	NA	66.9
1984-85	66.02	61.29	69.26	57.81	61.28	61.08
1990-91	62.24	54.71	57.06	53.32	62.48	60.92
1991-92	56.40	52.44	53.75	51.63	54.33	61.01
1992-93	59.69	50.55	53.58	51.14	49.86	60.51
1993-94	49.18	43.67	45.52	48.57	44.23	56.62
1994-95	52.58	46.59	48.55	52.62	54.67	59.20
1995-96	57.39	47.62	50.95	72.90	73.30	61.85
1996-97	53.64	44.10	47.25	55.91	71.55	57.34
1997-98	58.75	40.63	51.56	50.79	67.42	55.51
1999-99	46.13	41.37	43.02	49.56	63.04	55.49
1999-00	47.14	45.52	46.08	47.61	72.69	57.05
2000-01	44.58	46.68	45.91	49.74	72.64	58.53

Source : Worked out on the basis of earlier table.

The table exhibited that the private and foreign banks fared well in attaining C/D ratio than that of PSBs during 1994-95 to 2000-01. For

TABLE - 17
REGIONWISE CREDIT DEPOSIT RATIO

Region	*June 1969*	*Dec. 1980*	*Dec. 1985*	*March 1990*	*March 1993*	*March 1995*	*March 1999*	*March 2000*	*March 2001*
Northern	65.1	69.1	47.4	47.6	58.0	53.8	49.4	49.6	63.1
North Eastern	67.2	63.0	43.0	70.0	44.7	31.2	33.7	30.6	28.1
Eastern	52.8	55.0	48.2	52.6	50.5	43.4	38.0	37.2	36.9
Central	50.1	49.4	48.1	49.8	46.7	37.2	36.8	36.8	33.4
Western	73.2	70.1	69.3	63.7	60.5	63.2	67.0	74.6	75.0
Southern	78.5	80.9	76.7	83.2	71.5	76.10	68.7	66.8	65.8
India	71.9	66.9	65.6	60.7	58.9	57.3	54.8	56.0	58.5

Source : RBI, Banking statistics, Basic statistical Returns, various issues.

PSBs it has gradually declined during the post reform period against the pre reform era. The C/D ratios for foreign banks declined to 54.67 per cent in 1994-95 from 66.9 per cent in 1980-81. It further increased to 72.64 per cent. Thus, the performance of PSBs is regarded as unsatisfactory may be due to stringent rules imposed on bank under the reform measures. Table-17 depicts the region-wise scenario of C/D ratio. It is clear that the C/D ratios have been declining in almost all the regions of the country except western region. The declining rate in backward areas like NER, Eastern regions etc. are more significant than that of other regions. The ratios of western region increased from 70.1 per cent in 1980-81 to 75.0 per cent in March 2001. Thus the bank credit has been siphoned off from the backward region to comparatively well off region.

District-wise Classification of C/D Ratio

Table-18 exhibited the district-wise classification of bank deposits and credit by size of C/D ratio. During 1990-92 only few number of districts (28 in 1990 and 27 in 1992 out of 454 and 478 respectively) attained less than 20 per cent C/D ratio and such number has been increased to 105 out of 565 district in March 2000. Similar was the trend in the next size group of 20-30 per cent C/D ratios, where in the number of district shot up from 49 in March 1990 to 130 in March 2000. The number of district enjoying C/D ratio of 60 per cent and above drastically came down 101 in March 2000 from 177 in March 1990.

Though there has been a 60 per cent C/D ratio prescription of RBI for the rural branches only 242 districts out of 447 accounting about 50 per cent have attained the stipulated norms in March 1990 which has sharply declined to only 147 districts out of 548 in March 2000.

Thus poor infrastructure along-with other economical hazards thwarted the pace of growth of economy as a whole. Lower growth in the rural areas has further fuelled by the step motherly attitude of the banks without supplying required amount of credit.

A cursory glance at the list of districts appearing in the low range of C/D ratios suggests that above mentioned deterioration may have taken place primarily because of constricted banking activities in Jammu and Kashmir and some states in North Eastern Region (NER) in recent period. But a large number in the list also belongs to well off states like West Bengal, Bihar and UP. Interestingly some of the deposit generating districts in the relatively advanced states like Gurgaon, Rewari, Rohtak and Sonepat

TABLE – 18

DISTRICT WISE DISTRIBUTION OF BANK DEPOSITS & CREDIT BY SIZE OF CREDIT DEPOSIT RATIO

(Amount Rs. in crores)

C.D. ratio range	*March 1990*				*March 1992*				*March 2000*			
	No. of District	*Deposit Amount*	*Credit Amount*	*C.D. ratio*	*No of. District*	*Deposit Amount*	*Credit Amount*	*C/D ratio*	*No. of District*	*Deposit Amount*	*Credit Amount*	*C/D ratio*
All India level												
<20	28	2537	417	16.4	27	5917	934	15.8	105	99410	15391	15.5
20 – 30	49	14887	3813	25.6	54	16788	4295	25.6	130	114239	28827	25.5
30 – 40	71	17686	6140	34.7	69	24369	8542	35.1	97	98177	33810	34.4
40 – 50	60	30677	14190	46.3	83	24730	11050	44.7	85	64125	28881	45.0
50 – 60	69	19967	10771	53.9	82	45156	24362	54.0	47	49596	27705	55.9
60 – 100	142	75693	57303	75.7	142	106959	72472	67.8	87	262314	179958	68.6
> 100	35	10142	11492	113.3	21	14766	15369	104.1	14	141314	147255	104.2
Total	454	171590	104128	60.7	478	238689	137026	57.4	565	829176	461830	55.7
Rural areas												
<20	31	2117	320	15.1	30	4482	607	13.6	96	33725	4893	14.5
20 – 30	33	2845	745	26.2	34	2818	718	25.5	97	25532	6307	24.7
30 – 40	51	4727	1636	34.6	55	5623	1936	34.4	78	15912	5422	34.1
40 – 50	43	3246	1450	44.7	62	5551	2473	44.6	63	11662	5323	45.6
50 – 60	47	2351	1280	54.4	51	335	1800	54.0	67	9597	5260	54.8
60 – 100	140	6780	5274	77.8	151	9431	7198	76.3	114	17867	13835	77.4
> 100	102	4149	5459	131.6	89	5064	5943	117.3	33	5252	7317	139.3
Total	447	26217	16167	61.7	472	36308	20678	57.0	548	119549	48359	40.5

Source : Worked out on the basis of districtwise data in RBI, Banking Statistics, Basic Statistical Return (BSR), respective issues.

in Hariyana, Bilaspur, Mandi and Simla in Himachal Prodesh, Amritsar and Gudraspur in Panjab, Udupi of Karnataka and Kollam and Thiruvananthapuram in Kerala joined the same band wagon of low C/D ratio range (EPW Research Foundation, 2002).

The Progress of Public Sector Banks at a Glance

The progress of PSBs on the basis of the foregoing discussion pertaining to pre and post financial sector reform is summarised in the accompanying Table-A. The table demonstrated that total number of banks remained same after 1991 while there was quantum jump in the number of bank offices. It has increased from 7015 in June 1969 to 40933 on March 1991 and further to 46318 in March 2001.The branches of the SBI group jumped from 2462 in June 1969 to 13561 in March 2001. On the other hand, the same has increased in case of nationalised banks from 4134 to 32757 during the same period under consideration.

The number of population per office on the other hand was 64000 in June 1969. It declined dramatically to 14000 in March 1991. However, there was slight increase to 15000 on March 1997 but then the same remain unchanged till 2001. The amount of deposits of PSBs rose to Rs. 210811 crores in 1991 from Rs. 40222 crores in 1969 and further increased significantly by about four times to Rs. 830314 crores on March 2001. The amount of deposit per office has also increased dramatically during the post financial sector reform period. It rose from Rs. 5.05 crores in 1991 to Rs. 19.83 crores on March 2001. This indicated the efficiency of banking sector in mobilizing deposits from the economy as a whole. As regards to the advances per offices, the PSBs had failed to catch up the growth rate of deposits. This has been clearly revealed by the parameter of Credit/Deposit ratio significant indicator of banking activity. The ratio has significantly dwindled from 57.06 per cent on March 1991 to 51.56 per cent on March 1998, further to 45.91 per cent on March 2001. With a view to attain the main objective of nationalisation of banks, i.e., diversification of pattern of lending in favour of priority sector in particular, PSBs have only made spectacular achievements. Its share in priority sector lending has significantly increased from mere a 14.6 per cent on June 1969 to 32.1 per cent on March 1991 and further to 43.6 per cent on March 2001. However, the foregoing analysis revealed that the share of priority sector lending of all SCBs have declined particularly during post reform period. The reason may be attributed to the shyness of 42 foreign

TABLE – A
COMPARATIVE PROGRESS STATEMENT OF PSBS DURING THE PRE & POST FINANCIAL SECTOR REFORMS

Sl. No.	*Important Banking indicators*	*Pre-reform Progress as on*			*Post reform progress as on*		
		June 1969	*March 1981*	*March 1991*	*March 1997*	*March 1998*	*March 2001*
1	Number of Public Sector Banks		27	27	27	27	27
	SBI groups		8	8	8	8	8
	Nationalised Banks	14	19	19	19	19	19
2	Number of offices of PSBs	7015	30583	40933	44756	45013	46318
	State Bank group	2462	17308	11887	13112	13109	13561
	Nationalised banks	4134	15309	29046	31904	31904	32757
3	Population-wise percentage share of PSBs -						
	Rural	17.6	51.2	58.0	52.0	51.2	49.4
	Semi-urban	40.8	22.9	18.8	21.5	21.6	22.0
	Urban	23.3	14.8	13.6	14.6	15.0	15.7
	Metropolitan	18.3	11.1	9.5	11.9	12.2	12.9
4	Average Population per office ('000)	64	29	14	15	15	15
5	Deposits of PSBs (in crores)	4666	40222	210811	426367	504064	830314
	of which SBI groups deposits		12179	65494	140861	166060	304185
	NBs deposits		28043	145317	285506	338004	526129
6	P.C. share of PSBs deposits to total commercial banks deposit.		94.5	93.0	82.8	81.7	80.9

(Contd. Table-A)

Sl. No.	*Important Banking indicators*	*Pre-reform Progress as on*			*Post reform progress as on*		
		June 1969	*March 1981*	*March 1991*	*March 1997*	*March 1998*	*March 2001*
7	Advances of PSBs (crores) of which SBI groups advances NBs advance.		29.88	105524	220251	259903	381230
8	Pc share of PSBs advances to total advances of CBs.		87.0	89.9	79.9	80.1	77.5
9	Deposits of PSBs per office (crores)		1.20	5.05	10.42	12.36	19.83
	Advances of PSBs per office (crores)		NA	2.02	5.58	6.53	9.51
10	Per capita deposits (Rs.)		452	2360	6839	7359	9770
	per capital advances (Rs.)		208	618	3356	3759	5228
11	PSBs advances to Priority sector (crores)	441	12769	42276	79131	91319	127807
12	Share of PSBs Priority Sector advances to total bank credit	14.6	43.4	32.1	37.8	41.7	43.6
13	Credit-deposit ratios of PSBs (in Pc.)	77.5	73.06	57.06	47.26	51.56	45.91
14	C/D ratios of SCBs	71.9	78.2	6092	57.34	55.51	58.53

TABLE - B
POSITION OF PUBLIC SECTOR BANKS DURING PRE & POST REFORM PERIOD.

(figures in per cent indicate growth)

Bank group	*Pre Reform Period (1980-81 to 1990 – 91)*						*Post Reform Period (1990-91 to 2000 – 2001)*					
	Bank Offices		*Deposits*		*Advances*		*Bank offices*		*Deposits*		*Advances*	
	Cgr	*Cv*	*Cgr*	*Cv*	*Cgr*	*Cv*	*Cgr*	*Cv*	*Cgr*	*Cv*	*Cgr*	*Cv*
Public Sector Banks	2.71	8.36	20.62	29.2	14.94	46.69	1.03	2.99	17.72	43.5	15.42	39.14
I. SBI group	4.57	18.43	45.30	76.0	18.41	56.05	0.93	2.75	19.49	36.0	15.44	38.70
II Nationalised Banks	6.27	5.61	32.41	42.8	13.60	43.34	0.87	2.82	21.43	53.8	16.28	40.27
Private Sector Banks	- 0.19	8.38	23.84	60.6	-	-	3.52	10.32	45.75	74.4	42.67	69.22
Foreign Banks	0.07	0.51	37.35	82.9	-	-	2.12	10.98	14.38	36.1	23.67	55.15
Total of Scheduled Commercial Banks	2.24	6.84	36.42	51.5	21.01	48.38	1.25	7.82	19.24	46.1	17.57	42.96

Cgr = Compound growth rate, Cv = Co-efficient of variation (defined earlier)

Source : Self-compiled from the previous tables.

banks and 31 old and new private banks to lend the priority sector over the time. Thus, the PSBs have made a significant contribution in the monetary system of the country during the post reform period. The effectiveness of PSBs has been justified so far by the progress of various lending activities viz. mobilisation of deposits, extending of credit, credit to priority sector; agriculture, small scale industries, weaker and marginal borrowers, etc.

The position of PSBs in the banking scenario during pre and post financial reform is presented in the following Table – B. The analysis of **cgr** and **cv** of PSBs exhibited that the PSBs performed well in respect of branch expansion during pre reform era but in the post reform years, branch expansion performance was comparatively lower among the SCBs. The performance of PSBs in terms of deposits mobilisation is comparatively low and that too lower in the post reform period. However, it is slightly above the foreign banks during post reform period. Further, the rate of deposit mobilisation revealed by **coefficient of variation** indicated that PSBs ranked at the bottom during pre reform era, which has been significantly increased during subsequent years of post reform period. The lower growth rate of deposits in PSBs over the period indicated lack of professionalism in management and stringency imposed on them by the central bank from time to time. The position of PSBs in respect of performance in advances was not significant as compared to private and foreign banks during the post reform era.

References

1. Thingalaya, N. K. 1987. *Banking Development in India since Independence*, Pigmy Economic Review, (August) 33 (1) : 1.
2. Chandrasekhar, K. 1985. *History of Indian Banking* in Subrahmanya S. (Ed) Trend & Progress of banking in India, Deep & Deep Publications, p. 3.
3. All India Rural Credit Survey Committee, 1954, Government of India.
4. Rangaswamy, B. 1985. *Public Sector Banking in India*, New Delhi. pp. 8-9.
5. Chandrasekhar, K. *Ibid* p. 13.
6. Chandrasekhar, K. *Ibid* p. 14.
7. Bilgrani, S.A.R. 1982. *Growth of Public Sector Banks*, Deep & Deep Publications, New Delhi. p. 17.

8. Chandha, B. L. 1994. *Changing Phases of India Banking Since 1969; Emerging Scenario*, Pigmy Economic Review, (Nov. Jan) 38 (2) : 3.
9. Pandey, K. L., 1968. *Development of Banking in India Since 1949*. Calcutta Scientific Book Agency. p. 80.
10. Reserve Bank of India : 1977. *Committee's Report on Financing of Public Sector Banks*, RBI (Raj, J. as Chairman).
11. Mithani, D. M. 1991. *Money, Banking, International Trade and Finance*. Himalaya Publishing Home. Delhi.
12. Rual, R. K., 1997. *Industrial Finance in India*. op. cit.
13. Ramala, K.S. and Nagi, K.S., 1994. *Sickness in Small Scale Industries ; Problems & Prospects, New Trends in Indian Industries*. Vol. 2, Chugh Publications, Allahabad.
14. Hartough, K.J. 1994. *Entrepreneurial Bankers; The Banker's Personal Action Plan for Building a Profitable Small Business Portfolio*. Probus Publishing, Chicago.
15. Kohli, R. 1997. *Directed Credit and Financial Reforms*. op.cit.

4

Performance of Public Sector Banks : An Empirical Study (Deposits, Advances and C/D ratio)

The Public Sector Banks in India have made spectacular achievements in attaining the objectives of bank nationalisation in 1969. There is a quantum jump of bank offices from 7015 in June 1969 to 46318 in March 2001. The amount of deposits per office increased dramatically during post reform era from Rs. 1.2 crores in 1969 to Rs. 19.83 crores in March 2001. This indicated the efficiency of banking sector in mobilizing deposits from the economy as a whole. However, the advances per office have not grown at the same pace. It, further, has been supplemented by the declining trend of credit deposit ratio from 57 per cent in March 1991 to 45.9 per cent in March 2001.

With this backdrop an attempt has been made to assess the performance of existing PSBs in the area under study. In this respect 12 PSBs operating in the three districts have been considered and their activities were assessed over a period of 15 years, i.e., 1985 to 2000. Further, the performance of banks has been compared in two time periods, i.e., pre-reform period upto 1991 and post-reform period on the basis of some specific financial indicators. The operational activities in terms of branch expansions, deposit mobilizations, credit channelisation, C/D ratios, population served per bank were reviewed and compared between said two periods using statistical method and financial tools.

TABLE – 1
DISTRICTWISE BRANCH EXPANSION AS ON DECEMBER IN BARAK VALLEY

Districts	**1983*	*1984*	*1985*	*1986*	*1987*	*1988*	*1989*	*1990*	*1991*	*1992*	*1993*	*1994*	*1995*	*1996*	*1997*	*1998*	*1999*	*2000*	*Change in number Pre ref-orm*	*Change in number Post ref-orm*
Cachar	49	54	56	72	72	73	75	70	69	69	69	69	69	69	70	71	70	71	20	2
Karimganj	22	24	38	39	39	44	47	52	52	53	55	53	53	53	53	53	53	53	30	1
Hailakandi	–	–	–	–	–	–	–	18	19	19	20	20	20	20	20	23	23	23	1	4
Total	71	78	94	111	111	117	122	140	140	141	144	142	142	142	143	147	140	147	51	7

Source : Lead Bank Office; United Bank of India; Cachar, Karimganj & Hailakandi districts.

* Prior to 1983, Karimganj and Hailakandi was the part of erstwhile Cachar district which enjoyed independent district status on 1983 and 1989 respectively. Thus for brevity of analysis and comparison 1983 is taken as base.

Growth of Bank Branches

The bank nationalisation witnessed a spectacular achievement in the banking system through the expansion of bank branches. The establishment of more rural branches undoubtedly has served the twin objective of mobilization of rural deposits and channelisation of credit to the rural areas. However, the pace of acceleration of deposit mobilisation depends on the economic and industrial infrastructure of higher magnitude as well as creating greater awareness among rural populace for effective use of bank credit. Otherwise rural deposit would continue to be siphoned off to urban centres (Raul,1997)[1]. Therefore, the credit absorption capacity in the rural areas largely depends on the availability of required infrastructure.

During pre-bank nationalisation period, the banking activities in backward region particularly in North-Eastern Region (NER) was in the low ebb with limited lending activities. In 1949, there was only 32 number of bank branches in Assam. The total credit deployed in the whole state was Rs. 4.29 crores while the developed states like West Bengal received the lion share of Rs 145.22 crores (30.7 per cent) followed by Maharashtra with 129.04 crores (27.4 per cent), Tamil Nadu Rs 53.25 crores (11.2 per cent). (RBI,1954).

Under this backdrop banking scenario in the districts under study may be reckoned with their performance in the context of the country as a whole. The branch expansion in the districts under study is presented in the Table - 1.

It is revealed that during post-reform period there are only few new branches came up in the Cachar and Karimganj districts. While the branch expansion is comparatively higher in the Hailakandi district. The coefficient of variation (**cv**) is used to compare the inter district of branch expansion during the pre and post reform era.

	Pre-Reform (1983-1990)	*Post-Reform (1991-2000)*
CV_K	25.7	0.5
CV_C	14.8	0.9
CV_H	-	7.5
CV_T	20.4	1.6

Source : Self calculated on the basis of Table - 1.

It has been observed that during the pre-reform era, cv. of branch expansion of Karimganj district is 25.7 per cent as against 14.8 per cent in Cachar district. This registers rapid growth of bank branches in Karimganj district.

GINI'S COEFFICIENT

		1985			1991			2000	
Districts	*Population* in Lakhs*	*Bank offices in number*	*Population pressure per office '000*	*Population* in Lakhs*	*Bank offices in number*	*Population pressure per office '000*	*Population* in Lakhs*	*Bank offices in number*	*Population pressure per office '000*
Cachar	10.86 (49.3)	30 (44.7)	36.2	12.2 (48.8)	46 (53.4)	26.5	14.7 (48.8)	50 (52.6)	29.4
Kari mganj	7.12 (32.3)	27 (40.3)	26.3	8.3 (33.2)	29 (33.7)	28.6	10.0 (33.2)	30 (31.6)	33.3
Hailakandi	4.03 (18.4)	10 (14.9)	40.3	4.5 (18.0)	11 (12.9)	40.8	5.4 (18.6)	15 (15.7)	36.0
Total	22.01 (100)	67 (100)	32.8	25.0 (100)	86 (100)	29.1	30.2 (100)	95 (100)	37.8
G.C.C.		**2.25**			**(–) 6.43**			**(–) 4.07**	

Figures in the parentheses indicate percentage to total

*estimated by expert committee on population projection, Registrar General of India.

Source : (1) Directorate of Economics and Statistics, Government of India.

(2) Lead Bank offices, United Bank of India, Cachar, Karimganj and Hailakandi districts

$$* \; GCC = \frac{1}{100} \cdot (X_1 \cdot Y_2 - X_2 \cdot Y_1) + (X_2 \cdot Y_3 - X_3 \cdot Y_2) + \cdots + (X_n \cdot 100 - Y_n \cdot 100)$$

where,

GCC = Gini's coefficient of concentration.

$X_1, X_2, \text{- - - - -} X_n$ = Subsequent cumulative percentage of population distributed over district and

$Y_1, Y_2, \text{- - - - -} Y_n$ = Subsequent cumulative percentage of bank branches distributed over district.

Further, the growth rate of branch expansion is negligible except Hailakandi district (cv =7.5) in the post-reform era. The reason may be attributed to the district Hailakandi has enjoyed independent district status from 1989 only. Further, in order to assess inter district disparities of branch expansion, we have calculated Gini's co-efficient of concentration (**GCC**) with a view to determine whether the bank branches are adequately serving the population.

The GCC has been calculated mainly for 1985, 1991, 2000 to find out the trends therein. The table (in page 122) exhibited the position of the districts in respect of population as well as branch offices.

The analysis reveals that the co-efficient (**GCC**) has increased over the period. In 1985, it was 2.25 then plummeted to 4.07 in 2000. This reveals that the existing bank branches are inadequate to serve the population in the districts under study. Therefore, major areas are still remaining not served by the banks and the rural masses are yet to access the banking services. It is further confirmed by the foregoing analysis relating to the population served by the bank branches. It has been observed that during 1985 population served per branch at all India average was 15,000 against 32,000 in the study area that has further increased to 37,000 in December 2000.

Deposit Mobilization

The extent and volume of deposit mobilisation, an important parameter of banking performance is presented in Table – 2.

It has been observed that in December 1985, the total bank deposits relating to all banks in Barak valley stood at Rs 8139 lakhs of which PSBs accounted only 89.0 per cent against the national average of 94.6 per cent. This suggests that the pace of deposit mobilisation in the valley is almost at par with the all-India level.

The percentage share of PSBs deposits however increased to 90.4 per cent in December 1991. During, 1985-91 total bank deposits of the valley increased by 3.20 times against 2.70 times at national level. Further, the post reform period witnessed an increase to the tune of Rs. 103245 lakhs in December 2000 accounting 87.7 per cent of total deposit of all banks operating in the districts. This has however been achieved against 81.3 per cent at the all India level. The scene of deposit culture of private

TABLE – 2
GROWTH OF DEPOSITS OF PSBs VIS-À-VIS OTHER BANKS IN BARAK VALLEY IN DECEMBER (1984 – 2000)

(Amount Rs. in Lakhs.)

Year	*Public Sector Banks*			*Cachar Gramin Bank*	*Private sector Banks*	*Total Banks*
	SBI group	*Nationalised Banks*	*Total*			
1984	NA	NA	6265	NA	NA	6265 (100)
1985	2021 (24.8)	5225 (64.1)	7246 (89.0)	201 (2.4)	692 (8.5)	8139 (100)
1986	2923 (29.9)	6230 (61.6)	8353 (82.6)	216 (2.1)	738 (7.3)	10107 (100)
1987	3635 (32.4)	6417 (53.3)	10052 (89.7)	421 (3.7)	727 (5.5)	11200 (100)
1988	5023 (33.1)	8350 (55.0)	13367 (88.1)	776 (5.1)	1031 (6.7)	15174 (100)
1989	5793 (28.5)	12457 (56.1)	18250 (90.0)	762 (3.7)	1265 (6.8)	20277 (100)
1990	6650 (30.9)	12434 (57.8)	19084 (88.2)	820 (5.1)	1605 (6.8)	21509 (100)
1991	6477 (24.8)	16917 (64.8)	23394 (90.4)	976 (3.7)	1736 (6.6)	26106 (100)
1992	7981 (27.2)	18329 (62.5)	26310 (89.7)	1183 (4.0)	1823 (6.3)	29316 (100)
1993	8781 (26.9)	20417 (62.6)	29198 (88.3)	1353 (4.5)	2053 (6.2)	32608 (100)
1994	10939 (28.6)	23757 (62.2)	34696 (89.9)	1561 (5.1)	1885 (5.9)	38142 (100)
1995	13018 (28.7)	27806 (61.7)	40824 (88.1)	2252 (6.1)	2696 (5.9)	45772 (100)
1996	15334 (29.3)	30822 (59.0)	46156 (88.3)	3311 (6.3)	2735 (5.7)	52202 (100)
1997	17310 (28.1)	38834 (61.2)	56144 (88.9)	3864 (6.0)	3604 (6.1)	63612 (100)
1998	22997 (28.9)	47581 (59.7)	70578 (89.1)	4841 (6.1)	4189 (5.9)	79608 (100)
1999	26637 (28.0)	56646 (59.5)	83283 (87.5)	6736 (7.1)	5105 (5.4)	95124 (100)
2000	27319 (24.9)	68713 (62.7)	96032 (87.7)	7213 (6.5)	6209 (5.6)	109454 (100)

NA = Not available

Source : Lead Bank Office, United Bank of India, Cachar, Karimganj & Hailakandi district.

banks in the districts is reverse against all India shares of private bank's deposits, which has declined to 5.6 per cent in December 2000 from 8.5 per cent in 1985. However, it has increased to 13.3 per cent in 2000-2001 from 3.5 per cent in 1984-85 at the national level.

A comparison of growth of bank deposits may be revealed by compound growth rate (**cgr**) both in pre- and post-reform period. This can further be verified with co-efficient of variation (**cv**). The bank group-wise results of cgr and cv are obtained as under –

CGR AND CV OF BANK DEPOSITS (1985-2000)

Periods	*Value of*	*SBI*	*Nationalised Banks*	*PSBs Total*	*Cachar Gramin Bank*	*Pvt. Sector Bank*	*Total*
Pre-reform (1985-1990)	Cgr	38.6	34.8	40.6	45.1	28.6	21.2
	Cv	58.52	50.62	36.6	49.4	33.2	35.1
Post-reform (1991-2000)	Cgr	20.3	28.9	31.8	48.9	42.3	19.8
	Cv	46.6	47.7	48.3	48.3	38.9	48.1

Source : Self calculated on the basis of Table – 2.

The growth of deposits of PSBs during the pre-reform era (cgr = 40.6) was better than that of post-reform era (cgr. = 31.8). In case of private banks it was however better in the post-reform (cgr = 42.3) pre-reform (cgr = 28.6). It could thus be inferred from the above analysis that the reform measures have played a little in mobilising deposits in the area under study.

Channelisation of Credit

The growth of bank advances in the study area is furnished in the Table - 3.

The table delineated that the total bank advances in the valley was Rs. 3456 lakhs in 1985 of which the PSBs hold 89.5 per cent and the balance by private banks and Cachar Gramin banks.

The growth of bank advances in the area under study further has been assessed with compound growth rate in the pre (1985-91) and post reform (1991-2000) era respectively (origin at 1985 and 1991). The **cgr** of advances obtained as under -

TABLE – 3
GROWTH OF ADVANCES OF PSBs VIS A VIS OTHER BANKS IN BARAK VALLEY AS ON END DECEMBER

(Amount Rs. in Lakhs)

Year	*SBI group*	*Nationalised Banks*	*Public Sector Banks*	*Cachar Gramin Bank*	*Private Banks*	*Total Banks*
1984	NA	NA	2462	NA	NA	2462 (100)
1985	1563 (45.2)	1532 (44.3)	3095 (89.5)	149 (4.3)	212 (6.2)	3456 (100)
1986	1872 (47.3)	1972 (49.8)	3414 (86.3)	258 (6.5)	282 (7.2)	3954 (100)
1987	2031 (40.9)	2265 (45.6)	4296 (87.2)	351 (7.0)	318 (6.5)	4965 (100)
1988	2344 (35.4)	3436 (57.4)	5780 (87.3)	485 (7.3)	350 (0.8)	6615 (100)
1989	2942 (31.1)	5487 (58.0)	8429 (89.5)	572 (6.0)	452 (4.8)	9453 (100)
1990	2714 (28.0)	5897 (60.8)	8611 (89.2)	591 (6.2)	483 (4.1)	9685 (100)
1991	2919 (27.8)	6206 (59.1)	9125 (88.6)	669 (6.3)	698 (6.7)	10492 (100)
1992	3027 (27.1)	6583 (60.2)	9610 (85.7)	802 (7.2)	792 (6.9)	71204 (100)
1993	3211 (27.1)	6889 (58.6)	10100 (84.9)	976 (8.3)	726 (6.5)	11802 (100)
1994	3437 (28.0)	7395 (59.8)	10832 (86.3)	896 (7.1)	784 (5.7)	12512 (100)
1995	4097 (26.1)	8283 (57.4)	12380 (87.4)	1120 (8.6)	908 (4.8)	14408 (100)
1996	4127 (25.1)	8816 (60.1)	12943 (84.2)	1214 (9.2)	786 (5.9)	14943 (100)
1997	3987 (25.3)	8931 (59.2)	12918 (84.6)	1395 (9.1)	961 (6.2)	15274 (100)
1998	5187 (26.2)	9945 (56.8)	12132 (86.5)	1481 (8.5)	870 (5.9)	17483 (100)
1999	4667 (24.7)	11112 (58.7)	15779 (83.5)	1934 (10.2)	1194 (6.0)	18907 (100)
2000	523 (24.3)	12982 (60.3)	18213 (84.6)	2058 (9.5)	1253 (5.9)	21524 (100)

NA = Not available

Figures in the brackets indicate per cent to total advances

Source : Lead Bank office, United Bank of India, Cachar, Karimganj and Hailakandi District.

GROWTH OF ADVANCES

Cgr	*SBI*	*NBs*	*PSBs*	*CGB*	*Pvt. B*	*Total banks*
Pre-reform						
(1985 – 91)	36.1	49.2	41.2	51.6	35.1	41.9
Post-reforms						
(1991 – 2000)	11.2	12.6	14.6	15.9	13.7	16.0

Source : Self calculated on the basis of Table-3.

It is evident from the analysis that reform package had not brought any positive change in the channelisation of credit in the study area. The Cgr of advances of all banks slipped from 49.9 in the pre reform years to 16.0 in post reform era. This may be due to the reduction of priority sector lending norms from 40 per cent to 10 per cent on the basis of recommendation of the committee on financial system. (GOI, 1991)[3]

To examine the nature of growth of deposit as well as the growth of advances incremental growth of each variable has been calculated in the post reform period (1991-2000). In this respect, following hypothesis has been framed to test whether the growth of incremental deposit is at the same level of incremental advances or, whether banks are deploying credit in the economy at the same rate what they are mobilising.

"There is no difference in the growth of incremental deposit as well as incremental credit"

To test this hypothesis Pearson's correlation co-efficient (r) between incremental deposit and incremental advances has been calculated. The result obtained as under –

'r' = 0.615, 't' = 2.206, $t_{0.01}$ (8 df.) = 2.306, $t_{0.05}$ (8 df.) = 3.355

The analysis manifests that positive correlation coefficient is statistically not significant at 1 per cent and 5 per cent level of significance. This implies that the banks in the study area are not deploying credit at the same rate what they have mobilised deposits from the area under study. This indicates further siphoning of fund from the area of the study to the other region. Further, this has been confirmed by the analysis of C/D ratio (mentioned hereafter) that majority of PSBs in the study area has not attained the C/D ratio of 60 per cent stipulated at the national level.

Districtwise Classification of Deposit

The underline principle of branch expansion is to mobilize more deposits. The PSBs in this respect have been mobilising rural savings and inculcate the savings habit among rural masses. The Table – 4 furnishes the districtwise position of amount of deposits and the growth of deposit per office of PSBs. The table exhibited the fact that the total deposit of PSBs in Cachar district increased from Rs. 6123 lakhs in 1985 to Rs. 51203 lakhs in 2000 representing a significant increase of Rs. 45080 lakhs during the period of fifteen years. The share of PSBs has also increased from Rs. 2970 lakhs to 24516 lakhs during the same period under consideration in Karimganj district and in case of Hailakandi district it has increased from Rs. 3158 lakhs in 1985 to Rs. 20313 lakhs in December 2000.

The deposit per branches of PSBs turned out to be Rs. 110.00 lakhs and Rs. 153.1 lakhs for Karimganj and Cachar district respectively in 1985 and Rs. 315.8 lakhs for Hailakandi district in 1989*. The same has swelled to Rs. 817.2 lakhs, Rs. 1024.1 lakhs and Rs. 1354.2 lakhs for Karimganj, Cachar and Hailakandi district in 2000 respectively. The notable feature is revealed from the analysis of PSBs deposit performance that the districts have witnessed significant growth rate in deposit as well as deposit per office, despite all impediments. This shows a close interaction of bank personnel and rural population during the reform era. However, in respect of the deposit per office, the PSBs of the area under study failed to maintain national trend. In 1985 the deposit per office in India was Rs. 150 lakhs, which increased to Rs. 505 lakhs in 1991 and further to Rs. 1983 lakhs in 2000-2001. Thus, additional bank branches under Lead bank scheme have taped the deposits from rural masses as well as the population of the districts as a whole and also endeavoured to cultivate the savings habit among them.

Further, an attempt has been made to assess the relationship between growth of deposits of PSBs both in the national level and in the study area. We employ in this respect the analysis of correlation co-efficient between incremental deposits of PSBs in India and incremental deposits in the districts under study viz., Karimganj, Cachar and Hailakandi during the post reform years. The **matrix of 'r' value** is presented as under-

---

* *The year 1989 has been taken as base for Hailakandi District as it has enjoyed its independent district status on 1989 only.*

TABLE - 4
DISTRICTWISE DEPOSITS OF PUBLIC SECTOR BANKS IN BARAK VALLEY (DECEMBER)

(Amount Rs. in lakhs)

	Karimganj			Cachar			Hailakandi			
Year	*Total deposits (Rs.)*	*No. of bank branches*	*Deposit per office (Rs.)*	*Total deposits (Rs.)*	*No. of banks branches*	*Deposit per office (Rs.)*	*Total deposits (Rs.)*	*No. of bank branches*	*Deposit per office (Rs.)*	*National level deposit per office (Rs.)*
1985	2970	27	110.0	6123	40	153.1	NA	NA	NA	150
1986	2312	27	85.6	6895	42	164.2	NA	NA	NA	251
1987	2831	28	101.1	7221	42	171.9	NA	NA	NA	292
1988	3292	28	117.6	9296	42	221.3	NA	NA	NA	346
1989	3918	28	139.9	11174	42	266.1	3158	10	315.8	400
1990	4530	28	161.8	10132	43	235.6	4422	10	442.2	456
1991	5801	29	200.0	12858	46	297.5	5052	11	459.2	505
1992	6672	29	230.0	13786	49	281.3	5857	11	532.5	599
1993	7681	29	264.9	15146	49	309.1	6377	12	531.4	697
1994	9017	30	300.6	17686	49	360.9	7988	12	665.7	698
1995	9874	30	392.1	22131	49	451.6	8819	12	734.9	798
1996	11858	30	395.3	24558	50	491.2	9740	13	749.2	879
1997	12160	30	405.3	31578	50	631.5	12659	13	973.7	1042
1998	15632	30	521.1	37889	50	757.8	17057	15	1137.1	1236
1999	18158	30	605.3	46090	50	921.8	19035	15	1269.0	1450
2000	24516	30	817.2	51203	50	1024.1	20313	15	1354.2	1693

Sources : Lead Bank Office, UBI, Cachar, Karimganj and Hailakandi.

CORRELATION COEFFICIENT OF INCREMENTAL DEPOSITS

	All India	*Karimganj*	*Cachar*	*Hailakandi*
All India	1.00			
Karimganj	0.818* (3.762)	1.00		
Cachar	0.852* (4.305)	0.493 (1.499)	1.00	
Hailakandi	0.801* (3.540)	0.751* (2.999)	0.690* (2.524)	1.00

**Indicates significant.* *Figures in parentheses indicate 't' value.* $t_{0.05}$ *(7df) = 2.365*

The above econometric analysis reveals that correlation coefficient in the districts under study and national level in respect of incremental deposit is statistically significant at 5 per cent level of significance. This indicates the banks in the district under study are mobilising deposit over the years at par with the national level. The correlation coefficient of inter district deposit mobilisation, on the other hand, shows that banks in the district are performing well even at the same pace of inculcating the saving habit in the population. Thus, a further analysis is required in respect of the factors influencing the growth of deposit of PSBs.

Determinants of Deposit Mobilisation of PSBs in the Districts

The deposit mobilisation is a significant indicator of bank performance. However, the pace of growth of deposit received by the bank is influenced by several factors. We in this respect have considered the factors like Gross Domestic Product, index of consumer prices, interest rate on deposit and branch expansion. To know the inter dependency among the variables we have fitted regression equation which is found to be –

$$\text{Y (Deposit)} = -9614.632 + 4411\text{E-02 Gdp} + 0.407 \text{ Indc} - 1691.538 \text{ Int} + 254.852 \text{ Br.}$$

SE. (22756.221) (007) (4.131) (1048.337) (433.177)

The other results obtained as under.

Variables	*β*	*'t' value*	*Sig.*	*F*	R^2	*Adjusted* R^2
β_0 (constant)	-	-0.423	0.683			
GDPs at current prices (Gdp)	0.928	5.963	0.000			
Index of consumer prices (Indc)	0.009	0.098	0.924	102.691 (000[a]) Sig.	0.979	0.969
Interest rate on deposit (Intd)	-0.137	-1.614	0.141			
Branch expansion (Br)	0.121	0.588	0.571			

Significant at p = 0.05.

TABLE – 5
DISTRICTWISE ADVANCES OF PUBLIC SECTOR BANKS IN BARAK VALLEY (DECEMBER)

(Amount Rs. in lakhs)

	Karimganj			*Cachar*			*Hailakandi*		
Year	*Total Advances*	*No. of Banks branches*	*Advances per office*	*Total Advances*	*No. of Banks branches*	*Advances per office*	*Total Advances*	*No. of Banks branches*	*Advances per office*
1985	1012	27	37.5	2083	40	52.0	NA	NA	NA
1986	1058	27	39.2	2786	42	66.3	NA	NA	NA
1987	1335	28	47.6	2961	42	70.5	NA	NA	NA
1988	1373	28	49.0	4407	42	104.9	NA	NA	NA
1989	2091	28	74.7	4630	42	110.2	1708	10	170.8
1990	2319	28	82.8	4440	43	103.2	1852	10	185.2
1991	2330	29	80.3	4601	46	100.1	2194	11	199.4
1992	2623	29	90.4	4581	49	93.4	2406	11	218.7
1993	2708	29	93.4	4741	49	96.7	2651	12	220.9
1994	2938	30	97.9	5204	49	106.2	2690	12	224.2
1995	3175	30	105.8	6118	49	124.8	3087	12	257.2
1996	3120	30	104.0	6669	50	133.4	3154	13	262.5
1997	2689	30	89.6	7032	50	140.6	3277	13	273.0
1998	3475	30	115.8	8257	50	165.1	3400	15	283.3
1999	2735	30	91.2	9411	50	188.2	3633	15	302.7
2000	3287	30	109.5	10312	50	206.2	4614	15	433.1

* PSB includes SBI and other nationalised banks.

Sources : Lead Bank Office, UBI, Cachar, Karimganj and Hailakandi.

The analysis shows that $R^2 = 0.979$. This indicates about 98 per cent variations in the deposit mobilization of PSBs in the districts is explained by independent variables. It is further confirmed by F ratio that turns to be statistically significant. This implies the independent variables like branch expansion, interest rates and gross domestic product are perfect determinants of dependent variable viz. deposit mobilisation. However β (beta) value of each of the independent variables is statistically not significant at 5 per cent level of significance except GDP at current prices indicating that variables have no direct impact on deposit mobilisation in the study area. In other words, it can be argued that growth of bank deposit is very much subjective and only depends on economic condition of the society.

Districtwise Classification of Bank Credit

The growth of advances measured in terms of advances per office of PSBs operating in the districts has been presented in the Table –5 as under. It has been observed that bank credit in the district is far behind than the national level credit of Rs. 810 lakhs per office as on March 2000. Moreover the districts except Hailakandi are yet to catch up the state's average credit of Rs. 238.4 lakhs per office as on March 1999 (NEIBM 1999).[4]

In order to assess the extent of credit channelisation by the banks in the districts under study, we have calculated inter district correlation coefficient among incremental advances per branch shown as under –

CORRELATION COEFFICIENTS OF INCREMENTAL ADVANCES PER BRANCH

	India	*Karimganj*	*Cachar*	*Hailakandi*
India	1.00			
Karimganj	– 0.496 (1.616)	1.00		
Cachar	–0.329 (0.985)	0.094 (0.267)	1.00	
Hailakandi	0.492 (1.599)	0.273 (0.863)	0.316 (0.943)	1.00

Figures in the parentheses indicate 't' value.
$t_{0.05}$ *(8 df) = 2.306*

The analysis manifests that correlation coefficient in respect of advances per office of district under study in the national context scenario turned to be negative. This implies that the districts are yet to catch up the national tempo of credit channelisation. In other words banks are deploying credit in some other areas without deploying them for the economic growth of the area from which they have mobilised funds.

Now bank's performance in terms of growth of deposit per office and advances per office has been measured by using correlation coefficient (r) pertaining to both pre and post reform era. The high correlation coefficient will undoubtedly indicate more savings habit of the people as well as higher volume of credit deployment in the district. The results are found as under.

Period	*'r'*	*'t' value (cal)*	*'t' value (tab)*	
			1 per cent.	*5 per cent.*
Pre Reform	$r_k = 0.89$	3.904*	4.604	2.776
(1985 – 91)	$r_c = 0.97$	7.980**	4.604	2.776
	$r_H = -$			
Post reform	$r_k = 0.54$	1.813	3.355	2.306
(1991 – 2000)	$r_c = 0.74$	1.111*	3.355	2.306
	$r_H = 0.71$	2.851*	3.355	2.306

K = Karimganj, C = Cachar, H = Hailakandi

* *Significant at* $t_{.05}$

** *Significant at* $t_{.01}$ *and* $t_{.05}$.

The analysis explores the existence of high positive 'r' value for all districts under study in the pre reform era. However, 'r' value in post reform period appeared to be statistically not significant for Karimganj district and significant only at 5 per cent level of significance for Cachar and Hailakandi district. This highlights that the performance of PSBs in respect of deposit mobilisation and credit deployment is not satisfactory during post reform era. The analysis also reveals inter district credit gap as well as variation in the deposit mobilisation during post reform years. On the other hand, insignificant correlation coefficient implies that there is a scope of expediting the pace of banking operation in the districts under study.

Credit Deposit Ratio

Credit deposit ratio is considered as dependable indicator of efficiency of bank's participation in the developmental process. It indicates the extent of bank deposits advanced to multifarious activities in the area.

Nambiar (1980)[5] articulated that low credit absorption capacity due to low infrastructural facilities in the area particularly in 'No industrial region' is the main hardle of increasing in C/D ratio. The commercial banks, financial institutions along with developing and implementing authorities of the area can only take a challenge against the congenital impediments to sustain the economic development of that area. C/D ratio is not an unbiased indicator since it depends on two variables viz, total deposits and total advances. It has been observed that banks may have to grant advances to the beneficiaries through several government-sponsored schemes. In this case with the increase of advances, the C/D ratio will increase with the deposit variable remaining constant. Sikidar (1990)[6] has aptly viewed that the C/D ratio should be looked into its segment and disaggregated forms and for extending advances the sources of fund are –

(1) deposits

(2) refinance from higher financial institution

(3) accretion of profit.

C/D ratio, thus, does not manifest relatively better financial position. In the financial sector reform regime, Mani and Chacko (2002)[7] viewed that any low C/D ratio is unhealthy and will adversely affect the profitability of banks and hence, suggested the need of a detailed enquiry into the dynamics of its entirety. Nandal and Singh (2002)[8] observed that due to larger quantum of deposits, banks have advanced credit to a large extent but C/D ratio has not been found satisfactory. They suggested there should be proper recovery of loan amount from the loanee in order to have satisfactory C/D ratio, otherwise banks would suffer causing harm to the economy as a whole. Bhagawati (1991)[9] articulated that banks in north-eastern region have not been able to increase their credit portfolio. As a result, bank's sensitiveness and effectiveness in planning bank advances is required for bringing a paradigm change in the competitive environment.

Since nationalisation, the C/D ratio remained at the low ebb in the state of Assam, and for NER as a whole. In December 1982, the C/D ratio of state Assam was 41.1 per cent, and NER achieved 41.2 per cent, which was far behind from the national average of 68.2 per cent (GOI, 1987)[10]. The credit Deposit ratios of each bank groups can be had the following Table -7.

TABLE – 7

BANK GROUPWISE CREDIT-DEPOSIT RATIOS IN BARAK VALLEY AS ON END MARCH

(Ratio's in percentage)

Year	*State Bank groups*	*Nationalised Banks*	*Cachar Grameen Bank*	*Public Sector Banks (SBI–NBs)*	*Private banks*	*Total banks*
1994	NA	NA	51.2	NA	91.2	47.9
1985	58.3	56.0	68.9	51.2	41.9	49.1
1986	61.2	62.5	62.3	40.5	30.2	50.2
1987	59.1	69.5	74.8	46.1	31.7	44.8
1988	53.2	51.2	69.4	46.5	35.5	46.9
1989	46.8	56.3	54.1	47.0	38.1	41.7
1990	42.0	53.3	'58.7	51.0	37.2	36.7
1991	38.5	48.1	59.8	38.5	35.1	30.7
1992	39.1	36.5	54.1	38.4	30.0	41.0
1993	37.8	32.3	46.2	36.9	25.1	35.8
1994	33.1	31.3	38.3	32.5	21.7	31.2
1995	30.4	28.1	33.3	32.3	35.0	30.2
1996	22.4	27.0	30.2	26.10	33.6	28.0
1997	19.5	32.9	31.8	22.3	27.1	22.9
1998	18.2	30.4	31.0	22.6	31.1	22.5
1999	17.0	22.4	34.1	20.8	25.0	25.8
2000	15.2	32.5	31.2	23.1	26.3	20.0

NA : Not available.

Source : Lead Bank office, Cachar, Karimganj and Hailakandi district: File Record.

TABLE – 8
DISTRICTWISE CLASSIFICATION OF CREDIT-DEPOSIT RATIO (END MARCH)

(Ratios in percentage)

District	*1985*	*1987*	*1989*	*1990*	*1991*	*1993*	*1995*	*1997*	*1999*	*2000*
Karimganj	50.9	44.8	48.1	50.5	48.9	35.8	34.5	21.3	22.0	19.8
Cachar	49.2	46.9	46.7	36.7	30.7	31.5	30.2	22.9	22.6	20.0
Hailakandi	NA	NA	NA	49.6	43.2	36.8	32.7	21.8	20.5	23.1
Barak valley	51.2	46.1	47.0	51.0	38.6	36.9	32.3	22.3	20.8	23.1
Assam average (State)	NA	57.9	53.0	53.1	45.2	42.8	38.0	35.2	31.1	NA
India average	68.7	65.5	65.1	66.0	54.2	56.7	59.2	57.3	55.8	NA

Source : *(i) Lead Bank office, UBI, Cachar, Karimganj and Hailakandi district.*
(ii) Government of India (2000) Basic Statistics for NER, NEC Publications, Shillong. pp. 184.
(iii) Banking Sector, NEC Secretariat, Shillong.

TABLE – 9

BANKWISE DETAILS OF DEPOSITS, ADVANCES AND CREDIT DEPOSIT RATIO OF ALL BANKS IN BARAK VALLEY AS ON END DECEMBER

(Amount Rs. in Lakhs and ratios in percentage)

Banks	1985			1991			1999		
	Deposits (Rs.)	Advances (Rs.)	C/D ratio	Deposits (Rs.)	Advances (Rs.)	C/D ratio	Deposits (Rs.)	Advances (Rs.)	C/D ratio
State Bank of India	2021	1563	58.3	6477	2919	38.5	26637	4667	17.0
United Bank of India	3019	828	51.3	7819	3609	39.1	31897	4538	21.0
Allahabad Bank	751	251	26.9	1403	351	18.2	2356	518	19.0
Punjab National Bank	423	123	33.2	1042	312	43.3	2759	555	28.0
Vijaya Bank	107	21	NA	445	90	20.2	1691	516	19.0
Central Bank of India	123	48	80.2	2509	712	43.6	6480	1724	26.0
Indian Bank	113	42	27.1	241	71	29.5	1231	247	19.0
Union Bank of India	NA	46	29.4	523	151	25.8	1768	428	18.0
United Commercial Bank	428	118	49.0	2039	560	47.8	4468	1669	27.0
Panjab & Sind Bank	94	42	17.9	253	56	21.9	665	169	24.1
Bank of Baroda	104	38	49.4	505	239	47.3	2982	567	20.0
Indian Overseas Bank	NA	NA	NA	NA	NA	NA	100	13	14.0
Purbanchal Bank	24	17	NA	NA	NA	NA	NA	NA	NA
Canara Bank	13	29	124.9	38	55	143.1	246	168	43.0
Public Sector Banks	**7246**	**3095**	**51.2**	**23394**	**9125**	**38.6**	**83283**	**15779**	**20.8**
Cachar Gramin Bank	201	149	68.9	976	669	59.8	6736	1934	34.1
Federal Bank	271	76	23.6	615	263	42.7	2986	460	14.0
Assam Co-op. Apex Bank	421	934	32.8	1121	192	34.4	2119	734	39.0
Total	**8139**	**3954**	**49.1**	**26106**	**10.492**	**36.7**	**95124**	**18907**	**25.8**

NA = Not available *Source : Lead Bank office, UBI, Cachar, Karimganj and Hailakandi districts.*

The table manifests that C/D ratio of each bank groups have declined both in pre and post reform era. The declining rate is more significant in PSBs than that of their private counterpart. In 1985, the ratio for PSBs was 51.2 per cent against 41.9 per cent for private banks, which slipped to 23.1 per cent and 26.3 per cent for PSBs, and private banks respectively in Dec. 2000.

The SBI however, witnessed a declining trend since 1987 and touched the bottom level at 15.2 per cent as on March 2000. Table-8 depicts the districtwise variations in C/D ratio.

It is evident from the table that the districts under study have failed to achieve national average of C/D ratio even the state average over the years and rate of decline is more prominent during post nationalisation era. The gravity of the situation could be understood by the fact that during 1996, Tamilnadu, Karnataka and Andhra Pradesh witnessed C/D ratio of 89.02 per cent, 69.68 per cent. and 80.82 per cent respectively against the average of the southern state 79.90 per cent (SLBC, 1996)[11]. The reason of significant declining of C\D ratio may be attributed to the mounting number of defaulters over the years, non recovery of loans, willful defaulters, lack of supervision of end use of bank credit, lack of implementation of bankable schemes , definitional change in NPAs and so on.

Table-9 presents individual bankwise C/D ratio. The table discerned that no banks operating in the districts achieved stipulated C/D ratio, i.e., 60 per cent rather they have witnessed a gradual-declining trend over the years. This exhibited poor credit absorption capacity of the entire area along with lack of entrepreneurial zeal to undertake viable projects.

Priority Sector Lending of PSBs

The banks, without insisting adequate security, have supplied advances to priority and other neglected sections of the society at a concession rate of interest. However, the banking statistics revealed that, this designated priority sector as well as neglected sections received about 15 per cent of the total bank credit at the time of bank nationalisation. On the later period, proportion of advances to the priority sector has increased from 15 per cent to 33.3 per cent in 1974 and further to 40 per cent in 1980. The commercial banks in general and PSBs in particular, have achieved the target and even surpassed it in quantitative terms. But in qualitative terms, there is an apprehension among the bankers that the advances to priority sector resulted in a loss of interest income due to highly subsidized lending rates. As a result, the profitability of banks has adversely affected besides maintaining additional manpower requirements for supervision of small loans, mounting overdues, poor recovery of advances and raising volume of NPAs. (Niranjana, 2002)[12].

The Narasimham Committee (1991)[13] on financial sector reform has drawn attention to the problem of low and declining profitability and stated that "there is need for gradual phasing out of the directed credit programme, i.e., the stipulations that 40 per cent of all credit should go to the priority sector should be scrapped. The priority sector should be redefined and the proportion shall be fixed at 10 per cent of the aggregate credit." Table – 10 presents the data on the total bank advances to the priority and non-priority sector for the period between 1984 and 2000 in the three districts of the valley.

The table reveals that the share of priority sector advances to total advances have been declined in three districts both in pre and post reforms era. It has been observed that the average annual growth (**agr**) of total advances was 16.0 per cent, 12.5 per cent and 4.1 per cent in the Karimganj, Cachar and Hailakandi district respectively in the pre reform period, which has sharply declined to 13.3 per cent. 8.0 per cent. and 3.8 per cent in the post reform era. The sectorwise growth of credit in the post reform period is comparatively lower than that of pre reform period.

Sectorwise Credit Deployment of Banks

The banks operating in the area, keeping in view of their aim and objectives for the economic development under the lead bank schemes, have made an effort in providing financial support to agriculture and small-scale sector. The sectorwise credit deployment in the district is shown in Table-11. The table reveals that agriculture is one of the single dominant sectors that absorbed major portion of the credit outstanding both in pre and post reform era. In March 1985, credit outstanding for agriculture was Rs 165.35 lakhs, Rs 226.96 lakhs, Rs. 131.01 lakhs for Karimganj, Cachar and Hailakandi district respectively. The same has increased to Rs 159.7 lakhs, Rs. 334.78 lakhs and Rs. 143.26 lakhs in March 2000 respectively for three districts.

TABLE – 10
BANK CREDIT OUTSTANDING BY ACTIVITY IN BARAK VALLEY AS ON END DECEMBER

(Amount Rs. in lakhs)

Year	Karimganj district			Cachar district			Hailakandi district		
	Priority Sector	*Non-Priority Sector*	*Total*	*Priority Sector*	*Non-Priority Sector*	*Total*	*Priority Sector*	*Non-Priority Sector*	*Total*
1984	502 (77.5)	145 (22.5)	647 (100)	1308(72.1)	507(28.9)	1815 (100)	Nil	Nil	Nil
1985	715(65.6)	375(34.4)	1090(100)	821(76.9)	545(231)	2366(100)	Nil	Nil	Nil
1986	1023(83.5)	206(16.5)	1229(100)	2108(72.1)	814(279)	2922(100)	Nil	Nil	Nil
1987	1208(81.5)	274(18.5)	1482(100)	2572(73.8)	911(252)	3483(100)	Nil	Nil	Nil
1988	1231 (727)	461(27.3)	1692(100)	3035(57.4)	1894(42.6)	4929 (100)	Nil	Nil	Nil
1989	1508(64.6)	826(35.4)	2334(100)	3135(57.2)	2113(428)	5248(100)	1224 (71.6)	484 (20.4)	1708 (100)
1990	1531(64.3)	850(36.6)	2381(100)	3011(65.8)	2029(342)	5040(100)	1293 (69.3)	569 (30.7)	1852 (100)
agr	13.3	22.5	16.0	10.0	17.3	12.5	2.8	8.3	4.1
1991	1403(57.0)	1056(43.0)	2459(100)	4256(57.6)	1018(42.4)	5274(100)	1484 (67.6)	710 (32.4)	2194 (100)
1992	1625 (592)	1120(40.8)	2745(100)	3029(59.1)	2046(30.9)	5075(100)	1589 (77.6)	457 (22.4)	2046 (100)
1993	1700(61.0)	1325(39.0)	3025(100)	3073(57.1)	2306(42.9)	5379 (100)	1834 (69.1)	817 (30.9)	2651 (100)
1994	1731(56.3)	1345(43.7)	3074 (100)	3180(56.3)	2466(43.7)	5646 (100)	1577(58.6)	1113 (41.4)	2690 (100)
1995	1693(47.4)	1878 (52.6)	3571(100)	3772(57.7)	2585(42.3)	6357(100)	1780(576)	1307 (42.4)	1336 (43.3)
1996	2010(55.8)	1593(44.2)	3603(100)	4384(58.1)	3161(41.9)	7545(100)	1791(56.7)	1363 (43.3)	3154 (100)
1997	2022 (614)	1167(36.6)	3189(100)	4025(57.0)	4200(43.0)	8225 (100)	1682(51.3)	1595 (48.7)	3277 (100)
1998	2038(50.8)	1975(49.2)	4013(100)	4987(52.5)	4511(47.5)	9498(100)	1695(498)	1705 (50.2)	3400 (100)
1999	1875(58.6)	1324(41.4)	3199(100)	5595(49.0)	5821(51.0)	11416(100)	1945(535)	1688 (46.5)	3633 (100)
2000	2159(60.9)	1386 (39.1)	3545 (100)	5294(47.0)	6060(53.0)	11354(100)	2300(498)	2314 (50.2)	4614 (100)
agr	4.2	2.3	3.3	3.1	14.7	8.0	7.2	5.6	3.8

Figure in the parentheses indicate percentage to total credit of the respective district.
agr = Average Annual Growth Rate
Source : Lead Bank office, UBI, Cachar, Karimganj and Hailakandi districts.

TABLE – 11
SECTORWISE DEPLOYMENT OF BANK CREDIT UNDER ANNUAL CREDIT PLAN IN BARAK VALLEY AS ON MARCH (1986 – 1999)

(Account in Nos. and amounts Rs. in thousands)

Year	SECTORS							
	Agricultural & Allied activities		*SSI & Rural Artisans*		*Trade & Services*		*TOTAL*	
	Account	*Amount*	*Account*	*Amount*	*Account*	*Amount*	*Account*	*Amount*
Karimganj district								
1983	3910	16535	509	4192	617	7127	5036	27854
1984	3903	17504	750	6922	697	11940	5350	36366
1985	4823	11212	823	7175	723	9508	6369	27895
1986	2301	9272	683	6376	1691	10517	4675	26165
1987	2728	100081	696	10580	1722	8736	5056	29397
1988	3388	9717	797	5054	1609	10784	5794	25555
1989	3432	15101	813	12912	1755	15056	6000	43063
1990	3681	15152	820	10528	1538	15739	6258	41035
1991	3950	15696	828	8445	1434	15463	6212	39504
1992	3539	15897	803	6390	1287	8757	5629	31044
1993	3884	21918	922	12778	1468	17005	6274	51001
1994	3797	18668	787	12374	1407	16736	5891	48378
1995	4132	21132	784	21285	1290	24832	6206	67249
1996	2496	24349	817	23541	1393	20800	4706	68690
1997	2560	26965	743	15833	1638	27754	4941	70602

(Contd.)

(Contd. Table-11)

(Account in Nos. and amounts Rs. in thousands)

Year	SECTORS							
	Agricultural & Allied activities		SSI & Rural Artisans		Trade & Services		TOTAL	
	Account	Amount	Account	Amount	Account	Amount	Account	Amount
1998	2189	26565	773	16954	1624	34393	4586	77912
1999	1444	15419	484	8771	1448	30339	3376	54529
2000	1238	15977	565	10571	1836	45026	3639	71574
Cachar district								
31-12-83	8118	22696	1277	7876	1248	11407	10643	41976
30-9-84	8767	30843	1674	12687	1637	24905	12080	68435
31-12-85	1957	5316	812	6332	324	4103	3093	15751
31-12-86	2545	10162	839	8797	435	11502	3819	30461
31-12-87	2582	7770	1033	10177	315	6209	3930	24156
31-12-88	2792	10361	1213	14368	376	8206	4381	32935
31-12-89	NA	34565	NA	10315	NA	16191	NA	60871
31-12-90	6399	24983	4059	7640	2333	31263	7791	68886
31-12-91	6987	29391	118	9077	2557	21719	9662	60187
31-12-92	2809	22530	801	7629	2351	19231	5961	49390
31-3-93	3218	19878	916	9636	1495	16439	5629	45953
31-12-94	2808	22530	816	6258	1490	21467	5099	54255
31-3-95	2369	14673	624	14019	1635	31118	4628	59810
30-12-96	2159	19609	952	20090	2022	40784	5133	80433

(Contd.)

(Contd. Table-11)

(Account in Nos. and amounts Rs. in thousands)

Year	SECTORS							
	Agricultural & Allied activities		*SSI & Rural Artisans*		*Trade & Services*		*TOTAL*	
	Account	*Amount*	*Account*	*Amount*	*Account*	*Amount*	*Account*	*Amount*
30-9-97	2255	29517	648	19839	2869	65709	5772	115065
30-9-98	2136	34412	796	24190	2965	79623	5890	135323
31-12-99	2350	32378	1265	37584	3126	94407	6741	164369
31-3-00	2450	33478	1528	39281	3028	83408	7006	156167
Hailakandi district								
1989	2420	13101	613	10912	1534	13036	4567	37049
1990	1430	12910	703	11301	1434	14181	3567	38392
1991	2351	13560	729	15318	1287	9281	4367	38159
1992	1839	13816	713	12162	1391	13260	3943	39510
1993	2836	20968	823	12003	1407	11589	4319	44569
1994	3121	16312	729	10928	1218	24892	5068	52132
1995	2639	21862	613	24139	1123	23689	4106	69690
1996	2416	18674	580	21017	1359	12536	4355	52227
1997	1938	26312	728	12829	1439	18390	4105	57913
1998	1539	22392	791	15312	1408	17890	3738	55594
1999	2560	21831	865	18316	1506	27831	4931	67978
2000	1961	14326	871	15109	1458	26091	3490	55526

Source : Lead Bank Office, United Bank of India, Cachar, Karimganj and Hailakandi district.

The growth of bank credit in different sectors may be assessed by compound growth rate (cgr) of bank credit sanctioned during pre and post reform period. For this we have assumed the linear regression line Y = a + bt (y = total credit sanctioned corresponding to year (t) origin at 1983 and 1991 in pre and post reform period respectively). The results obtained are summarised as under.

Period	*District*	*Agriculture & Allied*	*SSI & Rural artisans*	*Trade & service*	*Total credit*
Pre-reform	Karimganj	-2.42	6.63	5.38	7.91
(1983-90)	Cachar	1.71	-1.20	10.31	9.23
	Hailakandi	-	-	-	-
Post-reform	Karimganj	0.43	2.45	9.23	11.28
(1991-2000)	Cachar	3.84	13.08	11.58	15.08
	Hailakandi	1.29	0.32	6.05	2.71

-Could not be calculated due to non-availability of comparable data

Source: Self calculated on the basis of Table-11.

The inter sector growth rate analysis in the pre reform era, reveals that there is a significant decrease in respect of credit sanctioned in agriculture & allied activities (cgr = -2.42) while small scale sector (cgr = 6.63) and trade & service (cgr = 5.38) accounted an increasing trend in Karimganj district. On the other hand, district Cachar experienced a negative growth rate of credit sanctioned in small sector (cgr = –1.20) followed by an increasing trend of agriculture & allied activities (cgr = 1.71) and trade & service (cgr = 10.31). It is therefore evident from the growth rate analysis that the reform process had made a positive impact on the sectorwise credit deployment. Both Karimganj & Hailakandi districts achieved highest growth rate in respect of trade and service (cgr = 9.23) and (cgr = 6.05) while district Cachar witnessed highest growth in SSI sector (cgr = 13.08) followed by agriculture and allied activities (cgr = 3.84).

The inter district growth rate analysis shows that the SSI and agriculture sector received comparatively less attention than that of trade and services in the post reform era. This may be due to the negative attitude of banks towards the proposals submitted by small entrepreneurs and the farmers. As they had bitter experience of sanctioning more loan to these sectors since the volume of overdue have mounted over the years.

References

1. Raul, R. K. 1997. *Industrial Finance in India*. op.cit. pp. 111-112.
2. RBI 1954. *Banking Monetary Statistics of India*. July. p. 274.
3. Govt. of India. 1991. *Report of the Committee on the Financial System*. op. cit.
4. North-Eastern Institute of Bank Management. 1999. Guwahati, Assam.
5. Nambiar, P.C.D. 1980. *Banking Policy; which direction*. Commerce 1980, Vol. 13, Sept. 20.
6. Sikidar, S. 1990. *Economic Development of Tribal India*. Ashish Publishing House, New Delhi pp. 160.
7. Mani, K.P. and Chacko, J. P. 2002. "Performance of Commercial Banks in Kerala; An Autopsy" *Banking and Financial Sector Reforms in India*, Deep and Deep Publications, New Delhi pp. 445-457.
8. Nandal, R. S. and Singh, A. 2002. *Banking Infrastructure in Harayana*. Banking and Financial Sector Reform in India, Deep & Deep Publication Private Ltd. pp. 457.
9. Bhagawati, S. K. 1999. *Credit Deposit Ratio of Commercial Banks; A Case Study of North Eastern Region*. Journal of North Eastern Council. [April, June] 19 (2) : 14 – 19.
10. Government of India. 1987. *Basic Statistics of North Eastern Region*, NEC Publications, (Ministry of Home Affairs), Shillong.
11. State Level Banker's Committee (SLBC) Reports, 1996.
12. Niranjana, S. and Anbumani, V. 2002. *Social objectives and Priority sector lending*. Banking and Financial Sector Reforms in India, Deep & Deep Publications, pp. 231.
13. Narasimham, M. 1994. *Financial Sector Reform : The Unfinished Agenda*. Platinum Jubilee Conference Volume, Indian Economic Association, Indira Gandhi Institute of Development Research, Bombay.

5

Profitability in Public Sector Banks : An Appraisal

Introduction

In the previous chapters an assessment has been made regarding operational activities of PSBs in terms of branch expansion, deposit mobilization, advances and C/D ratio particularly in the context of aligning banking activities with international standard. It has been observed that PSBs are facing a severe competition in deposits mobilisation owing to opening up the floodgate to the private and foreign sector banks during the reform regime. Moreover, huge non-performing assets (NPAs) over the years eroded the net worth of the banks and ultimately became a grave concern of the management. As a result, the profitability of banking sector, an essential requirement for the healthy operation and survival, had come under severe pressure. This chapter, therefore, is devoted to study the profitability performance and operational flexibility of banks during pre and post reform era pertaining to a period of 20 years, i.e., from 1980-81 to 2000-2001. The study also has identified some of the exogenous and endogenous factors affecting the profitability of the public sector banks in the context of financial sector reform. The following operational hypothesis in this respect has been framed:

> "Profitability of PSBs has not been in the upward trend following the measures of deregulation with clear commercial goals."

Profit and Profitability : The Conceptual Framework

Profit, "invisible hand" (Adam Smith)[1], ensures the prosperity of an organisation. It is the fundamental objective of every business as well as motivating force behind the running of a firm. Opinions differ sharply with regard to the definition of profit. But in general it is the difference between total revenue and total cost over a period of time (Gupta, 1977)[2]. There is mostly universal agreement with the definition that profit is primarily a residue or surplus of prices over expenses of production or leaving above costs (Hasan, 1975)[3].

Profit may be accounting profit, economic profit and social profit. Accounting profit* is calculated by taking explicit costs while economic profit** is derived at after taking both explicit and implicit costs into consideration (Angadi, 1987)[4]. Social profit is the difference between social benefit and social cost. It is yet difficult to find out social profit due to absence of an accurate measuring concept.

Profitability is the ability of a given investment to earn return from its use. It is otherwise known as earning power of concerned investment. It is an appropriate tool by which the performance and efficiency of a firm or industry is judged. Higher degree of profit earning capacity ensures prosperity of the concern. Like profit, there are accounting profitability and value added profitability. In accounting profitability*** relative change is measured by measuring the output as proportion of the input and comparing with the result of the similar firm, while value added profitability is measured by the excess of turnover plus income from services over the cost of bought in-goods or services (Gupta, 1989)[5].

Profitability in Banks

Profitability in banks is measured by relating profit to working fund/ total assets/income/ deposit etc. (Seshadri, 1980)[6]. Banks are being commercial organisation and like any such organisation, all of their activities should be directed towards earning profit. Essentially, banks must give a fair return on capital after providing adequately for business risks. In addition they should generate sufficient funds for survival, and perform their socio-economic activities entrusted on them. This has warranted banks to earn profit.

TABLE - 1
INCOME, EXPENDITURE AND PROFIT OF PSBs VIS-A-VIS OTHER BANKS (1980 –2001)

(Amount Rs. in Crores)

Year	Income					Expenditure					Profits				
	Public Sector Banks					*Public Sector Banks*					*Public Sector Banks*				
	SBIs	*NBs*	*Total*	*Pvt. Banks*	*Foreign Banks*	*SBIs*	*NBs*	*Total*	*Pvt. Banks*	*Foreign Banks*	*SBIs*	*NBs*	*Total*	*Pvt. Banks*	*Foreign Banks*
1980	1323	2512	3835	137	127	1310	2469	3779	135	121	13	43	46	2	6
1981	704	3125	4829	171	152	1688	3075	4763	169	140	16	48	64	2	12
1982	2023	3676	5699	204	177	2010	3619	5629	201	165	13	57	70	3	12
1983	2278	4232	6510	247	210	2252	4172	6424	243	193	26	60	86	3	16
1984	2783	5304	8087	307	259	2757	5247	8004	303	238	26	57	83	4	21
1985	3280	6312	9592	369	303	3245	6229	9474	363	278	35	83	118	5	24
1986	3792	7457	11249	436	384	3750	7308	11056	428	343	42	151	193	8	41
1987	4518	8792	13310	521	482	4463	8585	13048	510	443	55	207	262	10	40
1988	7066	13459	20525	785	799	6955	13205	20160	769	723	111	254	365	16	76
1989	7074	13660	20734	767	988	6957	13475	20402	749	876	117	185	302	18	112
1990-91	8302	15927	24229	908	1473	8152	15706	23857	877	1324	150	221	371	31	149
agr	23.6	21.8	22.4	23.8	31.2	22.6	21.7	23.8	23.4	30.2	31.8	30.0	33.6	39.1	52.3

Contd.

	Income					*Expenditure*					*Profits*				
	Public Sector Banks					*Public Sector Banks*					*Public Sector Banks*				
	SBIs	*NBs*	*Total*	*Pvt. Banks*	*Foreign Banks*	*SBIs*	*NBs*	*Total*	*Pvt. Banks*	*Foreign Banks*	*SBIs*	*NBs*	*Total*	*Pvt. Banks*	*Foreign Banks*
1991-92	13429	21018	34447	1342	2469	13183	20458	33641	1270	2038	245	560	.805	72	430
1992-93	13963	22126	36088	1879	4009	13683	25774	39457	1879	4857	280	-3648	-3368	60	-842
1993-94	13909	34686	37311	2353	4085	13553	29111	41660	2203	3511	357	-6589	-6232	153	1092
1994-95	15948	27000	43657	2173	4666	15101	26730	42541	1863	3969	846	269	1115	310	697
1995-96	20566	33074	53641	5331	6084	19773	34235	54008	4774	5335	793	-1160	-367	558	749
1996-97	23277	37983	61260	7356	7608	21569	36538	58108	6670	6942	1707	1445	3152	686	666
1997-98	24871	42831	67702	9449	8697	22411	40263	62674	8607	8067	2459	2567	5027	842	629
1998-99	29349	99500	78850	11492	9719	27883	47712	75696	10784	9191	1465	1788	3253	709	527
1999-00	34014	56896	90911	13689	10329	31335	54459	85794	12528	9361	2679	2437	5116	1161	967
2000-01	39372	64126	103498	16595	11983	37150	62031	99181	15433	1138	2221	2095	4316	1162	944
agr	14.0	12.8	11.4	23.3	17.8	8.6	9.8	14.6	20.6	17.6	24.6	15.2	18.6	33.8	10.4

SBs = State Bank of India and its associates, NBs = Naionalised Banks

Pvt. = Pvt. banks includes both new and old private banks.

Sources : *Financial Analysis of Banks, Vol. I & II, Indian Bank's Association, Bombay.*
Report on Trend and Progress of Banking in India – 94-95 pp. 24, 2000-2001. pp. 34, 35.

The profitability is the most important indicator of overall financial performance. The level of efficiency, productivity, and cost effectiveness is reflected through the bank's profit figure. In short, the profit of a bank can be considered as a composite index of the bank's performance in its various areas of operation (Angadi and Devraj, 1983)[7]. Therefore, banks in India, at the present juncture have to ensure a balance between social banking and profitability and earn a fair return to justify their existence.

Since nationalisation, banks acted over enthusiastically in observing norms much to the margin of their profits and profitability (Verma, 2002)[8]. But it was realised that adequate profits were an essential requirement of survival and healthy operation of the banking system. It is, in this context, PEP Committee (1977)[9] observed that the profitability of the banking system had come under severe pressure due to increased costs and comparatively lower earnings. The Narasimham Committee (1991)[10] also indicated erosion in the profitability of banking sector. The committee further observed that the directed credit programmes and directed investments strained the operational flexibility of banks leading to dwindling in their earnings.

Rangarajan (1992)[11] observed continuous declining trend in profitability of public sector banks. Using the Risk-Return Approach (RRA), Anagol and Das (1997) viewed that PSBs are lagging behind in the context of performance of foreign bank during 1992-95. Under this situation particularly where the PSBs are struggling hard for achieving higher degree of performance, an attempt has been made to analyse the performance of PSBs in terms of profitability in the national level banking scenario.

Bank Groupwise Profitability Performance : The Growth Rate Analysis

A bank groupwise income, expenditure and profits of all banks and the average annual growth **(agr)** are presented in Table – 1. It is found that during pre banking sector reform (1980 to 1990-91), there was 11.6 times increase in the income of foreign banks accounting an **agr** of 31.2 per cent. The PSBs recorded 6.3 fold (agr = 22.4) and private banks, 6.6 fold (agr = 23.8) increase in their respective income. The table discerns that during pre banking sector reform regime, the growth of expenditure of foreign banks (agr = 30.2 per cent) was higher than that of PSBs (23.4 per cent) and private banks (28.8 per cent). In case of PSBs, the volume

TABLE – 2
COMPONENT WISE INCOME, EXPENDITURE & PROFIT OF PSBs IN THE PRE-REFORM PERIOD (1980-1991)

(Amount in Rs. crores)

Year	Income			Expenditure				
	Interest & Discount	*Other income*	*Total (1+2)*	*Interest Paid*	*Establishment Expenses*	*Other expenses*	*Total (4+5+6)*	*Profits (3-7)*
	1	2	3	4	5	6	7	8
1980	3416 (89.0)	419 (11.0)	3835 (100)	2515 (66.5)	917 (24.3)	347 (9.2)	3779 (100)	46
1981	4341 (89.9)	487 (10.1)	4829 (100)	3254 (68.3)	1080 (22.6)	428 (8.9)	4763 (100)	64
1982	5165 (90.6)	535 (9.4)	5699 (100)	3889 (69.1)	1228 (21.8)	504 (9.0)	5629 (100)	70
1993	5937 (91.2)	573 (8.8)	6510 (100)	4392 (68.4)	1439 (22.4)	593 (9.2)	6424 (100)	86
1994	7415 (91.7)	672 (8.3)	8087 (100)	5418 (67.7)	1877 (23.4)	709 (9.1)	8004 (100)	83
1995	8799 (91.7)	793 (8.3)	9592 (100)	6403 (67.6)	2227 (23.8)	843 (8.9)	9473 (100)	118
1996	10226 (90.9)	1023 (9.1)	11249 (100)	7552 (68.3)	2487 (21.6)	1016 (9.3)	11054 (100)	193
1997	12102 (90.9)	1208 (9.1)	13310 (100)	9056 (69.4)	2752 (21.1)	1240 (9.5)	13048 (100)	262
1998-89	18658 (90.9)	1867(9.1)	20252 (100)	1408 (69.9)	4243 (21.3)	1835 (9.1)	20162 (100)	365
1989-90	18909 (91.2)	1825(8.8)	20734 (100)	14414 (70.0)	4097 (20.0)	1890 (9.3)	20401 (100)	302
1990-91	21960 (90.6)	2269(9.4)	24229 (100)	16999 (71.3)	4695 (19.6)	2163 (9.1)	23857 (100)	371
Cgr	**25.0**	**19.6**	**27.3**	**28.1**	**20.6**	**26.2**	**26.5**	**28.8**

Figure in the parentheses indicate percentage to total

Source : RBI, Report on Trend and Progress of Banking in India, Various Issues.

TABLE – 3
COMPONENT WISE INCOME, EXPENDITURE AND PROFIT OF PUBLIC SECTOR BANKS IN THE POST REFORM ERA (1991-2001)

(Amount in Rs. crores)

Year	Income			Expenditure				Profits
	Interest & Income	Interest income	Total (1+2)	Interest expanded	Other operating Expenses	Provisions & contingencies	Total (4+5+6)	(3-7)
	1	2	3	4	5	6	7	8
1991-92	30756(89.3)	3691 (10.7)	34447 (100)	21022 (62.4)	7882 (23.4)	4740(14.0)	33644 (100)	803
1992-93	32110 (88.9)	3978, (11.1)	36088 (100)	24112 (61.1)	8908(22.5)	6437(16.3)	39457 (100)	(-) 3369
1993-94	32466 (87.0)	4845 (13.0)	37311 (100)	22107 (53.0)	10041(24.1)	9512(22.8)	41660 (100)	(-) 4349
1194-95	37881 (86.7)	5806 (13.3)	43657 (100)	21763 (51.1)	12427(29.2)	8351(19.6)	42541 (100)	1116
1995-96	46532 (86.7)	7108 (13.3)	53665 (100)	30960 (57.3)	15144(28.0)	7903(14.6)	54008 (100)	(-) 434
1996-97	53900 (87.9)	7360 (12.1)	6126 (100)	36338 (62.5)	16034(27.6)	5735(9.8)	58108 (100)	3152
1997-98	59066 (87.2)	8635 (12.8)	67702 (100)	40164 (64.1)	17273(27.6)	(5236)8.3	62674 (100)	5029
1998-99	69417 (88.0)	9432 (12.0)	78850 (100)	4783 (63.3)	20450(27.1)	7306(9.6)	75596 (100)	3254
1999-00	79459 (87.4)	11497 (12.6)	90900 (100)	55375 (64.5)	22494(26.2)	7926(9.2)	85786 (100)	5114
2000-01	90984 (87.9)	12515 (12.1)	103498 (100)	61692 (62.2)	28013(28.2)	9476 (9.5)	99182 (100)	4316
Cgr	**14.7**	**15.8**	**13.7**	**15.1**	**15.7**	**9.4**	**14.6**	**6.5**

Figures in the parentheses indicate per cent. to total.

Source : Report on Trend and Progress of Banking in India, various issues.

of income swelled from Rs. 3835 crores in 1980 to Rs. 24229 cores in 1990-91 in contrast the expenditure increased from Rs. 3779 crore to Rs. 23857 crore during the same period. The profit margin of PSBs was lowest among other bank groups. The average annual growth of profits of PSBs was 33.6 per cent while the private banks (39.1 per cent) and foreign banks (52.3 per cent) topped the list.

The performance of banks during post reform period 1991-92 to 2000-01, has also been assessed on the basis of average annual growth (agr) of expenditure, income and profits. PSBs recorded 2.93 fold (agr = 11.4), pvt bank 3.05 fold (agr = 23.3) and foreign banks 6.9 fold (agr = 17.8) increase in income during the period under consideration. The growth of expenditure in PSBs is higher than that of income while it is lower in case of foreign and private banks. In respect of growth of profits, the superiority of private banks (agr = 33.8) during the post reform period has been observed.

It is clear from the above analyses that during the post reform era, PSBs in particular, have failed to achieve higher level of profitability, than that of their competitors private and foreign sector banks. This requires a detailed analysis specially to address the strength and weakness of PSBs in respect of earning of higher degree of profits.

Profitability of Public Sector Banks : The Component-wise Analysis

The component-wise growth of income, expenditure and profit of PSBs is presented in Table 2 and 3 pertaining to the pre and post reform periods respectively. A comparison of the growth of income, expenditure and profit is made on the basis of compound growth rate (cgr) for which we have assumed origin at 1980 and 1991-92 for pre and post reform era respectively.

The table depicts that both interest income and interest paid in absolute terms have been increased. Interest income accounted 6.4 times increase from 1980 to 1990-91 (pre-reform) while interest paid registered 6.8 times increase during the same period. During 1991-92 to 2000-01 (post reform), the interest income increased by 3.0 times while interest paid recorded a 2.7 times only. This indicates PSBs have not performed well during post reform era than that of pre-reform era. It is also noticed that the lion share of about 90 per cent of total income was contributed by interest income in the pre-reform years while about 87.9 per cent of interest income constituted the total income in 2000-01. The share of interest paid

TABLE – 4
WORKING RESULTS OF PUBLIC SECTOR BANKS VIS-À-VIS OTHER BANKS IN THE POST REFORM PERIOD (1991-2001)

(Amount in Rs. crores)

	Public Sector Banks				*Private Sector Banks*			
Parameters	*1992-93*	*1995-96*	*1998-99*	*2000-01*	*1992-93*	*1995-96*	*1998-99*	*2000-01*
A. Income	34447	53641	78850	13498	1879	5331	11492	16595
	(11.5)	(10.6)	(10.2)	(10.1)	(11.2)	(11.3)	(10.9)	(10.3)
(a) Interest income	30756	46533	69417	90983	1677	4590	10034	14498
	(10.2)	(9.2)	(9.0)	(8.8)	(9.1)	(9.7)	(9.5)	(8.9)
(b) Other income	3691	7109	9432	12514	202	742	1459	2099
	(1.3)	(1.4)	(1.2)	(1.2)	(1.8)	(1.7)	(1.4)	(1.3)
B. Expenditure	33644	54008	75596	99182	1879	4774	10784	15433
	(11.2)	(10.7)	(9.8)	(9.6)	(10.1)	(9.8)	(10.2)	(9.4)
(a) Interest Exp.	21027	30961	47839	61692	1154	3172	7865	10691
	(7.0)	(6.1)	(6.2)	(6.0)	(6.4)	(6.7)	(7.4)	(6.5)
(b) Provision & Contingencies	4735	7904	7307	9476	183	469	768	1686
	(1.6)	(1.6)	(1.0)	(0.9)	(0.8)	(1.0)	(0.7)	(1.0)
(c) Other operating exp.	7882	15144	20450	28013	482	1133	2151	3055
	(2.6)	(2.9)	(2.7)	(2.7)	(2.2)	(2.3)	(2.0)	(1.8)
C. Operating profit	5427	7536	10506	13793	213	1027	1476	2849
	(1.8)	(1.5)	(1.4)	(1.3)	(1.4)	(2.4)	(1.5)	(1.7)
D. Net Profit	904	– 367	3253	4317	60	558	709	1162
	(0.3)	(–.07)	(0.4)	(0.4)	(0.9)	(1.5)	(0.8)	(0.7)
E. Total Assets	301529	506047	770145	1029770	16776	17176	104006	163379

Figure in the parentheses indicate percentage to total assets.
Source : Report on Trend and Progress of Banking in India, various issues.

TABLE – 4
WORKING RESULTS OF PUBLIC SECTOR BANKS VIS-À-VIS OTHER BANKS IN THE POST REFORM PERIOD (1991-2001)

(Amount in Rs. crores)

	Foreign Banks				All Scheduled Banks			
Parameters	*1992-93*	*1995-96*	*1998-99*	*2000-01*	*1992-93*	*1995-96*	*1998-99*	*2000-01*
A. Income	4009	6085	9719	11984	41977	65058	100062	132078
	(12.3)	(12.8)	(12.7)	(11.8)	(11.1)	(10.8)	(10.5)	(10.2)
(a) Interest income	3700	4960	7860	9471	37489	56082	87312	114951
	(11.6)	(10.5)	(10.3)	(9.3)	(9.3)	(9.4)	(9.2)	(8.9)
(b) Other income	309	1125	1859	2513	4489	8975	12750	17127
	(2.1)	(2.3)	(2.4)	(2.5)	(1.4)	(1.5)	(1.3)	(1.3)
B. Expenditure	4851	5336	9191	11039	46127	64118	95572	125654
	(11.1)	(11.4)	(12.0)	(10.8)	(10.3)	(10.7)	(10.1)	(9.7)
(a) Interest Exp.	2570	3186	5200	5768	27836	37319	60905	78152
	(6.5)	(6.7)	(6.8)	(5.7)	(6.1)	(6.2)	(6.4)	(6.0)
(b) Provision & Contingencies	1423	837	1245	2160	8043	9210	9320	13323
	(1.9)	(1.8)	(1.6)	(2.1)	(1.6)	(1.5)	(1.0)	(1.0)
(c) Other operating exp.	858	1312	2745	3110	10148	17589	25346	34179
	(2.1)	(2.7)	(3.5)	(3.0)	(3.0)	(2.9)	(2.7)	(2.6)
C. Operating profit	1021	1587	1773	3105	NA	10149	13811	19747
	(3.4)	(3.4)	(2.3)	(3.0)	–	(1.7)	(1.5)	(1.5)
D. Net Profit	– 842	749	527	945	– 4150	939	4490	6424
	(– 1.8)	(1.6)	(0.7)	(0.9)	(– 1.0)	(0.2)	(0.5)	(0.5)
E. Total Assets	31896	47430	76567	101824	3520201	699162	950718	1294974

Figure in the parentheses indicate percentage to total assets.
Source : Report on Trend and Progress of Banking in India, various issues.

and establishment expenses to total expenditure were 66.5 per cent and 24. per cent respectively in 1980. During the period 1980-2001, the share of interest paid has been decreased by 62.2 per cent while establishment expenses increased by 28.2 per cent. The other operating expenses remained around 9.2 per cent throughout the period. As a result, the quantum of profit of PSBs was Rs. 46 crores in 1980 swelled to Rs. 371 crores in 1990-91 accounting a 8.0 times hike during the pre reform years. The total volume of profits of PSBs in the initial year of reform (1991-92) was Rs. 803 crores but during next two consecutive years they recorded a loss of Rs. 3369 crores, and Rs. 4349 crores respectively but in 1995-96 it was declined to a loss of Rs. 434 crores. Thereafter, the profit increased to Rs. 4316 crores in 2000-2001 recording 6.6 times increase from 1991-92.

The compound growth rate of income and expenditure shows that in the pre reform era the growth of income of PSBs (cgr = 27.3) was higher than that of expenditure (cgr = 26.2). However, the PSBs lost its credibility for maintaining higher growth in income (13.7 per cent) than expenditure, (14.6) during post reform period. It is also clear that growth of interest income (cgr. = 25.0) was higher than non-interest income (cgr. = 19.6) during pre-reform while post reform period experienced a higher growth of non-interest income (cgr. =15.8) than that of interest income (cgr. = 14.7). The total expenditure of PSBs registered a rapid growth than income. Interest paid also recorded a higher growth (cgr. = 15.1) than interest income (cgr. = 14.7).

As a result, the growth of profit of PSBs during the post reform was comparatively much lower (cgr. = 6.5) than that of the pre reform era (cgr. =28.8). This may be due to the introduction of prudential norms on income recognition and provisioning norms since 1992-93.

The Performance of PSBs : A Comparison with Other Private and Foreign Banks

In order to measure the efficiency of banks, we have considered an important parameter, i.e., proportion of income, expenditure and operating profit to the total assets. This is an important performance indicator widely accepted by the banks. A comparative analytical figures of working result for all banks groups are presented in Table – 4. The table shows that during the post reform period between 1991-92 to 2000-2001 the PSBs witnessed a low percentage of profits to total assets in contrast to private and foreign banks. The reason of low profitability of public sector banks may be attributed to higher interest spread (interest income minus interest paid). This may be due to greater contribution to priority sector lending and comparatively lesser involvement of private sector lending. The foreign banks, on the other hand, are not only bias towards the trade and industry but the pattern of credit allocation also reveals the pre-dominance of high yielding private corporate sectors. Around 93 per cent of the total credit advanced by foreign banks was in favour of private corporate sectors, the corresponding figure for PSBs is around 50 per cent during the post reform years (Keshari et. al. 1994)[13].

Profitability of PSBs : Ratio Analysis

With a view to measure the profitability of the banks we have employed ratio analysis technique over the financial data pertaining to the period from 1985 to 2000 comprising of 16 years. The following commonly used ratios are selected for measuring the profitability performance of the banks.

(I) Interest earned ratio (e) $= \dfrac{\text{Total Interest earned}}{\text{Volume of business}} \times 100$

(II) Interest paid ratio (p) $= \dfrac{\text{Total Interest paid}}{\text{Volume of business}} \times 100$

(III) Manpower expenses ratio(m) $= \dfrac{\text{Manpower expenses}}{\text{Volume of business}} \times 100$

(IV) Other establishment expenses ratio(o)

$$= \frac{\text{Other establishment expenses}}{\text{Volume of business}} \times 100$$

(V) Non-Interest income ratio(n) $= \dfrac{\text{Non–interest income}}{\text{Volume of business}} \times 100$

(VI) Spread ratio(s) = Interest earned ratio – interest paid ratio (e – p)

(VII) Burden ratio (b) = Manpower expenses ratio + other establishment expenses ratio – non-interest income ratio (m + o – n), and

(VIII) Profitability ratio (p) = Spread ratio – burden ratio (s – b)

TABLE – 5

PROFITABILITY RATIOS OF PSBs VIS-A-VIS OTHER BANKS

Year	*Interest earned ratio (e)*			*Interest paid ratio (p)*			*Spread ratio (s = e – p)*			*Man power expenses ratio (m)*		
	PSBs	*Pvt.*	*FB*	*PSBs*	*Pvt.*	*FB*	*PSBs*	*Pvt.*	*FB*	*PSBs*	*Pvt.*	*FB*
1985-86	6.9	4.9	8.4	4.1	3.2	5.3	2.8	1.7	3.1	1.5	1.2	1.1
1987-88	6.1	7.9	9.8	4.2	4.6	4.5	1.9	3.3	5.3	1.4	1.7	1.3
1990-91	7.2	7.6	9.9	5.8	4.8	3.7	1.4	2.8	6.2	1.6	1.2	1.2
1995-96	7.6	8.3	9.4	5.1	5.9	6.0	2.5	2.4	3.4	1.3	2.0	0.9
1996-97	7.9	8.6	9.6	5.0	5.8	6.1	2.9	2.8	3.5	2.3	1.2	0.9
1998-99	8.0	7.6	10.2	5.2	6.2	6.5	2.8	1.4	3.7	2.1	1.7	0.8
2000-01	8.1	8.1	10.8	5.3	6.2	6.8	2.8	1.9	4.0	2.5	2.1	0.9

Year	*Other establishment exp. ratio (o)*			*Non-interest income ratio (n)*			*Burden ratio (b = m + o – n)*			*Profitability ratio (p = s – b)*		
	PSBs	*Pvt.*	*FB*	*PSBs*	*Pvt.*	*FB*	*PSBs*	*Pvt.*	*FB*	*PSBs*	*Pvt.*	*FB*
1985-86	0.8	0.9	2.9	0.6	0.7	1.6	1.7	1.6	2.4	1.1	0.1	0.7
1987-88	0.9	0.8	3.4	0.7	0.8	2.1	1.6	1.7	2.6	0.3	1.6	2.7
1990-91	0.7	0.7	3.1	0.8	0.9	2.0	1.5	1.0	2.3	–0.1	1.8	3.9
1995-96	0.8	0.7	1.6	0.9	1.3	2.2	1.2	1.4	0.3	1.3	1.0	3.1
1996-97	0.9	0.8	1.7	1.5	1.5	2.2	1.6	0.5	0.4	0.9	2.3	3.1
1998-99	0.7	0.6	1.9	1.1	1.7	2.3	1.7	0.6	0.4	1.1	0.8	3.3
2000-01	0.9	0.8	2.5	1.2	1.6	2.3	2.2	1.3	0.9	0.6	1.0	3.1

PSBs = public sector banks, Pvt. = Private sector banks, FB = foreign banks

Source : Self Calculation on the basis of earlier tables.

TABLE – 6
COMPONENTS OF PROFITABILITY OF PSBs

(Rs in crore)

Year	*Profits (crores)*	*Priority Sector (crores)*	*Estab. expenses (crores)*	*Burden (crores)*	*Spread (crores)*	*Credit Deposit ratio*	*Ratio of fixed deposit to Current deposit*
1991-92	805	43033	7882	4191	5103	53.75	3.73
1992-93	-3352	44741	8908	4930	7998	53.58	3.61
1993-94	-6232	45517	10041	5196	10360	45.52	3.59
1994-95	1115	52403	12427	6621	12581	48.55	3.58
1995-96	-367	61809	15144	8036	15572	50.85	4.25
1996-97	3152	68925	16034	8674	17562	47.25	4.21
1997-98	5027	79131	17273	8638	18908	51.56	4.65
1998-99	3253	91319	20450	11018	21578	43.02	3.99
1999-00	5116	107200	22494	10975	24084	46.08	4.83
2000-01	4316	127801	28013	15498	19292	45.91	4.82

Source : Self computed based on earlier tables.

The above mentioned ratios were calculated and presented in Table-5. It is evident from the table that the interest earned ratio of PSBs is hovering around 7.4 per cent during the period under consideration. The interest paid ratio, on the other hand of the PSBs and private banks was 5 per cent while it was 5.6 per cent in the foreign banks. The comparative performance of foreign banks was better in respect of higher spread ratio. However, other establishment expenses ratio of the foreign banks was relatively higher than that of PSBs and private banks. Moreover, the PSBs have generated more employment avenues over the years. As a result, it topped the list in respect of man- power expenses ratio that has resulted in their higher burden ratio on average. The PSBs however, have experienced lower profitability than private and foreign banks over the years. On the other hand, they have recorded on an average yearly profit of Rs. 0.1 per hundred-rupee volume of business while foreign banks recorded on average Rs 3.0 per hundred-rupee volume of business. Thus, it can be argued that though PSBs have accounted good quantum of profit during the post reform period but the undeniable fact remains that the foreign banks have still achieved a better profitability than the Indian segments in the banking industry.

Factors Influencing the Profitability of PSBs

The foregoing discussion discerned that the profitability of the banking system had come under severe pressure due to increased costs and comparatively lower earnings. In this respect an attempt has been made to identify the factors influencing the profitability of PSBs. Both exogenous and endogenous factors affecting the profitability of the PSBs have been considered. They include, priority sector lending, pre-emption of deposits in the form of CRR and SLR, establishment costs, spread of commercial banking in rural areas, composition of bank deposits viz, ratio of fixed deposit and current deposit, spread, burden and so on. The accompanying Table – 6 exhibits the position of aforesaid variables during 1991 – 2001.

To assess the interdependency among the factors we have used following multi regression model.

$$\pi = b_0 + b_1 PSL_t + b_2 (C/D)_t + b_3 (FD/CD)_t + b_4 E_t + b_5 S_t + b_6 B_t + U_t$$

where,

π	=	Profit
PSL	=	Priority Sector Advances
C/D	=	Credit-Deposit ratio
FD/CD	=	Ratio of fixed deposit to current deposits
E	=	Establishment expenses
S	=	Spread
B	=	Burden and
b_o	=	Intercept
and b_1	=	(i = 1,2,3, ...6) = Co-efficient of regression parameters.

Here our a priori assumptions are given as under:

$$\frac{d\pi_t}{dPSL_t} < 0,$$

$$\frac{d\pi_t}{d(C/D)_t} > 0,$$

$$\frac{d\pi_t}{d(FD/CD)_t} < 0,$$

$$\frac{d\pi_t}{dE_t} < 0,$$

$$\frac{d\pi_t}{dS_t} > 0,$$

and $$\frac{d\pi_t}{dB_t} < 0$$

The following regression equation is obtained

***Y(π)* = 12617.815 + 1621E-02 PSL– 0.702E + 9.207 E-03B + 0.658S – 136.615 C/D – 839.724 FD/CD**

SE [20715.578] [0.116] [1.486] [0.036] [1.409] [581.389] [6681.763]

The ANOVA of dependent variables is shown below-

ANOVA ; PROFITABILITY OF PSBs

	d.f.	*SS*	*MSS*	*F*	*Sig.*
Regression	6	13443688	2240614.648		
Residual	3	22087111	7362370.205	0.304	0.900[a]
Total	9	35530798	-		

Note : *SS = Sums of Squares*
MSS = Mean Sum Squares.

The other estimation obtained as under :

REGRESSION CO-EFFICIENTS

Factors	*b value*	*'t' value*	*Sig.*	*R^2*	*Adjusted R^2*	*SE*
1. b_0 (intercept)	-	0.609	0.585			
2. Priority Sector lending (PSL)	0.236	0.139	0.898			
3. Establishment expenses (E)	-21.239	-0.473	0.669			
4. Burden (B)	0.150	0.253	0.817	0.378	-0.865	2713.36879
5. Spread (S)	21.035	0.467	0.672			
6. Credit deposit ratio (C/D)	-0.252	-0.235	0.829			
7. Fixed deposit/ current deposit (FD/CD)	-0.214	-0.126	0.908			

It has been revealed from the above econometric analysis that F ratio (0.304) is statistically not significant at 5 per cent level of significance. This indicates the entire regression is not significant. In other words there are certain other variables having greater influence on the profitability of PSBs which were not considered in this model.

In order to assess the influence of individual factors on profitability we have conducted 't' test on individual regression co-efficient (b). The analysis shows that none of the co-efficient is significant at 5 per cent level of significance. However, negative regression coefficient (b) of establishment expenses (– 21.239), C/D ratio (– 0.252) and ratio of fixed deposit and current deposit (– 0.214) implies that the higher volume of establishment expenses, more exposure of banks towards lending activities and management of time and demand deposits are major deterrent of profitability of banks.

Profitability of PSBs : The Empirical Analysis

The foregoing analysis regarding profitability of public sector banks exhibited that the banks were remained profitable during post reform era on the basis of parameters i.e., the average annual profits per hundred-rupee volume of business. However, they have failed to catch up the level of performance achieved by the private as well as foreign sector banks. The gravity of the situation may be revealed by the fact that return on assets (ROA), the most telling measure of banks performance, was 0.4 for PSBs against 0.5 for foreign banks in 2000-01. (RBI, 2001)[14]. Further, net profit or spread ratio (the difference between interest earned and interest paid) usually considered as true measure of core operation of banking sector turned upturn than the PSBs. The spread as per cent of volume of business was 1.5 per cent for PSBs while the same for foreign banks was 4.0 per cent.

With this backdrop, an attempt has been made hereunder to analyse the profitability of PSBs in the study area particularly to test whether the banks are achieving their desired performance during the post reform era.

Bank-wise Growth in Income

Bank-wise income of PSBs in the area under study is presented in Table-7. The income of all PSBs has been increased in absolute term during 1993-2000. In regard to the growth of income, Union Bank of India is on the top position. There is 6.26 times increase in income of Union Bank of India followed by Indian Banks (6.21 times), State Bank of India (6.06 times), Vijaya Bank (5.91 times), United Bank of India (4.97 times), Allahabad Bank (3.92 times), and Punjab National Banks (3.89 times) during the period.

Bank-wise Growth in Expenditure

A bank-wise comparative position of the expenditure of PSBs is presented in Table-8. It is evident from the table that United Commercial Bank (UCO) witnessed a high growth rate in expenditure. There is 15.5 times increase of expenditure in UCO bank followed by Indian Bank (9.56 times), Union Bank of India (6.56 times), Vijaya Bank (5.36 times), State Bank of India (4.06 times), United Bank of India (3.49 times) throughout the period. The growth of expenditure of PSBs (3.93 times) however as a whole is quite impressive while compared to the growth of income (5.44 times) during 31.3.92 to 31.3.2000. This implies the banks under the study

TABLE - 7

BANK WISE INCOME GROWTH OF PSBs IN BARAK VALLEY

(Amount Rs. in Lakhs)

Banks	*31.3.92*	*31.3.93*	*31.3.94*	*31.3.95*	*31.3.96*	*31.3.97*	*31.3.98*	*31.3.99*	*31.3.00*
1. State Bank of India	NA	711.0	937.0	1235.0	1406.0	2596.0	3001.0	3208.0	4309.0
2. United Bank of India	NA	837.0	959.0	1436.0	1908.0	3565.0	3021.0	3479.0	4164.0
3. United Commercial Bank	NA	26.3	27.3	69.1	71.8	75.2	82.5	84.0	123.0
4. Punjab National Bank	NA	18.2	21.3	30.0	38.1	42.6	67.2	68.9	70.8
5. Indian Bank	NA	4.6	6.2	12.8	16.3	19.2	22.3	22.1	28.6
6. Union Bank of India	6.2	7.9	10.6	12.3	18.7	21.6	22.3	35.8	49.5
7. Vijaya Bank	12.2	14.9	20.2	29.2	43.0	62.5	67.7	81.2	88.2
8. Allahabad Bank	9.6	10.6	12.6	21.1	19.6	25.6	27.9	25.6	41.6
Total	**NA**	**1630.5**	**1994.2**	**2845.5**	**3521.5**	**6407.7**	**6289.6**	**7004.6**	**8874.7**

Source : Statements of Income & Expenditure, Zonal offices of respective banks.

TABLE - 8
BANKWISE EXPENDITURE GROWTH OF PSBs IN BARAK VALLEY

(Amount Rs. in Lakhs)

Banks	31.3.92	31.3.93	31.3.94	31.3.95	31.3.96	31.3.97	31.3.98	31.3.99	31.3.00
1. State Bank of India	NA	678.0	913.0	1050.0	1105.0	1706.0	2516.0	2703.0	3708.0
2. United Bank of India	NA	759.0	839.1	1282.0	1539.0	1859.0	3206.0	2548.0	2929.0
3. United Commercial Bank	NA	24.2	25.2	74.9	102.0	203.8	255.2	316.6	375.0
4. Punjab National Bank	NA	15.1	18.6	15.6	25.2	30.2	38.6	52.2	48.6
5. Indian Bank	NA	3.2	5.2	6.8	12.3	18.1	25.2	26.1	30.6
6. Union Bank of India	NA	5.1	6.1	5.2	10.1	13.5	20.6	21.3	33.4
7. Vijaya Bank	24.7	31.1	42.8	62.1	90.6	119.0	46.9	154.4	166.7
8. Allahabad Bank	4.8	8.2	13.1	23.2	18.2	23.1	5.2	28.6	37.8
Total	**NA**	**1523.9**	**1863.1**	**2519.8**	**2902.4**	**3972.7**	**6233.7**	**5850.2**	**7329.1**

NA = Not available

Source : Statements of Income & Expenditure, Zonal offices of respective banks.

TABLE - 9
BANKWISE PROFIT OF PSBs IN BARAK VALLEY

(Amount Rs. in Lakhs)

Banks	*31.3.92*	*31.3.93*	*31.3.94*	*31.3.95*	*31.3.96*	*31.3.97*	*31.3.98*	*31.3.99*	*31.3.00*
1. State Bank of India	NA	33.0	24.0	185.0	301.0	980.0	485.0	505.0	601.0
2. United Bank of India	NA	78.0	12.0	153.0	369.0	625.0	810.0	931.0	1135.0
3. United Commercial Bank	NA	2.1	2.1	(-) 5.0	(-) 30.2	(-) 128.6	(-) 172.7	(-) 232.6	(-) 252.0
4. Punjab National Bank	NA	3.1	2.7	14.4	11.9	12.4	28.6	16.7	22.2
5. Indian Bank	NA	1.4	1.0	6.0	4.0	1.1	2.9	4.0	(-) 2.0
6. Union Bank of India	NA	2.8	4.5	7.1	8.6	8.1	1.7	14.5	16.1
7. Vijaya Bank	(-) 12.5	(-) 16.2	(-) 22.5	(-) 32.9	(-) 46.5	(-) 56.5	(-) 79.0	(-) 73.2	(-) 78.5
8. Allahabad Bank	4.8	2.4	0.7	(-) 2.1	1.4	2.4	2.7	(-) 3.0	3.8
Total	**NA**	**106.6**	**24.5**	**325.5**	**619.2**	**1353.9**	**1073.4**	**1162.4**	**1445.6**

NA = Not available.

Source : Statements of Income & Expenditure, Zonal offices of respective banks.

area are earning considerable profits over the years. The detail discussion has been made hereafter.

Bank-wise Growth of Profit

Profit is the chief barometer of the efficiency and productivity of a bank. It is taken to be an important objective for survival and growth of an enterprise. The excess of income over expenditure forms the profit. Stated otherwise, it is the difference between spread and burden for a commercial bank. Due to high growth of expenditure of UCO Bank and Indian Bank, profitability of these banks has suffered during post reforms years. The gravity of the situation can be exhibited in the following Table – 9.

As on 31-3-2000, UCO Bank, Indian Bank and Vijaya Bank had incurred a loss of Rs 252.0 lakhs, Rs. 2.0 lakhs and Rs. 78.5 lakhs respectively. During 1993-2000, except these three banks, other PSBs in the districts under study have turned out to be profitable. In this context, it may be mention worthy that Verma Committee (1999)[15] identified of these three banks as weak (on the basis of accumulation of net loss). Thus in the study area these three banks are also suffering a loss and UCO bank witnessed a worse off position. Its volume of loss of Rs. 5 lakhs on 31.3.1995 swelled to Rs. 252 lakhs on 31.3.2000. On the other hand Vijaya Bank incurred a loss of Rs. 12.5 lakhs on 31.3.1992 which increased to Rs. 78.5 lakhs as on 31.3.2000. However Indian Banks earned profit except in the financial year ended on 31.3.2000.

Profitability Performance : The Growth Rate Analysis

An analysis of the growth of income, expenditure and profits may be made with average annual growth rate (**agr**) and co-efficient of variation (**cv**) in the post reform period. The results obtained are presented in Table - 10. It is revealed that the growth of profits of United Bank of India (UBI) is highest (**agr** = 25.7) followed by Allahabad Bank (**agr** = 23.1), United Bank, (**agr** = 23.1), Vijaya Bank (**agr** = 21.0), State Bank of India (**agr** = 18.8) and Punjab National Bank (**agr** = 17.1). Two of the banks viz, United Commercial Bank and Indian Bank experienced a negative growth rate. The growth rate of profits of PSBs as a whole is 21.9 per cent in the districts under study which is higher than the growth in national level of 18.6 per cent. The growth scenario and their relevant **cv** values indicate that the banks in the districts are satisfactorily discharging their duties though the pace of opening up of branches in rural areas have

TABLE – 10

BANKWISE AVERAGE ANNUAL GROWTH (AGR) AND CO-EFFICIENT OF VARIATION (CV) (1993-2000)

Banks	*Income*		*Expenditure*		*Profits*	
	agr	*cv*	*Agr*	*Cv*	*agr*	*cv*
State Bank of India	20.6	55.4	21.1	55.9	18.8	74.0
United Bank of India	17.2	49.9	14.5	46.7	25.7	76.9
United Commercial Bank	17.3	42.0	25.4	73.4	(–)31.1	98.8
Punjab National Bank	17.1	41.6	13.5	50.8	17.1	58.8
Indian Bank	18.2	46.9	23.1	65.1	(–) 26.9	180.6
Union Bank of India	18.3	47.2	20.2	53.1	21.6	56.2
Vijaya Bank	18.1	48.6	18.6	48.9	21.0	78.2
Allahabad Bank	16.8	39.4	17.2	51.2	23.1	59.0
All Banks	**18.8**	**51.6**	**17.8**	**49.8**	**21.9**	**69.5**

Source : Self calculated on the basis of Tables – 7, 8 and 9.

considerably slowed down over the years. Moreover, the financial sector reform initiated in 1991 offered a level playing field to PSBs to excel them to do better than they have ever done before.

Besides, to examine the relationship between the volume of business and profitability growth we have calculated incremental volume of business and incremental profits from 1993 to 2000. In this respect we have framed the hypothesis "Incremental volume of business have no direct and positive bearing on the profitability of banks."

The hypothesis is examined by the correlation coefficient (r) analysis. The result found as under.

r = 0.914; 't' (cal) = 5.046; 't' (tab) at 5 df.; 5 per cent = 2.517; 1 pc = 4.032

The 'r' value between the volume of business and profits is 0.914. This association is highly positive and statistically significant both at 5 per cent and 1 per cent level of significance. It suggests that volume of business have a direct bearing on the volume of profits of PSBs in the study area. Thus the null hypothesis is rejected.

Component-wise Profitability Analysis

The component wise data relating to income, expenditure and profits of PSBs are presented in Table – 11. It is revealed that throughout the reform years, interest earned accounted more than 2/3 rd of the total income. While the share of interest paid increased from 59.1 per cent in March 1993 to 82.2 per cent in March 2000. It is also clear that interest earned recorded 5.4 times increase while interest paid recorded 6.7 times increase during the period. Although the share of interest paid have been increased over the period so as in the case of share of establishment expenses. On the other hand, operating expenses have been decreased from 26.1 per cent to 15.3 per cent and 14.8 per cent to 2.5 per cent respectively during the same period under consideration. The PSBs in the district are absolutely depending on loans and advances as source of income. The growth of income and expenditure of PSBs may further be analysed by the cgr and cv. It has been observed that cgr for interest paid is higher (39.1) than interest earned (36.6).

The growth rate of other establishment expenses (cgr = 13.6) is lower and other operating expenses are (cgr = – 2.2) negative. As a result, the profitability of PSBs increased from Rs. 106.6 lakhs in March 1993 to Rs.

TABLE – 11

COMPONENTWISE INCOME, EXPENDITURE AND PROFIT OF PSBs IN BARAK VALLEY (1993-2000)

(Amount Rs. in Lakhs)

	Income			Expenditure				
Year	*Interest income*	*Other income*	*Total*	*Interest expenses*	*Estab. & Staff expenses*	*Operating expenses*	*Total*	*Profit/ Loss*
31.3.93	1138.1 (69.8)	492.4 (30.2)	1630.5 (100)	901.2 (59.1)	398.5 (26.1)	224.2 (14.8)	1523.9 (100)	106.6
31.3.94	1320.9 (66.2)	673.3 (33.8)	1994.2 (100)	1023.5 (54.9)	401.2 (21.5)	438.4 (23.5)	1863.1 (100)	24.5
31.3.95	2021.6 (71.0)	823.9 (29.0)	2845.5 (100)	1328.6 (52.7)	945.2 (37.5)	246.0 (9.8)	2519.8 (100)	325.5
31.3.96	2505.2 (71.1)	1016.3 (28.9)	3521.5 (100)	2016.2 (69.5)	821.0 (28.3)	65.2 (2.2)	2902.4 (100)	619.2
31.3.97	5003 (78.0)	1404.1 (22.0)	6407.7 (100)	2521.5 (63.5)	1051.7 (26.5)	399.5 (10.0)	3972.7 (100)	1353.9
31.3.98	5106.2 (81.2)	1183.4 (18.8)	6289.6 (100)	4526.1 (72.6)	1523.1 (24.4)	184.5 (3.0)	6233.7 (100)	1073.4
31.3.99	5098.5 (72.8)	1906.1 (27.2)	7004.6 (100)	4129.0 (70.6)	1321.6 (22.5)	399.6 (6.8)	5850.2 (100)	1162.4
31.3.00	6197.1 (69.8)	2677.6 (30.2)	8874.7 (100)	6021.6 (82.2)	1120.9 (15.3)	186.6 (2.5)	7329.1 (100)	1445.6
Cgr	**36.6**	**37.0**	**34.9**	**39.1**	**13.6**	**-2.2**	**35.7**	**177.3**
CV	**52.8**	**50.1**	**51.6**	**48.2**	**43.7**	**45.8**	**41.2**	**69.6**

Figure in the parentheses indicate percentage to total

Source : Zonal offices of the respective bank,. Barak Valley.

1445.6 lakhs in March 2000 recording 13.6 fold increase. The high rate of growth of (cgr =177.3) profit of PSBs is due to the reduction in establishment and operating expenses in the area. However, the improvement of content and nature of regulation, corporate governance systems in banks, risk management, transparency in operation is needed for further strengthening the banking operation.

In order to examine the impact of total earnings on the profitability of PSBs incremental growth of total income and incremental profits has been calculated in the post reform period (1993-2000). In this context our hypothesis is "incremental flow of total income has a direct and positive impact on the profitability of PSBs".

The hypothesis is tested with the help of correlation coefficient (r) between incremental income and incremental profits. The result obtained as under –

r = 0.890

't' value (cal) = 5.510

't' value (tab) at 5df.

5 per cent = 2.571

1 per cent = 4.032

The correlation coefficient is found to be 0.890. It is being highly positive and significant at both 5 per cent and 1 per cent level of significance. Hence, the hypothesis is found to be valid in the area under study. It indicates that total earnings have a direct impact on bank profit and increase in total income certainly resulted in a rise of profit.

Further to assess the relationship between the growth of expenditure and the volume of profits of PSBs in the area under study, the analysis of correlation coefficient 'r' between incremental expenditure and incremental profits has been employed. In this respect our hypothesis is "Incremental expenditure has a negative impact on the banks profitability". The result obtained as under

r = – 0.173

't' value (cal) = 0.392

't' value (tab) at 5df.

5 per cent = 2.571

TABLE - 12
PROFITABILITY RATIOS OF PSBs IN BARAK VALLEY IN THE POST REFORM PERIOD (1993-2000)

(Ratios in percentage)

Year	*Interest earned ratio (a)*	*Interest paid ratio ratio (b)*	*Spread ratio* (c = a - b)	*Establishment & manpower ratio (d)*	*Non-interest income (e)*	*Burden ratio (f = d - e)*	*Profitability ratio (p = c - f)*
1993	2.9	2.3	0.6	1.0	1.2	(-) 0.2	0.8
1994	2.9	2.2	0.7	0.8	1.5	(-) 0.7	1.4
1995	3.8	2.5	1.3	1.8	1.5	0.3	1.0
1996	4.2	3.4	0.8	1.4	1.7	(-) 0.3	1.1
1997	7.2	3.7	3.5	1.5	2.0	(-) 0.5	4.0
1998	6.0	5.2	0.8	1.8	1.4	0.4	0.4
1999	5.1	4.2	0.9	1.3	1.9	(-) 0.6	1.5
2000	5.4	5.2	0.2	0.9	0.9	0	0.2
Grand Mean	**4.7**	**3.6**	**1.1**	**1.3**	**1.5**	**(-) 0.2**	**1.4**

Source : Self calculated on the basis of earlier tables.

The negative 'r' value is not statistically significant at 5 per cent level of significance. It indicates that the banks have not yielded higher profit due to an increase in expenditure over the years in the area under study. Thus the hypothesis is found to be true indicating thereby that incremental expenses have mounted over the years and not resulted in increasing profits. The reason may be attributed to involvement of excess staff in the branches and volume of businesses has not increased over the years.

Analysis of Profitability Ratio

An attempt has been made hereunder to workout various ratios for measuring the profitability performance of PSBs in the districts under study during the post reform period. The profitability ratios are calculated by relating various components of income, expenditure and manpower to a common denominator, i.e., volume of business for the period 1993-2000.

The profitability ratios are worked out and presented in Table – 12. The interest earned ratios of PSBs in the districts on average was 4.7 per cent, while interest paid ratio was 3.6 per cent during 1993-2000. As a result, the spread ratio stood at 1.1 per cent which is lower than that of the national levels (2.3 per cent). The lower spread ratio indicates the bank's inability of mobilising low cost fund or not -advancing loans at higher rates. Higher non- interest income ratio (1.5 per cent.) in comparison to the establishment expenses ratio (1.3 per cent.) pushes the burden ratio (establishment expenses ratio minus non- interest income ratio) to the negative (– 0.2 per cent) region. The variations in spread ratio and negative burden ratio through out the period affected the banks' profitability. The profitability ratio (spread ratio minus burden) in the districts except in 1997 were nowhere at the national level. PSBs in the districts recorded on an average yearly profit of 0.2 per hundred-rupee volume of business in 2000 against 0.6 per hundred-rupee volume of business at the national level in 2000-01. This indicates that PSBs in the district could not compensate the provision and contingencies, which includes provisions for non-performing assets.

Influencing Factors on Profitability of Banks in the Study Area

In order to assess the factors affecting the profitability of PSBs in the district, unlike in the national level, regression analysis have been employed taking into consideration of various factors like priority sector lending, C/D ratio, establishment expenses, spread, burden, and deposits

TABLE - 13
DETERMINANTS OF PROFITABILITY

(Figures in Rs in lakh)

Year	*Profit (Lakhs) (Y)*	*Priority Sector advances (Lakhs) (PS)*	*C/D ratio (per cent) (C/D)*	*Establishment exp. (Lakhs) (EST)*	*Burden (Lakhs) (B)*	*Spread (Lakhs) (S)*	*Deposit (Lakhs) (D)*
31.3.93	106.6	6607	36.9	398.5	– 94.0	236.9	30551
31.3.94	24.5	6488	32.5	401.2	– 272.1	397.4	36257
31.3.95	325.5	7245	32.3	945.2	121.3	693.0	43076
31.3.96	619.2	8185	26.0	821.0	– 195.3	489.0	49467
31.3.97	1353.9	7729	22.3	1051.7	– 352.4	2482.1	60008
31.3.98	1073.4	8720	22.6	1523.1	339.7	580.1	75419
31.3.99	1162.4	9415	20.8	1321.6	– 584.5	969.5	90019
31.3.00	1445.6	9753	23.1	1120.9	– 1556.7	175.5	103245

Source : Self-calculated and self-compiled from various earlier tables.

as independent variables and profit earned as dependent variable. The regression equation has been fitted over the data pertaining to the period of 8 years, 1993-2000, exhibited in Table – 13.

The linear regression equation is obtained as –

Y (Profit) = 1124.707 + 0.188 PS + 1.115 C/D + 0.174 EST

SE. [5186.100] [0.518] [71.647] [1.861]

+ 0.123 B + 0.200 S + 7.007 E - 08 D

[0.068] [0.362] [0.035]

The other relevant results are obtained as under -

Variables	*β*	*'t' value*	*Sig.*	*F*	R^2	*Adjusted* R^2	*SE*
β_0(Constant)	-	0.247	0.864				
Priority Sector lending (PS)	0.200	0.267	0.884				
Credit deposit ratio (C/D)	0.044	0.057	0.963				
Establishment expenses (EST)	0.123	0.093	0.041*	3.698	0.957	.698	312.03712
Burden (B)	0.126	0.127	0.010**	(.378[a]) Sig.			
Spread (S)	0.305	0.827	0.560				
Deposits (D)	0.352	0.210	0.162				

*** Significant at 5 per cent and 1 per cent level of significance.*

Dilating upon the table, it is revealed that variation in the dependent variable viz. profits of PSBs in the districts is explained about 96 per cent by independent variables (R^2 = .957). However, the F ratio is not statistically significant. This implies that independent variables viz. establishment expenses burden, spread, and deposits may not be considered as perfect determinants of dependent variable as per the study area is concerned. This may be due to data coverage as only 8 years from the post reform era have been covered. However, β (beta) value of each of the, independent variables indicates some different results. The establishment expenses and burden have turned to be statistically significant. This indicates that the mounting expenses of banks have eroded their profitability in the study area. Thus, an urgent step are warranted to arrest the unbridled volume of expenses in comparison to the volume of business made by the banks in the study area over the period under consideration.

Notes

* Accounting Profit = $(E_A + E_s) - (I_c + O_c)$.

where E_A = Earning from assets, E_s = Earning from other services.

I_c = Interest cost, O_c = Operating cost.

** Economic Profit = $(E_A + E_s) - (I_c + O_c) + S_c + K_c)$

where S_c = Solvency cost

K_c = Opportunity cost of capital and reserve

*** Accounting Profitability $= \frac{\text{Accounting profit}}{\text{Capital employed}} \times 100$

Data relating to Fixed Deposit and Current Deposit is not available in the area under study. Hence, total deposit, is considered as independent variable instead of ratio of Fixed Deposit to Current Deposit as used in national level.

References

1. Adam Smith ; The Wealth of Nations.
2. Gupta, L. N. 1977. *Profitability and Public Sector*. Oxford and IBH Publishing Co., New Delhi, p. 23.
3. Hasan, Z. 1975. *Theory of Profit*. Vikash Publishing House Private Ltd., New Delhi, p. 9.
4. Angadi, V. B. 1987. *Integrated Approach to Study of Banks Profitability*. Prajyan. (Oct-Dec). XVI (4) : 524.
5. Gupta, M. C. 1989. *Profitability Analysis; An Empirical Approach*. Pointer Publisher, Jaipur, pp. 7, 8, 9.
6. Seshadri, J. H. 1980. *An Economic Analysis of Profitability in Commercial Banks*. Prajnan, (July – Sept), IX : 215.
7. Angadi, V.B and Devraj, V.J. 1983. Productivity and Profitability of banks in India. Economic and Political Weekly, (Nov – 26). 18 (48).
8. Verma Saveeta, & Verma Satish, 2002. Determinants of Profitability of SBI groups, other Nationalised Banks and foreign banks. Banking & financial sector Reforms in India, Deep & Deep Publications, pp. 321.

9. PEP Committee popularly known as Productivity, Efficiency and Profitability Committee appointed by RBI under the chairmanship of J.C. Lathur, submitted its report on 1977.
10. Government of India, 1991. *Report of Committee on financial system, Ibid.*
11. Rangarajan, C. 1992. *Banking and Profitability.* in Choudhury C. M. (eds) Dynamics of Indian Banking, Printwell, Jaipur.
12. Anagol, M. and Das. M. R., 1997. *Foreign vs Domestic Banks in India ; Post Reform years*, in Subramanium, K. and Velayudhan T. K. (eds) Banking Reforms in India. Managing Change, Tata McGraw Hill, New Delhi.
13. Keshri, P.K. and Paul, M.T. 1994. *Relative Efficiency of Foreign & Domestic Banks* : Economic and Political Weekly Vol. 29, (26 January).
14. RBI, Report and Progress of Banking in India, 2000-01.
15. Government of India, 1999. *Report on the committee on restructuring of Public Sector Banks* popularly known as Verma Committee.

6

Productivity in Public Sector : An Analysis

In the previous chapter it has been seen that the profitability of PSBs had come under severe pressure due to increase in the operational cost. It is imperative, therefore, that the banks should gain strength as well as attain competitiveness by marshalling its existing resources effectively with a view to survive in the competitive economic environment. Logically an assessment of the productivity of PSBs during the banking sector reform regime is urgently required. In the present chapter, an attempt has been made to study the effectiveness of reform measures on the banking activities. In this respect, the parameters like labour productivity, branch productivity, cost responsiveness and return on working fund (ROWF) were used and compared their magnitude between pre and post reform regime.

Introduction

Bank, as a business concern, cannot overlook the profitability aspect since profit signifies efficiency. For the long term survival and growth of banks, profit is imperative. Public sector banks have, of late, demonstrated a remarkable ability to adjust to the new operating environment and acquired a high level of business strength.

Productivity is one of the factors affecting the profitability among others like expansion of banks' operation in the areas characterized by deployment of funds is non-profitable coupled with higher overhead expenses, increase in sickness in industrial units, mounting of NPAs over the years etc. Higher the productivity results in propor-tionately lower in the establishment cost. On the other hand, higher productivity indicates that, along smaller transactions a bank does high volume of transactions too. In contrast, lower productivity increases relative operational cost and often becomes the cause of losses as intermediary returns are directly related to the productivity.

Definition

Productivity is universal and simple concept refers to an organisation's effectiveness in using all its resources viz labour, financial resources, fixed assets and premises. It indicates the relationship between output and input expended in any work situation (Monga, 1992)[1]. In this respect Peter Drucker (1980)[2] articulated "without productivity objectives, a business does not have direction. Without productivity measurement, it does not have control." Productivity is an efficiency index that measures the rate of output per unit of input like man, material, machine, money and space. It explains the efficiency in the use of factors of production employed by an organisation. Productivity is the corner stone of banking growth and economic development. In simplest sense, it means efficiency and effectiveness of services. In fact, productivity is an essential part of self-improvement and achievement of excellence, which is a part of the dynamic society. Optimum productivity is attained when there is a balance between all factors of production that yield maximum output for least effort (Choudhary, 1998)[3]. *The productivity measures the extent to which the actual input consumption exceeds the minimum input necessary to produce the actual input level.* The minimum input consumption is determined in a manner consistent with other current knowledge of the available production technology (Diwan, 1997)[4] but there are difficulties in measuring productivity in service industries where quality of services assumes greater importance.

Productivity Ratios for Banks

A bank is a financial institution generating a stream of financial services in order to sustain a stock of assets and liabilities. The financial services are produced, delivered and consume instantaneously. In the process, the consumer is exposed to an experiential quality that is part of the service. In case of banks, the distinctions between input and output is not clear (Asthma and Srinivas, 1997)[5]. One aspect of productivity is the measurement of business (deposit + advances) per branch and per employee and the other aspect is cost responsiveness and return on working fund (Angadi, 1984)[6].

The productivity ratios of banks are worked out by relating the total deposits, total advances and the total business (deposit plus advances) of the banks to the total number of branches and also total number of employees. The following are the commonly used ratios measuring productivity of the banks have been considered for the purpose of the analysis.

Labour Productivity

1. Deposits per employee $= \dfrac{\text{Total Deposit}}{\text{No. of Employee}}$

2. Advances per employee $= \dfrac{\text{Total Advances}}{\text{No. of Employee}}$

3. Business per employee $= \dfrac{\text{Deposit + Advances}}{\text{No. of Employee}}$

4. Deposit per branch $= \dfrac{\text{Total Deposit}}{\text{No. of branches}}$

5. Advances per branch $= \dfrac{\text{Total advances}}{\text{No. of branches}}$

6. Business per branch $= \dfrac{\text{Deposit + Advances}}{\text{No. of branches}}$

Cost responsiveness (CR) measures degree of cost effectiveness that reflects the bank's profitability to a greater extent. "In the context of regulated interest rate structure, the profits of a bank have a greater bearing on profitability than the spread management" (Angadi, 1984)[7]. In case of bank and other service industry the earnings (yields) may be considered as output while relevant operating costs may be termed as input. Therefore, the productivity of a bank can be evaluated by CR, which is defined as :

$$\text{CR} = \frac{\%\ \text{variation in cost}}{\%\ \text{variation in earning}}$$

The return on working fund shows the productivity of capital employed in a bank and is defined as –

$$\text{ROWF} = (\text{Profit /working fund}) \times 100$$

Bank Group-wise Classification

The bank group wise productivity ratios relating to labour productivity and productivity per branch are presented in Table - 1. The table shows that the average labour productivity measured either by deposits, advances or total business per employee is lowest in PSBs than that of foreign and private banks. The deposits per employee of PSBs increased from Rs. 10.2 lakhs in 1985-86 to Rs. 104.1 lakhs in 2000-01, which are lower than the foreign, and private banks. In case of the foreign banks, it has been increased steadily from Rs. 32.8 lakhs in 1985-86 to Rs. 416.7 lakhs in 2000-01. The advances per employee also increased to Rs. 47.8 lakhs in 2000-01 from Rs. 9.3 lakhs in 1985-86. As a result the total business per employee of PSBs has also registered a lower growth than that of foreign and private banks. During the period 1985-2001, the average business per employee for PSBs was Rs. 61.1 lakhs, the corresponding figure for private and foreign bank was Rs. 93.9 lakhs and Rs. 300.3 lakhs respectively. This lower labour productivity may be attributed to the national level trade union that opposed the move of modernisation, automation and computerisation and getting regular pay hike without corresponding increase in productivity (Pedgaonkar, 2002)[8].

The average productivity of branches of PSBs in terms of deposits, advances and total business was higher than private banks but much lower than the foreign banks during the pre reform years. However, PSBs in this respect did not achieve significant mark in the banking activities during post reform years (1991 – 2001). The total business per branch of PSBs was Rs. 1874.9 Lakhs, in the context of Rs. 3905.1 lakh for private banks and for foreign banks Rs. 53782.1 lakh in 2000-01. Moreover, the average deposit per branch was around Rs. 783.5 lakhs for PSBs and Rs 825.1 lakhs for private banks during 1985 to 2001. Similarly, the average business per branches of PSBs was much lower than that of the private and foreign banks. The average business per branch for PSBs was increased from Rs. 344.7 lakh in 1985 –86 to a meager amount of Rs. 356.1 lakhs in 1990-91 further to Rs. 1874.9 lakh in 2000-01. This has indicated that PSBs during the reform regime are performing comparatively better as its volume of business per branch has increased by almost two fold. On the other hand, it has increased by about 4 times in case of private sector banks during the same period under consideration. Further in case of the foreign bank, the volume of business per branch jumped more than by 7 times from Rs. 7871 lakh in 1990-91 to Rs. 53782.1 lakh in 2000-01. Moreover, advances

TABLE – 1 (a)
PRODUCTIVITY RATIO OF PUBLIC SECTOR BANKS VIS-À-VIS OTHER BANKS (1985-2001)

(fig in Rs. in Lakhs)

	Deposit per employee			*Advances for employee*			*Total Business per employee*		
Year	*PSBs*	*Pvt.*	*FB*	*PSBs*	*Pvt.*	*FB*	*PSBs*	*Pvt.*	*FB*
1985-86	10.2	12.7	32.8	9.3	7.5	23.6	17.1	17.6	36.3
1986-87	14.1	15.2	37.1	10.6	12.1	24.3	20.3	16.2	61.3
1987-88	16.2	16.5	40.5	11.3	8.3	31.6	27.3	25.1	71.2
1990-91	24.0	16.0	50.0	12.6	9.3	35.6	36.1	25.2	87.6
1995-96	38.5	71.6	237.8	20.9	37.7	174.8	62.0	88.9	412.6
1996-97	47.9	83.7	281.1	24.7	46.8	192.2	76.1	86.3	481.4
1998-99	68.7	131.4	313.1	29.6	66.3	130.0	90.3	196.5	513.0
2000-01	104.1	197.6	416.7	47.8	98.3	302.6	151.8	295.8	719.4
Grand mean	**40.5**	**68.1**	**176.1**	**20.7**	**35.7**	**114.3**	**61.1**	**93.9**	**300.3**

Source : Self calculated on the basis of

(i) RBI, Statistical tables relating to banks in India, Vol-1987, 1991, 1997-98, 2000-2001.

(ii) RBI, Basic statistical Return, Vol. 1987, 1991 and 1997.

TABLE – 1 (b)
PRODUCTIVITY RATIO OF PUBLIC SECTOR BANKS VIS-À-VIS OTHER BANKS (1985-2001)

(fig in Rs. in Lakhs)

	Deposit per bank branch			*Advances per bank branch*			*Business per branch*		
Year	*PSBs*	*Pvt.*	*FB*	*PSBs*	*Pvt.*	*FB*	*PSBs*	*Pvt.*	*FB*
1985-86	269.8	78.1	2739.3	126.3	91.2	1971.19	344.7	291.2	4710.4
1986-87	298.6	91.3	3155.4	139.6	106.5	2072.7	351.2	341.6	5228.1
1987-88	392.0	172.6	3681.7	181.2	120.9	2720.1	361.2	356.2	6839.2
1990-91	455.2	219.3	4675.6	257.8	128.5	3195.7	356.1	347.8	7871.3
1995-96	782.9	696.7	17694.7	326.7	358.6	13003.4	961.2	1039.2	30698.1
1996-97	952.6	1143.8	21246.5	429.1	639.6	15203.9	1444.7	1783.4	34308.1
1998-99	1324.2	1590.9	27020.9	569.7	860.9	11220.9	1891.2	2736.6	41306.2
2000-01	1792	2607.9	31152.6	823.1	1297.3	22629.5	1874.9	3905.1	53782.1
Grand mean	**783.5**	**825.1**	**13920.8**	**356.7**	**450.4**	**8957.2**	**948.2**	**1350.1**	**23092.8**

Source : Self calculated on the basis of

(i) RBI, Statistical tables relating to banks in India, Vol. 1987, 1991, 1997-98, 2000-2001.

(ii) RBI, Basic statistical Return, Vol. 1987, 1991 and 1997.

per branch of PSBs during the pre reform regime increased by two fold from Rs. 126.1 lakh in 1985-86 to Rs. 257.8 lakh in 1990-91. The same, on the other hand, has been increased by about 4 times during the post reform period in case of PSBs. However the incremental rate of advances per branch was higher in case of both private and foreign banks where the latter topped the table.

Bank-wise Classification

The bank-wise productivity performance of PSBs is presented in Table-2. The table discerns that the **Corporation Bank** comparatively performed well during year March 1998 and March 1999. **Oriental Bank of Commerce**, in contrast, showed highest business per employee of Rs. 318 lakh at the end of March 2002. UCO Bank, Vijaya Bank and Central Bank of India accounted comparatively less business throughout the period 1997-2002. Among the State Bank group, the business per employee of the State Bank of Patiala is on the top. In absolute term it increased from Rs. 91.23 lakh in March 1997 to Rs. 194.34 in March 2002, while the State Bank of Bikaner and Jaipur accounted less business per employee, which was increased from Rs. 63.24 lakhs in March 1997 to Rs. 105.19 lakhs in March 2001.

Further, coefficient of variation (**cv**) of individual bank revealed a wide variation in the per employee business in case of Andhra Bank (45.2 per cent) followed by Bank of Maharashtra (54.1 per cent), Syndicate Bank (36.7 per cent) and Central Bank of India (31.1 per cent). However, among three weak banks identified by Verma Committee (1999) on the basis of available information,

Indian Bank (23.0 per cent) has yet to gain its momentum in its operation, while UBI (27.9 per cent) and UCO Bank (32.5 per cent) are performing comparatively better during the year under consideration. The evidence suggests that all PSBs have not performed well in the post reform period as well as did not gain momentum in their businesses. The causes of wide variation of the volume of per employee business of individual banks may be attributed to mismanagement on the part of the PSBs in regard to the human resource planning and deficiencies in the proper positioning of existing employees.

Analysis of CR and ROWF

The productivity of banks can also be measured by the parameter viz, cost responsiveness (CR) and return on working fund (ROWF). The

TABLE – 2
BANKWISE PRODUCTIVITY : BUSINESS PER EMPLOYEE

(Amount in Rs. Lakhs)

Sl. No.	*Name of the bank*	*March 1998*	*March 1999*	*March 2001*	*March 2002*	*Coefficient of variation*
	Nationalised Group					
1	Allahabad Bank	77.00	90.00	129.00	153.00	27.0
2	Andhra Bank	67.69	81.14	153.62	195.96	45.2
3	Bank of Baroda	117.24	134.75	166.11	222.76	25.0
4	Bank of India	99.14	96.15	184.26	218.74	35.6
5	Bank of Maharashtra	78.91	90.62	164.77	291.44	54.1
6	Canara Bank	102.33	116.88	190.67	214.88	30.5
7	Central Bank of India	66.38	79.55	110.38	148.77	31.3
8	Corporation Bank	141.50	185.02	245.31	290.44	26.4
9	Dena Bank	101.00	126.00	207.00	221.00	31.3
10	Indian Bank	87.73	97.87	136.00	156.00	23.0
11	Indian Overseas Bank	90.79	103.78	141.40	175.41	25.9
12	Oriental Bank of Commerce	134.80	169.70	263.20	318.00	32.9
13	Punjab & Sind Bank	92.76	111.49	168.08	181.67	26.9
14	Punjab National Bank	75.65	89.58	141.95	167.76	31.6
15	Syndicate Bank	53.26	88.83	133.68	155.12	36.7
16	UCO Bank	56.00	73.00	97.00	134.00	32.5
17	Union Bank of India	96.98	112.94	183.23	214.75	32.0
18	United Bank of India	72.01	81.46	120.00	144.00	27.9
19	Vijaya Bank	72.00	89.86	122.83	169.38	32.6
	State Bank Groups					
1	State Bank of India	75.44	93.64	136.58	173.01	31.7
2	State Bank of Bikaner & Jaipur	63.24	74.17	105.19	129.42	28.0
3	State Bank of Hyderabad	90.00	109.00	165.00	166.04	25.4
4	State Bank of Indore	75.02	80.52	126.00	171.00	34.3
5	State Bank of Mysore	62.35	70.75	112.15	124.96	28.7
6	State Bank of Patiala	91.23	106.67	143.45	194.31	29.6
7	State Bank of Saurashtra	77.35	92.80	123.87	152.12	25.8
8	State Bank of Travancore	89.81	99.97	157.32	178.78	28.5

Source : RBI, Trend and Progress of Banking in India, Various Issues.

following table demonstrates comparative productivity position of different group of banks on basis of the aforesaid parameters.

The table exhibits the cost responsiveness of banks during 1983-2001. Generally, a high CR results in a lower productivity and vice versa. The average cost per unit of output (earnings) increases, if the percentage increase in cost (input) is higher than in earnings (output) over a period of time and vice versa. It has been observed that there is a sudden spurt in CR for all the bank groups in 1992-93 owing to adherence of provisions in the banking sector reforms. This is followed by a decline in 1994-95 and 1995-96. The CR of PSBs touched the bottom level in 1994-95. During 1998-2001, the CR was on increasing trend. It reached 1.15 in 1998-99 and declined to 0.84 in the next year further increased to 1.06. However, foreign banks did not fare comparatively well in this respect during the post reform period.

The return on working funds (ROWF) enables us to know overall profitability of the working funds. It shows the productivity of capital employed. By and large, an increasing trend is noticed in the return on the working fund over the period under consideration in case of private banks. However, the PSBs failed to achieve the international standard of ROWF, which would be at least more than unity. The PSBs experienced a negative balance of ROWF in both the years 1992-93 and 1993-94. While both foreign banks and private banks have done remarkably well during post reform period. It may further be observed that all three groups of banks made an effort to improve their productivity in the reforms years and succeeded in repairing their bottom line by recovering operating costs. Besides, the productivity is still low compared to international standard*. However, the foreign banks have out performed the PSBs and private banks during entire period. The comparative position of PSBs was low in the post reform era indicating thereby that PSBs achieved less profit than foreign and private banks.

However, earning profit was never an issue of PSBs. Besides, meeting of obligations under the schemes like high priority sector advances, issue of Kishan Credit Card along with providing personal insurance package to all cardholders to cover them against accidental death or permanent

* According to International Standard, Return on assets (ROA) should be greater than 1 per cent but Indian domestic banks have less than 1 per cent.

TABLE – 3
PRODUCTIVITY RATIO : TO CR AND ROWF

Year	*Cost responsiveness*			*Return on working fund*		
	PSBs	*Pvt. Banks*	*Foreign Banks*	*PSBs*	*Pvt. Banks*	*Foreign Banks*
1982	NA	NA	NA	0.12	0.13	0.81
1983	1.01	0.99	0.96	0.11	0.11	0.79
1984	1.01	0.98	1.01	0.09	0.11	0.90
1985	0.98	1.03	0.97	0.11	0.15	0.94
1986	097	0.93	0.85	0.15	0.15	1.34
1987	0.98	1.05	1.56	0.17	0.19	1.14
1988-89	1.00	0.98	0.79	0.19	0.25	1.34
1989-90	1.31	1.03	0.84	0.13	0.25	1.54
1990-91	0.99	0.98	0.99	0.18	0.35	1.50
1991-92	0.97	0.90	1.05	0.27	0.57	1.57
1992-93	3.62	1.12	7.34	-1.00	0.34	- 2.88
1993-94	1.60	0.89	6.83	-1.15	0.57	1.51
1994-95	0.13	0.77	0.89	0.25	1.16	1.60
1995-96	0.14	0.71	1.86	0.36	1.20	1.31
1996-97	0.53	0.69	1.91	0.38	1.31	1.70
1997-98	0.71	0.92	1.03	NA	NA	NA
1998-99	1.15	1.06	1.09	NA	NA	NA
1999-00	0.84	0.79	1.31	NA	NA	NA
2000-01	1.06	0.79	1.53	NA	NA	NA

Source : Indian Banks Association Bulletin, various issues.
RBI, Statistical Tables relating to banks in India, various issues.

disability. PSBs are required further to earmark 5 per cent of their net bank credit to women entrepreneurs and that should be achieved by March 2004. Moreover, they cannot close any rural branch on the plea of non-availability of staff and volume of business. In spite of all compulsions PSBs have emerged as stellar performer in recent years.

Bank's Productivity: An Empirical Analysis

The foregoing analyses clearly demonstrated that efforts are being made to improve the productivity of PSBs during the reform era but they are yet to achieve the International Standard. In the following paragraph an attempt has been made to analyse the productivity performance of PSBs in the area under study. To analyse the productivity of PSBs in the districts under consideration we have considered both labour productivity and branch productivity during the period 1985 – 2000.

Labour Productivity

We have considered widely used parameter like deposit per employee, advance per employee and business per employee, to measure the labour productivity. The accompanying Table-4 exhibited the productivity ratio of PSBs in the districts under study.

The deposit per employee in the districts increased from Rs. 24.99 lakh in 1991 to 68.84 lakh in 2000. Similarly, the advances per employee and total business per employee have also increased from Rs. 9.75 lakh and Rs. 34.74 lakh to Rs. 13.06 lakh and Rs. 81.90 lakh respectively during the period under consideration. It has further been observed that, the three indicators of labour productivity are in the increasing trend during the post reform years. The average deposit per employee (Rs. 47.56 lakh) and business per employee (Rs. 61.7 lakh) in the district level exceeds the national average of Rs. 40.5 lakh and Rs. 61.1 lakh respectively during same period. However, in respect of average advances per employee (Rs. 11.2 lakh) the districts are yet to catch up the national average of Rs. 20.7 lakh. This indicated that rate of deployment of bank credit in the gainful venture in the districts is far less than that of mobilisation of deposits. Thus there is an ample scope of deploying credit if profitable ventures are made available.

Branch Productivity

The parameters like deposit per branch, advances per branch and business per branch are used as measures of branch productivity. It is

TABLE - 4

PRODUCTIVITY RATIO OF PSBs IN BARAK VALLEY AS ON MARCH (1985-2000)

(Amount Rs. in Lakhs)

	Labour productivity			*Branch productivity*		
Year	*Deposit per employee*	*Advance per employee*	*Business per employee*	*Deposit per branch*	*Advance per per branch*	*Business per branch*
	NA	NA	NA	135.7	46.2	181.9
	NA	NA	NA	179.8	82.6	273.6
	24.99	9.75	34.74	279.0	106.1	378.1
	36.45	11.05	47.50	443.74	136.0	584.7
	47.10	10.80	57.94	606.4	139.8	742.6
	60.40	11.45	71.89	876.6	166.1	1042.8
	68.84	13.06	81.90	1010.8	191.7	1202.6
Grand mean	**47.56**	**11.2**	**61.7**	**504.6**	**124.0**	**629.5**

NA = Not available.

Business = deposits + Advances.

Source : Self compiled on the basis of deposits, advances, employees and number of branches.

observed from the table that the average productivity per branch in terms of deposits, advances and total businesses has considerably increased. The deposits per branch increased from Rs. 135.7 lakh in 1985 to Rs. 279.0 lakh in 1991 further to Rs. 1010.8 lakh in 2000. Thus during the post reform regime rate of growth of deposit per branch is much higher than that of pre-reform period. The advance per branch has also increased from Rs. 46.2 lakh in 1985 to Rs. 106.1 lakh further to Rs. 191.7 lakh in 2000. Similarly, business per branch although increased from Rs. 181.9 lakh to Rs. 1202.6 lakh throughout the period and the banks achieved about 4 times growth during the post reform era. However, average productivity (around Rs. 629.5 lakh) is much lower than the national level productivity per branch of Rs. 948.2 lakh during the years under comparison.

Bank-wise performance

The bank-wise productivity in terms of volume of business per employee during post reform period (1991-2000) is presented in Table–5.

The table discerns that United Bank of India achieved highest per employee business while Canara Bank witnessed the lowest during the period 1991-2000. The business per employee of United Bank of India increased to Rs. 81.3 lakh in 2000 from Rs. 31.9 lakh in 1991. The same for Canara Bank was Rs. 12.3 lakh in 1991, increased to Rs. 51.6 lakh in 2000. Although United Commercial Bank and Allahabad Bank have shown comparatively better performance with regard to the business strength per employee in the first phase of banking sector reform (the figure being Rs. 48.2 lakhs and Rs. 41.2 lakhs respectively in 1995). They have however, failed to maintain such comparative business strength in the second phase of the reform. The business per employee of UCO Bank and Canara Bank reached to Rs. 52.3 lakh and 61.2 lakh respectively in 2000, which was comparatively lower than the other PSBs in the districts under study. During 1991-2000, the Indian Bank ranked first with regard to the growth of business per employee which recorded 3.47 fold increase. This is followed by State Bank of India (3.15), United Bank of India (2.9), Union Bank (2.76), Vijaya Bank (2.56), Canara Bank (2.40), Punjab National Bank (2.37), Bank of Baroda (2.35), Punjab & Sind Bank (2.60), Central Bank of India (2.41), Allahabad Bank (1.97), United Commercial Bank (1.7) respectively.

Apart from this, the volume of business per employee of individual banks in the study area is much lower than the national level of business

TABLE – 5
BANK WISE BUSINESS PER EMPLOYEE IN THE BARAK VALLEY (AS ON MARCH)

(Amount in Rs. Lakhs)

Sl. No.	*Name of Banks*	*1991*	*1995*	*1996*	*1997*	*1998*	*1999*	*2000*	*CV*
1	State Bank of India	22.3	31.2	41.9	45.3	47.8	59.8	70.1	32.9
2	United Bank of India	31.9	41.3	51.6	52.1	63.1	68.2	81.3	27.7
3	United Commercial Bank	29.2	48.2	41.3	45.9	49.0	50.2	52.3	16.1
4	Punjab National Bank	30.2	33.6	35.7	40.2	41.2	68.7	71.8	34.4
5	Indian Bank	17.1	23.6	28.9	30.3	40.3	56.1	59.3	40.8
6	Union Bank	24.9	28.6	47.5	49.5	60.4	63.2	68.9	31.5
7	Vijaya Bank	31.3	41.3	47.2	49.3	60.2	79.1	80.3	27.1
8	Allahabad Bank	31.0	41.2	45.1	53.2	59.2	60.3	61.2	23.8
9	Central Bank of India	28.3	39.1	51.3	63.0	65.1	67.3	68.3	19.3
10	Punjab and Sind Bank	22.8	29.3	36.1	48.2	51.2	59.2	60.3	30.9
11	Bank of Baroda	21.3	29.7	32.3	39.5	40.1	42.9	50.1	24.1
12	Canara Bank	21.0	21.3	37.2	39.1	48.2	49.6	51.6	30.9

Source : Self-calculated on the basis of the data obtained from Lead Bank Office, UBI.

per employee. In order to identify variation in the business per employee we have used co-efficient of variation (**cv**). Higher the **cv** higher is the productivity of the banks. It is revealed that Punjab National Bank (34.4 per cent), State Bank of India (32.9 per cent), Indian Bank (40.8 per cent) and Union Bank of India (31.5 per cent) are performing well than the others in the districts during the period 1991-2000.

The bank-wise branch productivity further has been calculated on the basis of the business per branch and presented in Table – 6.

The table manifests that all bank branches have attained higher growth in business over the years. The State Bank of India topped the list followed by Allahabad Bank, Indian Bank, Union Bank and so on in March 2000. The business per branch for State Bank of India was Rs. 182.0 lakh in March 1985 which was increased to Rs. 138.1 lakh accounting a 7.58 fold increase in March 2000 while Allahabad Bank recorded 6.79 fold increase in business per branch during the same period. In terms of growth of business per branch in March 2000 over 1985 the Bank of Baroda ranked first (10.9 fold) followed by Indian Bank (10.6 fold), Central Bank of India (10.5 fold), UCO Bank (8.4 fold), Canara Bank (7.9 fold), Union Bank (7.5 fold), Punjab National Bank (6.9 fold), United Bank of India (6.4 fold), Vijaya Bank (6.3 fold), Punjab & Sind Bank (6.3 fold) respectively.

Further, analysis of **cv** also suggests that Union Bank (64.1 per cent), fared well over the years followed by Bank of Baroda (59.1 per cent), State Bank of India (53.8 per cent), Canara Bank (53.4 per cent), Allahabad Bank (52.6 per cent), Indian Bank (51.2 per cent), Central Bank of India (50.2 per cent) and United Commercial Bank (50.1 per cent) and so on. It may therefore be argued that the branch productivity has gradually been increased during the post reform years in the valley under study.

Interrelationship Between Per Employee Income, Expenditure and Productivity

Attaining higher competitiveness in the present environment is the buzzword. Banks, consequent upon the reform measures, have attempted during post reform at achieving higher degree of productivity by following the strategy of enhancing volume of business per branch as well as per employee through reduction of expenditure.

The accompanying Table – 7, shows that both income per employee and branch along with expenditure have increased over the years. On the

TABLE – 6
BANKWISE BUSINESS PER BRANCH IN THE BARAK VALLEY (AS ON MARCH)

(Amount in Rs. Lakhs)

Sl. No.	*Name of Banks*	*1991*	*1995*	*1996*	*1997*	*1998*	*1999*	*2000*	*CV*
1	State Bank of India	182.0	371.0	483.2	698.2	832.2	1080.2	1381.1	53.8
2	United Bank of India	163.7	381.7	531.6	782.3	930.1	1030.2	1050.6	45.7
3	United Commercial Bank	152.3	392.0	583.1	756.1	872.6	1131.2	1284.6	50.1
4	Punjab National Bank	171.7	381.6	614.2	697.0	881.3	981.6	1181.3	46.1
5	Indian Bank	123.3	375.1	591.3	703.1	921.6	989.3	1295.6	51.2
6	Union Bank	171.2	380.1	514.3	892.3	831.7	1050.6	1282.1	64.1
7	Vijaya Bank	181.3	351.2	493.1	753.1	856.0	1157.5	1138.3	49.8
8	Allahabad Bank	193.5	342.6	431.9	771.0	912.6	1016.1	1312.9	52.6
9	Central Bank of India	156.3	314.3	636.1	683.1	821.2	941.6	1231.6	50.2
10	Punjab and Sind Bank	167.1	328.7	568.7	781.3	914.0	1031.7	1051.3	46.5
11	Bank of Baroda	103.1	371.3	436.1	431.1	704.3	1131.8	1130.7	59.1
12	Canara Bank	121.3	348.3	681.2	538.2	705.7	938.6	1281.2	53.4

Source : Self-calculated on the basis of the data obtained from Lead Bank Office, UBI.

TABLE – 7
PER CAPITA AND PER EMPLOYEE INCOME, EXPENDITURE AND VOLUME OF BUSINESS

(Amount Rs. in lakhs)

Year	*Per capita Employee income*	*Income per bank branch*	*Per capita employee expenditure*	*Expenditure per bank branch*	*Per emoployee business*	*Business per bank branch*
31-3-1993	1.57	19.1	1.56	17.9	34.74	361.3
31-3-1994	1.81	20.9	1.70	21.6	42.18	509.0
31-3-1995	2.54	33.0	2.03	27.9	47.50	584.7
31-3-1996	3.12	40.5	3.01	32.2	60.44	734.5
31-3-1997	4.95	71.1	4.18	43.6	57.94	742.6
31-3-1998	4.55	69.8	4.53	67.7	68.67	953.5
31-3-1999	5.07	76.1	4.12	63.5	71.89	1042.8
31-3-2000	6.36	95.4	5.08	78.57	81.90	1202.6

Source : Self-calculation on the basis of earlier tables.

other hand, employee productivity (business per employee) has increased from Rs. 34.74 lakh on March 1993 to Rs. 81.90 lakh on March 2000. While bank productivity (business per branch) increased from Rs. 361.3 lakhs to Rs. 1202.6 lakh during the same period. However, to assess the interrelationship between the variables, correlation coefficient (r) has been calculated. The results are obtained as under –

Correlation Matrix

Marked correlation is significant at $p < 0.05$

N = 8 (Case-wise deletion of missing data)

Variables	*PEI*	*IPB*	*PEE*	*EPB*	*PEB*	*BPB*
PEI	1.00					
IPB	1.00*	1.00				
PEE	0.98*	0.98*	1.00			
EPB	0.94*	0.95*	0.95*	1.00		
PEB	0.94*	0.94*	0.94*	0.95*	1.00	
BPB	0.94*	0.95*	0.93*	0.97*	0.99*	1.00

PEI = Per Capita Employee Income

IPB = Income Per Bank Branch

PEE = Per Capita Employee Expenditure

EPB = Expenditure Per Bank Branch

PEB = Per Employee Business

BPB = Business Per Bank Branch.

The correlation matrix discerned that the **'r'** values between the variables are highly positive and statistically significant. Thus it can be argued that,

(a) Low level of per employee income is associated with low level of per employee business. It indicates there is a scope of increasing volume of business that would lead to increase in per capita employee income.

(b) With increase in the volume of expenditure there will be corresponding increase in volume of business. Thus, incentives to employees, automation of branches, facilities to the customers are prerequisite for growth of productivity of the employees and the branches in the districts.

Cost Responsiveness vs Productivity

The productivity of the banks in the study area may further be examined on the basis of the interrelationship between the parameter, cost responsiveness and profit as percentage of volume of business.

TABLE – 8
COST RESPONSIVENESS VS PRODUCTIVITY

Year	*Cost responsiveness*	*Profit as per cent to volume of business*
31-3-1994	0.932	0.23
31-3-1995	0.771	0.04
31-3-1996	0.566	0.56
31-3-1997	0.370	0.81
31-3-1998	-19.140	1.01
31-3-1999	0.536	1.17
31-3-2000	0.791	1.26

Correlation coefficient (r) = – 0.30.

It has been found that the CR in 1994 was 0.93, which has declined to 0.771 in 1995 then to 0.566 in 1996 further to the bottom of – 19.14 in March 1998 and then slightly increased during the corresponding year and reached to 0.791 in March 2000. This indicates that efforts have been made for increasing the level of productivity by reducing the average cost per unit of output (earnings) in the reform years. The profit as percentage of volume of business has increased in post reform years except in 1995. It was 0.23 in March 1993 swelled to 1.26 in March 2000. This explains that the profitability of PSBs has increased with the increase in the volume of business in the area under study during post reform era. The correlation coefficient between CR and profit as percentage to volume of business is found to be negative (r = – 0.30). It indicates that, the banks are becoming cost conscious over the years and gradually acquiring strength of competitiveness.

It could be inferred from the above analyses that PSBs are gradually accelerating the pace of their productivity in spite of initial shocks. But it is still at the low level in the national context. The analyses of various indicators of productivity revealed that there is wide disparity in profitability of PSBs in the districts. The reasons may be attributed to bankers apathy in lending due to mounting over dues, willful defaulters, lack of entrepreneurship zeal, lower contribution in the priority sector lending, non availability of viable proposals and the like.

References

1. Monga, R. C. 1992. *Dynamics of Productivity Management*, Productivity 33 (1).
2. Drucker, P.F. 1980. *Managing in Turbulent Times*, New York, Harper – Row.
3. Choudhary, A.K. 1998. *Bank Management*. Rajat Publication, New Delhi, pp. 172, 173.
4. Diwan, P. 1997. *Productivity and Technology Management*. A Pentagon Press Publication, Hari Nagar, New Delhi, pp. 34, 39.
5. Asthma, P. and Srinivas P. 1997. *Productivity in Commercial Banks*. Productivity, (Oct. Nov.) 38 (3) : 441.
6. Angadi, V. B. 1984. *Some Issues Relating to Productivity of Indian Scheduled Commercial Banks*. The Journal of the Indian Institute of Bankers, 58 (4) : 184
7. 198, *Ibid*., p. 185.
8. Pedgaonkar, S. L. 2002. *Competition ; The Rationale of Financial Sector Reform* in Banking and Financial Sector Reform in India, op. cit. pp. 380.

7

Non-Performing Assets : Nature and Trend—A Critical Assessment

Introduction

The banking sector reform measures, since 1991, heralded epoch-making changes for aligning banking activities with international standard. Earlier, profits were seldom a matter of serious concern to banks. Deposit mobilisation was the main goal. The public sector banks (PSBs) till early 1990s made reckless loans and advances. These by-gone days' philosophy has gone into oblivion in the financial sector reform regime. Profits became a driving force through cutting of operational costs, upgrading technology and customers' standards. The convergence, competition and consolidation, the trio is dominating the banking system. Since introduction of prudential norms on income recognition, asset classification and provisioning thereon from the financial year1992-93 as per recommendation of Committee on Financial System (Narasimham Committee-1) the banking operation in Indian context has undergone a gut wrenching changes. The pace of transformation has further been accelerated by the paradigm shift in respect of opening up the floodgates to foreign banks, allowing private banks to operate in the Indian banking arena, reduction in interest rates, raising the cap of foreign direct investment from 49 per cent to at least 74 per cent in private sector banks, extending benefits of Article 72 (A) of the Income Tax Act i.e., set off and carry forward of accumulated losses, lower cap on the lending rates for agriculture and small scale sectors, along with change of monolithic mindset of the workforce in the event of exposure of banking activities to the market forces where competition is the main mantra. However, huge amount of bank credit, catalysts of economic growth, has been tied as NPAs and not available for the productive purposes. The Public sectors banks alone were saddled with NPAs of nearly Rs 83000cr during 2000 though dwindled to Rs 55624 cr in 2002 but still that is mind-boggling. The growing NPAs menace is taking toll on efficiency and profitability of the banking sector. The Narasimham Committee-1 in this respect rightly expressed apprehension over the erosion in the quality of the asset portfolio of the banks. Thus proper management of NPAs is warranted for the economic growth of the country.

With this backdrop an attempt has been made to study the nature and substantial affect of the NPAs on the banking sector along with the measures adopted to arrest its growing menace. Both statistical and financial tools were applied over the financial data based on RBI bulletin to assess the significant impact on the banking activities.

NPA: What is it?

The Securitisation Reconstruction of Financial Assets and Enforcement of Security Interest Act, 2002 defined non performing assets *(NPAs) as "an asset or account of a borrower, which has been classified by a bank or financial institution as sub-standard, doubtful, or loss assets in accordance with the direction or guidelines relating to asset classification issued by the RBI".* An asset is, therefore, considered to have gone bad when the borrower has defaulted on principal and interest repayment for more than two quarters or 180 days (the *lag would get reduced to 90 days from March 31,2004 to conform international norms).* As per RBI guidelines NPAs consist of sub-standard assets, doubtful assets and loss assets. Any assets generally turned into NPAs when it failed to yield income during certain period. As a result, doubtful assets find its way from sub-standard assets after 18 months in Indian context against 12 months under the international norms and finally when it is found irrecoverable then it migrates to loss assets category. Banks are allowed to make full provisions for such assets 100 per cent of unsecured portion of doubtful assets plus 20-50 per cent of secured portion (depending on the period for which the account is doubtful) and a general 10 per cent (20 per cent under the international norms) of the outstanding balance in respect of sub-standard assets.

The central bank is in favour of implementing the time limit of 90 days instead of existing 180 days from April 2004 so that the banks would remain competitive in the context of their international exposure. With effect from March 31, 2005, banks will have to classify assets as 'doubtful', if they remained under the sub-standard category for 12 months (currently at 18 months). To help banks to overcome extra provisioning because of changes in asset classification, the central bank has allowed a phased provisioning: a minimum of 20 per cent each year over four years.

Calculation of NPAs

According to RBI directives, all banks are required to maintain NPAs both on gross and net basis. It is generally expressed in the percentage term,

NPAs= [(gross or net NPAs) / total advances] × 100

Where net NPAs= Gross NPAs – provision for NPAs

The aforesaid definition suggests that the ratio is designated as "non performing assets to total assets" but in reality it is worked out in case of credit only, i.e., non performing credit is related to total credit.

It has been observed that total bank credit in Indian context constitutes of about 70 per cent of total deposit received encompassing primary sector lending, commercial lending and compulsory pre-emption by the central bank. The later consists of cash reserve ratio (CRR) presently slashed to 5 per cent from earlier 5.5 per cent and statutory liquidity ratio (SLR) 25 per cent of net demand and time liabilities. *Section 42 of RBI Act 1934, provides that every scheduled bank is required to maintain CRR with RBI an average daily balance and the amount shall not less than 3 per cent of the net demand and time liabilities.* The RBI according to the act is empowered to increase CRR from time to time maximum up to 15 per cent of the net demand and time liabilities. Both, CRR and SLR are known as reserve instruments in the hands of the central bank to regulate the liquidity of the banking system. The portion of the total deposit as received by the banks is held with RBI in form of reserve requirements yields a return of about 6.5 per cent and 7.5 per cent for CRR and SLR respectively. Thus, the banks should include such investment while working out the ratio of NPAs as a per cent to total assets. In contrast the foreign countries have no compulsory pre-emption of high level of CRR and SLR, which probably resulted their lower ratio of about 2-3 per cent. It is argued in the fast changing banking scenario of the country specially in the context of aligning banking activities with international standard that Indian banks should aim at attaining such ratio of at least 5 per cent or at below level.

In international banking, while working out NPAs, collateral security is deducted for arriving at the NPA. These aspects of NPAs should carefully be reckoned with in the calculation and its comparison with international banks' NPAs.

* Break up of Rs. 100 deposited with banks.

Particulars	*Amount (Rs.)*	*Nature and yield*
a. In CRR (Pre empted by RBI)	5.50@	RBI, pays only bank rate i.e., 6.5% (varies from time to time)
b. In SLR	25.00	Yield 7.5% (used to deficit financing of Central Government)
c. Priority sector lending 40% Rs. (100 - 30.50)	27.80	Higher NPA risk
d. Commercial lending	41.70	Bank use its freedom.
Total	**100.00**	

@ *During mid tern review of monetary and credit policy in October 2001, The RBI has reduced CRR from 7.5% to 5.5%.*

The guidelines relating to provisioning requirement and overdue period can be seen in the regulatory framework presented in Table – 1.

Banks however, are advised to phase the provisioning against NPAs over the period and continuously improve their capital base.

Capital Adequacy Ratio (CAR)

The CAR was introduced from 1992 after acceptance of Narashimhan Committee Report, which recommended introduction of prudential norms by commercial Banks and Financials Institutions, in respect of Income Recognition, Assets Classification, prescribed by Bank of International Settlement (BIS). The motive behind was that the banks should attain its competitiveness as well as remain sound in their operation. They have to maintain minimum capital funds against their risk-weighted assets and other exposure on their risk-weighted assets and other exposure on an ongoing basis. The Basle Committee prescribed minimum 8 per cent capital adequacy standard with a view to regulate banking operation on a global basis in 1987. However it is open to national authorities to adopt more stringent requirements.

Banks in India are required to attain this ratio on an incremental basis in phased manner 9 per cent with effect from 31st March 2000 to 10 per cent from March 2001. The CAR is derived as under :

TABLE – 1
CHANGES IN REGULATORY FRAMEWORK

Variables	*1992-93*	*1993-94*	*1994-95*	*1995-96*	*1996-97*	*1997-98*	*1998-99*	*1999-00*	*2000-01*
1. CRAR (per cent of RWA)									
Domestic Bank with International Business	*	8	8	8	8	8	8	9	9
Other Domestic Banks	4	4	4	8	8	8	8	9	9
Foreign Banks	8	8	8	8	8	8	8	9	9
2. NPA (overdue period in quarter)									
Substandard assets[@]	4	3	2	2	2	2	2	2	2
Doubtful assets	8	8	8	8	8	8	8	8	6[#]
3. Provisioning requirements (in per cent)									0.25
Standard assets	-	-	-	-	-	-	-	0.25	
Substandard assets	10	10	10	10	10	10	10	10	10
Doubtful assets (Secured portion)	20-50	20-50	20-50	20-50	20-50	20-50	20-50	20-50	20-50
Doubtful assets (unsecured portion)	100	100	100	100	100	100	100	100	100
Loss assets	100	100	100	100	100	100	100	100	100

Notes : * *To achieve 8 per cent as early as possible and any case, before end-March 1994. The concept of past due (grace period of 30 days) was dispensed with effective April 1, 2001.*

\# *Reduced to 6 quarters effective March 31, 2001; reduced to 2 quarters effective March 31, 2004.*

@ *Reduced to one quarter effective March 31, 2004.*

Source : Reserve Bank of India, RBI Bulletin, various issues.

$$CAR = \frac{\text{Capital fund of the bank}}{\text{Risk weighted Assets (RWA)}} \times 100$$

Capital fund : Capital inclusive of tier-1 and supplementary capital respectively.

Tier-1 capital comprises; issued capital; subscribed and paid up capital ; statutory reserves, capital reserves, share premium, revenue and other reserves including investment fluctuation reserve and balance in profit and loss account.

Tier-II capital comprises; Unsecured, Redeemable and Non-Convertible debentures. The BIS in 1996, proposed to incorporate Tier – III capital in the current definition of capital fund i.e., Tier-I and - II capital, though RBI did not implement it.

However, the proposed accord, Basel – II, revised in January, 2000, will effect by 2005, has added operational risk in the RWA. It is defined as the risk of direct or indirect loss resulting from inadequate or failed internal processes, people and systems or from external events. However, it has been observed that operational risk will constitute approximately 20 per cent of overall capital requirements. Thus under the new method, RWA constitutes credit risk along with market risk and operational risk.

$$CAR = \frac{\text{Tier - I + Tier - II + Tier - III}}{\text{Credit risk + market risk + operational risk}}$$

Risk weighted Assets and other exposures may be calculated as

(Assets * Risk weight) + (Off balance sheet items i.e., contingent credit exposure * conversion factors)

However, the capital level considered adequate only to cover credit risk, i.e., the amount of capital that the bank will need to protect itself against default of any of its assets. This ratio incorporates different risk weightage for different asset types. For instance, investments in government securities carry zero risk weightage (i.e., they are credit risk free), which means that an institutions does not need to earmark any capital against holdings of government securities. While investment in corporate debt securities carry 10 per cent risk weightage, which means that the institutions has to maintain capital of 10 per cent of total such investment in that security against risk of this investment turning sour.

This apart, any investment is subject to market risk while risk free assets can lose value in the regime of rising interest rate. The RBI, therefore,

TABLE-2
CAPITAL ADEQUACY RATIOS OF PUBLIC SECTOR BANKS (BANK WISE)

Sl. No	*Name of the banks*	*1993-94*	*1994-95*	*1995-96*	*1996-97*	*1997-98*	*1998-99*	*1999-00*	*2000-01*
A	**SBI group (8 Banks)**								
1.	State Bank of India	12.90	12.77	11.60	12.17	14.58	12.51	11.49	12.8
2.	State Bank of Bikaner & Jaipur	4.58	4.15	9.33	8.82	10.65	12.26	12.35	12.4
3.	State Bank of Hyderabad	6.17	6.63	9.90	10.84	10.83	12.35	10.86	12.3
4.	State Bank of Indore	4.47	5.07	8.80	9.31	9.83	12.35	11.26	12.7
5.	State Bank of Mysore	4.62	3.60	8.81	10.80	11.61	10.23	11.56	11.1
6.	State Bank of Patiala	11.22	10.00	9.51	11.25	13.24	12.47	12.60	12.3
7.	State Bank of Saurashtra	5.26	5.24	12.38	12.14	18.14	14.35	14.48	13.8
8.	State Bank of Travancore	4.00	3.07	9.40	8.17	11.48	10.27	11.09	11.8
B.	**Nationalised Group (19 Banks)**								
9.	Allahabad Bank	Nil	4.92	9.68	11.00	11.64	10.38	11.51	10.5
10	Andhra Bank	Nil	4.36	5.07	12.05	12.37	12.02	13.36	13.4
11	Bank of Baroda	9.10	8.72	11.19	11.80	12.05	13.30	12.16	12.8
12	Bank of India	0.82	9.10	8.44	10.26	9.11	10.55	10.57	12.2
13	Bank of Maharashtra	Nil	6.02	8.49	9.07	10.90	9.76	11.66	10.6
14	Canara Bank	12.06	10.93	10.38	10.17	9.54	10.96	9.64	9.8
15	Central Bank of India	Nil	4.85	2.63	9.41	10.40	11.88	11.18	10.0
16	Corporation Bank	9.40	10.70	11.30	11.30	16.90	13.20	12.80	13.3
17	Dena Bank	6.68	7.41	8.27	10.81	11.88	11.14	11.63	7.7
18	Indian Bank	3.50	8.50	Nil	18.81	1.41	Nil	Nil	Nil
19	Indian Overseas Bank	1.69	8.42	5.95	10.07	9.34	10.15	9.15	10.2
20	Oriental Bank of Commerce	10.23	18.69	16.99	17.53	15.28	14.10	12.72	11.8
21	Panjab & Sind Bank	Nil	5.40	3.31	9.23	11.39	10.94	10.57	11.4
22	Panjab National Bank	8.00	9.07	8.23	9.15	8.81	10.79	10.31	10.2
23	Syndicate Bank	0.29	5.60	8.42	8.80	10.49	9.57	11.45	11.7
24	UCO Bank	-	8.10	7.83	3.16	9.07	9.63	9.15	9.6
25	Union Bank of India	9.71	8.28	9.50	10.53	10.86	10.09	11.42	10.8
26	United Bank of India	-	2.50	3.50	8.23	8.40	9.60	0.62	10.4
27	Vijaya Bank	5.71	9.58	Nil	11.53	10.30	11.00	16.61	11.5

Source : RBI, Trend and Progress of Banking In India, various issues.

announced guidelines for primary dealers (whose portfolios are purely risk-free securities) to maintain a 7 per cent capital against their holdings of government securities (Mecklai, 2001). This 7 per cent however is an adhoc number and would be vetted by the RBI. When portfolio risk is low, the institution could increase its portfolio and make much more return. Conversely high market volatility would only bring more risks.

Bankwise Achievement of Capital Adequacy Ratio

As regard to capital adequacy, all public sector banks barring Indian Bank and Dena Bank attained capital adequacy ratio of above 9 per cent as on March 31st 2001. Further, three banks Canara Banks, UCO Bank and Dena Bank fell short of the medium term capital adequacy target of 10 per cent while UCO Bank, and Indian Bank will be looking to the government for capital, others such as Indian Overseas Bank and Andhra Bank may approach the capital market to strengthen their capital base. Other banks are likely to seek refuge in tier II capital. The bankwise capital adequacy ratio are presented in the table (page 209).

Magnitude of NPAs

High level of NPAs is endemic to the Indian financial sector. It reflects country's poor bankruptcy laws as well. The mounting pressure of NPAs can be seen from the following chart.

The diagram exhibits that the PSBs are saddled with highest gross NPAs while in the percentage terms of net NPAs they are exerting well above the private banks. This fact has also been demonstrated in the following table :

YEAR WISE GROSS AND NET NPAS POSITION

(Rs in crore)

Year(as on March)	*Gross NPAs*		*Net NPAs*	
	Amount Rs	*Pc to gross advances*	*Amount Rs*	*Pc to net advances*
1996	39584	17.00	18928	8.91
1997	43577	17.84	20285	9.18
1998	45653	16.02	21232	8.22
1999	51710	15.90	24211	8.11
2000	53033	14.01	26187	7.42
2001	54773	12.41	27969	6.71
2002	56473	11.12	27958	5.81
2003	54066	9.41	24963	4.51

Source: Report on trend and progress on banking in India (various issues)

The reasons may be attributed to:

- Change in the composition of assets in favour of investment in government securities and other appropriate securities. This is reflected by the ratio of investment to credit which rose for all banks from 59 per cent in 1996-97 to 72 per cent in 2000-01. In the Economic Survey 2002-03 it has been observed that banks' investment in the government securities rose by a record 35 per cent to Rs 85738 cr during the current fiscal up to Jan 10, 2003 from Rs 63082 cr in the corresponding period last year and this was despite the fact that there has been sharp fall in yields on government securities. As against, the banks' investment in the govt-sec that amounts to 37.8 per cent of banks net demand and time liabilities as compared to the statuary stipulation of 25 per cent, the bank credit to commercial sector raised only 9.7 per cent till January 10 during this fiscal 2003, compared to 11 per cent in the previous period.
- Success on the part of banks in using one time settlement scheme.
- Bankers' apathy towards small and medium sectors while sanctioning loan as they are sitting on a pile of dubious loans many of which may have to be declared as NPAs as stricter norms for provisioning kick in.
- The enactment of Securitisation Act and its specific provision of debt recovery. The gross NPA to the percentage of gross advances and net NPA to net advances declined to 9.41 per cent and 4.51 per cent respectively in 2003 in comparison to its previous year.

However, the volume of net NPAs has squeezed over the years, which may be evident from the following table:

NET NPAs AS PERCENTAGE OF NET ADVANCES

As on March	*All banks*	*Public sector banks*	*Private sector banks*	*Foreign banks*	*Fls banks*
1997	8.1	9.2	5.4	1.9	8.0
1998	7.3	8.2	5.3	2.3	8.0

(Contd.)

(Table Contd.)

As on March	*All banks*	*Public sector banks*	*Private sector banks*	*Foreign banks*	*FIs banks*
1999	7.6	8.1	7.4	2.9	9.6
2000	6.8	7.4	5.4	2.4	9.8
2001	6.2	6.7	5.4	1.9	8.6
2002	5.5	5.8	5.2	1.9	8.4
2003	4.4	4.5	4.6	1.8	7.3
Coefficient of variation	19.66	22.41	15.79	15.53	10.54
Skewness	-.6565	-0.5436	1.9979	1.2107	.3635

Source: Report on trend and progress on banking in India (various issues)

It is evident that in the Indian banking scenario the position of the PSBs has considerably been consolidated over the years. The higher degree of coefficient of variation of PSBs signifies larger variation in the percentage of net NPAs to net advances during the period under consideration. The intensity of adverse effect of the NPAs on banking performance is gradually declining, which is revealed by the negative Skewness(-0.543). But, the net NPAs, in absolute term to the tune of Rs 32764cras on March 2003 though declined from Rs 35546cr in the previous year, is still mind-boggling. However the banking activities are expanding by leaps and bounds which may seen from the following facts.

GROWING IN EVERY SPHERE

(Figure in Rs cr.)

End March	*2001*	*2002*	*2003*	*Coefficient of variation(CV)*
Aggregate Deposits	876521	1012510	1188583	15.25
Domestic Credits	990458	1147161	1527712	22.61
No. of branches	67937	68195	68561	2.12

Despite the low interest regime the aggregate deposits in absolute terms have been swelling and domestic credits are expanding at a greater rate.

The PSBs generally dominate the banking system and hold about 80 per cent bank deposits, but they are not conducive to efficiency, innovation, fiscal prudence, investment and growth in modern increasingly integrated economic world. The PSBs framework does not foster effective innovation risk taking and commercial orientation. This is so because the bank management has no freedom in the matters of recruitment, promotion, remuneration and closure of non-remunerative branches. This, as a result, led to poor customer service. However it can not be denied that as per the government directives the PSBs are required to direct a significant part of lending about Rs. 28 per Rs. 100 of deposits, to priority sector- agriculture, small scale sector and other small scale borrowers which often turned into sour investment. The Economic survey 2002-03 revealed that the PSBs have performed well in terms of meeting the targets for priority sector lending. It accounted 43.1 per cent of deposits in the priority sector lending.

NPAs: its impact on Bank performance

As per the prudential norms, income should not be recognized on accrual basis. It should only be booked when it is received. Thus, in measuring the efficiency of banks, actual return on assets is considered as superior parameter than that of size of income in the balance sheet. The deleterious effects of NPAs on return on assets are:

- Current profit will decline with provisioning requirement
- The total size of interest income will decline as income is only recognized on receipt basis
- Higher provisioning requirements affect profits and accretion to capital fund
- Recycling of fund will be restricted and asset liability mismatch will be widened.

It has been observed that gross and net NPA as percentage of total advances have been moved down over the years. Still the NPA level can be considered as staggering magnitude in absolute terms costing the PSBs more than Rs.5000 crores annually by way of loss of interest besides servicing and litigation cost. The malady of high level of NPAs eroded the profitability of banks. It is in this respect hypothesized that *profitability at PSBs has taken a beating following deregulation.*

To test the same the profitability ratio defined as *net profit to total assets* has been considered as yardstick. The ratio for all PSBs (27) has been improved from minus 1 per cent of assets in 1992-93 to 0.6 per cent in 1999-2000.The profit of three loss making banks as identified by the Verma Committee, i.e., Indian Bank, United Commercial Bank (UCO) and United Bank of India if excluded, then the ratio rises to 0.7 per cent.This compares with the profitability of 34 private sector banks (old and new) of 0.9 per cent during same period under consideration. The profitability, which is explained by the composite ratio, defined as *spread ratio less burden ratio* (s-b) has not been improved over the years especially in comparison to their foreign counterpart.

Thus factors affecting the profitability need further analysis. In order to identify the interdependency among the variables, multiple regression equation has been fitted considering earning ratio [interest earning ratio (IER) *plus* non interest earning ratio (NON.INT) *less* interest paid ratio (IPR)] as dependent variable and ratio of net NPA to net advances (NPA), man power ratio (MPR) other establishment expense ratio (OTH. EXP), as independent variables.

We obtained following multiple regression:

Y earning ratio = *3.3157 - 0.3848 NPA + 0.36876MPR + 0.19589 OTH.EXP*

(SE) (5.4917) (.4415) (0.9990) (3.28825)

t- value 0.60377 -0.64877 0.60597 0.51914

p- level 0.58859 0.5627 0.5873 0.6395

R= 0.7793, R^2= 0.6074, Adj R^2 = 0.2148, F (3, 3) = 1.5472 $p<0.36429$

The analysis reveals that R^2 =. 6074.This implies that an about 61 per cent variation in the earning ratio is explained by the independent variables. However the F ratio is not statistically significant. It indicates that regression is not significant. This, on the other hand, implies that there are other exogenous variables contributing much in the overall earning of the banking sector, which have not been considered in the model. Provisioning against NPAs is one item in the computation of profit, the other key items are spread, operating expenses and other income, i.e., non fund based income which includes fees, commission for service provided, and profit on sale of investment, foreign exchange and derivative revenues. Further, the regression shows that the NPAs have a negative affect on the profitability of the banks, though statistically not significant. Moreover, the positive regression coefficient of manpower ratio implies that there is an ample scope of increasing profitability of the banks with proper use of strategic human resources.

However, in the wake of deregulation interest earned ratio and non interest income ratio has been rising, spread are healthy hovering around 3 per cent and other establishment ratio is at below 1 per cent, despite

TABLE – 3

FREQUENCY DISTRIBUTION OF NET NPAS OF PSBs VIS-À-VIS OTHER BANKS

Year	*PSBs*			*Old Pvt. Banks*			*New Pvt. Banks*			*Foreign Banks*		
	up to 10%	*10 to 20%*	*above 20%*	*upto 10%*	*10 to 20%*	*above 20%*	*upto 10%*	*10 to 20%*	*above 20%*	*upto 10%*	*10 to 20%*	*above 20%*
1995	2	15	10	-	-	-	-	-	-	-	-	-
1996	19	6	2	22	3	-	9	-	-	30	1	-
1997	17	9	1	22	3	-	9	-	-	36	1	2
1998	17	9	1	21	4	-	9	-	-	34	6	2
1999	18	8	1	17	5	-	9	-	-	27	11	3
2000	22	5	-	18	5	-		-	-	31	7	4
2001	22	5	-	16	4	1	8	-	-	31	6	5

Source : Trend and Progress of Banking in India various issues, RBI.

higher degree of profitability over the years has not been achieved. In this respect it may be argued that NPAs are not the sole factor in eroding the profitability of the banks as the net NPAs to net advances ratio has been declining over the years. This has further confirmed the influence of other exogenous factors in the bank's profitability. It therefore points out at the managerial aspect of the PSBs, which has not properly articulated the facts about the performance and their intrinsic strength. They further have not cultivated the fine art of managing investors' relationship and market perception.

Frequency Distribution of NPAs

The table exhibiting frequency distribution of net NPAs of PSBs vis-à-vis other private banks and foreign bank revealed that in 1995, 10 out of 27 PSBs accounted net NPAs of more than 20 per cent of their advances. While other 2 were placed of in below 10 per cent and 15 banks were within 10- 20 per cent net NPAs category. The position however, had undergone a sea change in the latter period where in 22 banks achieved the target of net NPAs less than 10 per cent and none of the PSBs found within category of above 20 per cent of net NPAs during 2001.

The position of private banks in this context is better as there is no banks found in the category of above 20 per cent of net NPAs of their advances. In 2001, only 3 old private banks out of 31 private banks accounted NPAs more than 20 per cent of its net advances. During 1995-2001, no new private banks witnessed NPAs above 10 per cent in their books whereas considerable number of foreign banks experienced net NPAs above 20 per cent of their advances.

It could be inferred from the analysis that the PSBs are continuously improving their operation in the reform regime as there is no banks fall in the category of net NPAs above 20 per cent of their advances during 2001. It is also evident that, by introducing 'net concept', RBI succeeded notably, i.e., the number of banks, showed low level of NPAs, however this may not be considered a genuine progress in the financial strength of PSBs.

Sector-wise Non-Performing Assets

The sector-wise analysis of NPAs of PSBs revealed that priority sector added up a large proportion about 50 per cent of total advances in March 1995 and slipped to 45.4 per cent in March 2001. In the non-priority sector, the same has been increased to 51.4 per cent in March from 46.5 per cent in March 1995.

TABLE – 4
SECTORWISE GROWTH OF NPAs

Growth rate	*Priority sector*			*Non-priority sector*			*Public sector*			*Total of PSBs*		
	SBIs	*NBs*	*Total*	*SBIs*	*NBs*	*Total*	*SBIs*	*NBs*	*Total*	*SBIs*	*NBs*	*Total*
b	386.39	543.32	924.82	982.23	1321.39	1911.39	53.29	-0.642	- 18.03	1291.12	1721.08	2854.28
Cgr	4.97	3.99	4.37	8.42	7.89	8.86	2.49	- 0.29	-1.31	6.95	5.84	6.24

Source : Self calculated.

TABLE – 5
POSITION OF NON-PERFORMING ASSETS OF PSBs VIS-À-VIS OTHER BANKS (END MARCH)

(Amount in Rs. crores)

	Public Sector Banks			*Pvt. Sector Banks*			*Foreign Banks*			*All Commercial Banks*		
Year	*NPAs Rs.*	*Advances Rs.*	*NPA as per cent to advances*	*NPAs Rs.*	*Advances Rs.*	*NPA as % to advances*	*NPAs Rs.*	*Advances Rs.*	*NPA as % to advances*	*NPAs Rs.*	*Advances Rs.*	*NPA as % to advances*
1997	43577	244214	17.8	2542	29959	8.5	1181	27525	4.3	473.00	301698	15.7
1998	45653	284971	16.0	3186	36753	8.7	1976	30972	6.4	50815	352696	14.4
1999	51710	325328	15.9	4643	44492	10.4	2201	31433	7.6	58555	401253	14.6
2000	53291	380077	14.0	4761	58249	8.2	2615	37432	7.0	60841	475758	12.8
2001*	54773	442134	12.4	6039	71237	8.5	3071	45395	6.8	63883	558766	11.4
b	3003.0	49094.6	-	856.9	10387.2	-	441.3	42193.8	-	4319.2	63719.8	-
Cgr	60.078	15.288	-	22.249	23.738	-	22.199	12.589	-	7.773	15.972	-

**Provisional*

Source : Trend and Progress of Indian Banking, 1998-99, pp. 72 and 1999-2000, pp. 77.

An analysis relating to the percentage change of NPAs over previous years revealed that fresh accretion of NPAs in the priority sector is comparatively less during 1995-2001. The **cv** analysis demonstrates that SBI group witnessed more variation in the quantum of NPAs over the years in all sectors, priority sector (10.30 per cent), non-priority sector (26.09 per cent) and public sector (24.72 per cent). The sector wise growth of NPAs of PSBs is exhibited in Table – 4.

The compound growth rate (cgr) of NPAs in non-priority sector is comparatively higher (8.86 per cent). The **'*b*'** and **cgr** became negative in the public sector. This reveals that the nationalised banks might not have considered fresh loan to the public sector due to further NPAs menace over the years.

Moreover, the overall **cgr** of NPAs during 1995-2001 in case of PSBs was 6.24 per cent. The non-priority sectors' **cgr** (8.86 per cent) overweighs the priority sector (4.37 per cent). Thus this sector is adding considerably fresh NPAs over the years.

On the other hand, higher NPAs in priority sector advances have pushed up the overall proportion of NPAs by three to four per cent. The reasons of higher proportion of NPAs in priority sector advances may be attributed to; the directed and pre-approval nature of loans sanctioned under sponsored programmes, lack of effective follow up due to large number of small accounts, absence of cost effective legal recovery measures, lack of repayment culture consequent on the loan waiver schemes, willful defaulters and so on.

A comparison of NPAs as per cent of advances of public sector, private sector and foreign banks is presented in Table - 5.

The table depicts that during 1997-2001, NPAs as percentage of advances has been declining in the PSBs. It has slipped to 12.4 per cent in March 2001 from 17.8 per cent in March 1997. The foreign banks and private banks witnessed swelling of NPAs both in percentage and absolute term.

The bank group-wise growth of NPAs and advances has been analysed with the help compound growth rate (cgr) for the period of 1997 to 2001. For this we have assumed linear regression line $Y = a + bt$ (Y = total amount of NPAs/advances to year (t) origin at 1997. The analysis revealed that the growth of NPAs of PSBs is higher (60.08 per cent) than private (22.45 per cent) and foreign banks (22.19 per cent). One worth

TABLE – 6
BANKWISE CLASSIFICATION OF NPAS AS A PROPORTION TO ADVANCES

(Per cent)

Sl. No.	Name of the banks	Gross NPA as a Proportion to Gross advances								Net NPA as a proportion to net advances					
		1993-94	1994-95	1996-97	1997-98	1998-99	1999-2000	2000-2001	CV	1996-97	1997-98	1998-99	1999-2000	2000-2001	CV
1.	State Bank of India	26.3	21.6	16.0	14.1	15.6	14.3	12.9	26.2	7.3	6.1	7.2	6.4	6.0	8.3
2.	State Bank of Hyderabad	21.9	15.8	19.2	19.0	16.0	16.1	14.0	14.1	11.4	10.9	8.8	7.3	7.8	17.7
3.	State Bank of Patiala	13.1	11.4	11.3	11.8	14.0	10.9	10.0	10.3	5.9	7.1	8.2	6.1	4.9	17.4
4.	State Bank of Travancore	13.7	11.1	14.5	20.0	18.5	14.4	11.4	20.9	8.8	12.2	10.8	8.6	7.7	17.0
5.	State Bank of Bikaner and Jaipur	18.2	17.2	13.8	11.7	16.1	16.2	12.9	14.6	7.9	7.2	10.5	10.1	7.8	15.3
6.	State Bank of Mysore	19.9	12.8	17.0	17.5	17.0	14.0	12.8	15.7	10.9	10.7	10.5	8.1	7.6	14.8
7.	State Bank of Saurashtra	16.1	10.7	14.8	14.8	15.5	13.7	14.5	11.4	6.0	6.6	7.7	7.8	6.9	9.6
8.	State Bank of Indore	16.1	10.6	15.8	15.1	14.7	10.8	9.1	20.4	11.3	11.0	10.1	7.5	5.9	23.1
9.	Allahabad Bank	24.7	26.0	24.0	23.2	20.1	19.1	17.6	13.3	14.8	15.1	12.5	12.2	11.2	11.6
10.	Andhra Bank	23.4	14.3	11.8	9.81	9.4	7.8	6.1	45.2	4.1	2.9	4.3	3.5	2.9	16.5
11.	Bank of Baroda	18.7	16.5	17.2	14.6	16.0	14.7	14.1	9.6	7.5	6.6	7.7	6.9	6.7	6.2
12.	Bank of India	30.0	21.0	11.8	11.6	11.9	12.9	10.2	43.1	6.9	7.3	7.3	8.6	6.7	9.3
13.	Bank of Maharashtra	36.2	25.7	20.7	17.4	16.0	12.6	12.3	39.0	7.1	8.7	8.7	6.8	7.4	10.5
14.	Canara Bank	18.1	12.5	20.3	18.7	18.3	10.4	7.8	29.6	9.3	7.5	7.1	5.3	4.8	18.3
15.	Central Bank of India	35.3	25.0	25.0	20.5	17.4	16.6	16.0	28.6	14.4	12.2	9.8	9.8	9.7	20.3
16.	Corporation Bank	7.3	4.9	9.9	7.6	5.7	5.4	5.0	25.8	3.6	2.9	2.0	1.91	1.9	27.1
17.	Dena Bank	22.5	17.0	15.1	13.7	12.4	18.2	25.3	24.5	9.9	8.3	7.7	13.4	18.3	23.0

(Contd.)

(Contd. Table-6)

Sl. No.	Name of the banks	Gross NPA as a Proportion to Gross advances								Net NPA as a proportion to net advances					
		1993-94	1994-95	1996-97	1997-98	1998-99	1999-2000	2000-2001	CV	1996-97	1997-98	1998-99	1999-2000	2000-2001	CV
18.	Indian Bank	26.8	24.1	39.1	38.9	38.7	32.8	21.7	22.3	25.2	26.0	21.7	16.1	10.0	30.3
19.	Indian Overseas Bank	31.6	23.6	15.8	13.4	13.3	13.2	11.8	38.8	7.6	6.2	7.3	7.6	7.0	8.3
20.	Oriental Bank of Commerce	6.0	4.1	7.4	6.2	6.3	5.5	5.2	16.4	5.6	4.5	4.5	3.8	3.5	10.9
21.	Punjab and Sind Bank	31.0	22.0	30.7	26.8	23.0	16.3	18.4	21.1	12.0	10.8	10.5	9.3	12.2	8.3
22.	Punjab National Bank	21.4	17.0	16.3	14.5	14.1	13.2	11.7	19.0	10.4	9.6	9.0	8.5	6.6	17.2
23.	Syndicate Bank	29.3	27.5	19.3	15.3	10.7	7.7	7.8	49.3	7.5	5.8	4.0	3.1	4.1	13.6
24.	UCO Bank	32.2	26.7	28.4	24.0	22.6	18.8	11.7	26.6	13.7	11.1	10.8	8.7	6.3	24.5
25.	Union Bank of India	12.9	9.4	10.4	11.2	12.4	12.3	11.2	10.0	7.0	7.7	8.7	7.9	6.8	8.9
26.	United Bank of India	35.1	29.1	36.2	33.5	32.4	27.6	21.5	15.4	19.2	14.1	14.7	12.7	10.4	20.5
27.	Vijaya Bank	21.1	13.4	18.7	15.2	13.7	11.5	10.0	24.5	9.5	7.6	6.7	6.6	6.2	16.1

*Provisional

Source : Report on Trend and Progress of Banking in India, pp. 210 Economic & Political Weekly, March 23, 1996- pp. 736.

nothing point in this respect is that the growth of NPAs of PSBs is higher than the growth of advances where as private banks experienced a uniform growth rate of both NPAs and advances.

Thus, the problem of NPA is multidimensional and unless the same is checked and the NPA level is brought down to the international standards of 2 to 3 per cent of total loan assets, it is bound to weaken the banking system. A major stumbling block for the banks to reduce their NPAs is the legal system prevailing in the country.

Bank-wise Classification of NPAs

From the foregoing discussion it is evident that the fresh accretion of NPA of every year added extra fat to the volume of NPAs. As in the absolute term it is going up while the percentage terms of NPAs in PSBs is coming down. Thus, the position of NPA of individual PSBs needs further study. In this respect, bank-wise NPA as per cent to advances (gross and net) has been demonstrated in the accompanying Table – 6. The table exhibited the position of NPAs of all banks during 1993-2001. It has been observed that except Dena Bank and Punjab & Sind Bank the ratios of net NPAs to advances has considerably been dwindled in 2000-01 from the previous year. The net NPAs to advances jumped from 13.4 per cent. in 1999-00 to 18.3 per cent in 2000-01 in case of Dena Bank while for Punjab and Sind Bank it has increased to 12.2 per cent in 2000-01 from 9.3 per cent. in the previous year. However, 21 of the 27 PSBs showed an increase in the ratio of gross NPAs to gross advances with more than 10 per cent while only 6 PSBs are showing ratio below 10 per cent of gross NPAs to advances. Further more, only 6 Banks accounted their NPAs below the internationally accepted level of 5 per cent of Net NPAs to net advances in 2000-01. The list includes, State Bank of Patiala, Andhra Bank, Canara Bank, Corporation Bank, Oriental Bank of Commerce and Syndicate Bank. This implies that the Banks are continuously improving their assets portfolio as well as their recovery position.

Measure to Contain NPAs

The problem of NPA is multidimensional and unless same is checked and its level is brought down to international standard of 2-3 per cent of total loan assets the whole banking sector will definitely loose its grip in the competitive market. It has been observed that in percentage term gross NPA has been declined from 13.91 per cent in 1999-2000 to 9.2 per cent in 2003-04 for nationalized banks. In case of PSBs, it has declined13.98

per cent to 9.36 per cent during the same period. The ratio of net NPA to net advances has dwindled to 4.77for nationalized banks and 4.54 per cent in case of PSBs during the same period.

DISTRIBUTION OF PUBLIC SECTOR BANKS BY RATIO OF NET NPA TO NET ADVANCES

(No. of Banks)

Financial year end	*March Up to10 per cent*	*Net NPA to 10pc – 20 per cent*	*Net Advances Above 20 per cent*
1995	2	10	5
1996	19	6	2
1997	17	9	1
1998	17	9	1
1999	18	8	1
2000	22	5	-
2001	22	5	-
2002	24	3	-
2003	25	2	-

However, recovery in absolute terms during each year has exceeded by fresh accretion of NPA. The gravity of real threat revealed from the fact that gross and net NPAs of PSBs which were at Rs. 41041 crores and Rs.19696 crores respectively during 1993-94 swelled to Rs. 54,773 crores and Rs. 27,968 crores respectively as on end of March 2001. Twenty-five out of 27 PSBs witnessed the downward trend in net NPAs as percentage of advances. However, only six PSBs during 2000-01 could achieve internationally accepted level of 5 per cent of net NPAs to net advances.

The table discerns that number of banks in the higher group of net NPA to net advances is declining over the years. McKinsey & Co, with a view to improve the asset quality portfolio, estimated that 35 to 40 per cent of Indian banks accounting about 40 per cent of banking business are extremely weak and the quantum of capital required for Indian banking system will range from Rs 45000 crores to Rs 70000 crores in next three years. About Rs 15000 crores to Rs 40000 crores would be required to clean up balance sheet and shoring up capital in the line with new norms laid down by Bank for International settlement (BIS). Furthermore, about Rs 12000-13000 crores would be needed for streamlining operations.

The government however, earmarked considerable amount as recapitalization for troubled Indian banks with a view to strengthening their basic operations. The efficacy of the government bail out in improving the efficiency of primary activities of the banks is a debatable issue. It has been evident that, three banks, Indian Bank, United Commercial Bank and United Bank of India which were identified by the Verma Committee as weak banks, have now managed to turnaround by intensifying recovery. The Indian Bank has managed to a substantial growth in its business. The return on advances has increased from 10.26 per cent in March '01 to 10.57 per cent in December' 02 and cost of deposit fell from 7.91 per cent to7.76 per cent during the same period. Gross profit has also swelled to Rs 103 crores (Apl-Dec'01) from Rs 57 crores in the same period in the previous year. About Rs 200 crores against the target of 295 crores has been recovered upto Feb. 2002. The United Bank of India has also managed well to bring their gross NPAs level. Its outstanding gross NPAs fell from Rs 602 cr in 2000-01 to Rs 542 cr in the next year.

Despite several recovery steps floated, accretion of NPAs on average of all banks is in the rising trend. A major stumbling block for the banks to reduce their NPAs is probably the prevailing legal system in the country. However the RBI/ government of India has been goading the banks to take steps for arresting the fresh increment of NPAs and creating legal and regulatory environment to expedite the recovery of existing NPAs of banks. The measures undertaken to encounter the menace of NPAs along with their efficacy can be summarised here under:

1. **Lok adalat Intitutions (LAIs)**: LAIs help banks to settle disputes involving accounts in 'doubtful' and 'loss' category with outstanding balance of Rs 5 lakhs. The DRTs are now empowered to organize lokadalats to decide in case of NPAs of Rs 10 lakhs and above. The PSBs has recovered Rs 40.38 crores as on September 2001 through this forum.
2. **Debt Recovery Tribunals** (DRTs): DRTs are established under section 3 (1) of the Recovery of Debts due to Banks and Financial Institutions Act, 1993. There are 22 numbers of DRTs across the country set up at the major metropolis; Kolkata, Delhi, Mumbai, Allahabad and Chennai. The PSBs till Sept. 2001 have recovered Rs 1864.30 crores only out of 9814 cases for Rs 6264.71 crores. Complexities of documentation and operational features of Indian Banking system impeded the recovery process. However, provision for placement of more recovery officers, training of tribunal

recovery officers about the intricacies of banking practices, penal provision for disobedience of tribunal orders, appointment of receivers with power of realization, protection and preservation of property will definitely add momentum in recovery of the NPAs.

3. **Circulation of information among defaulters**: The RBI circulates periodically in details about the willful defaulters of borrowers of banks and FIs. This is considered as caution list while considering fresh or additional credit limits by the banks and FIs.The RBI also publishes a list of borrowers with outstanding aggregating Rs 1 cr and above whom suits have filed to recover amounts as on 31 March on every year.

4. **Settlement Advisory Committees (SAC)**: RBI provides for setting up of an independent SAC to scrutinise as well as to recommend compromise proposals for NPAs. The banks in this respect are free to design and implement their own policies for recovery and write off incorporating compromise and negotiated settlement in respect of unresolved cases under the NPAs with the approval of their board. The guidelines have urged the banks to go for lump sum settlement up to Rs 5 crores of non-performing loans and one leeway has been provided in cases where the borrowers are unable to pay the entire one time go. In such cases at least 25 per cent of the settled amount to be taken upfront while the balance will be recovered in installments within a period of one year.

5. **Assets Reconstruction Companies (ARCs):** ARCs, in the private sector regulated by the RBI, were set up with authorized capital of Rs 2000 crores and initial paid up capital Rs 1400crs. It will negotiate with banks and FIs for acquiring distressed assets and develop markets for such assets. It will buy the NPA of banks and financial institutions at the pre-determined value and issue Redemption bonds of fixed return. The ARCs are the centralized agencies for resolving bad loans. They are further expected to help the promoting institutions to spruce up the balance sheet by taking bad loans off their books. The guidelines, issued by the RBI to operational the provisions of the Securitisation Act, cover wide range of activities include registration and operations of ARCs, financing the activities,

permissible business, operational structure, transfer financial assets.

Sections 7 (1) and 7 (2) of the Securitisation Act provide specific guidelines enabling ARCs to

- Securitise NPAs
- Issue security receipts to qualified institutional buyers (QIBs) include, FIs, Insurance Companies, banks asset management companies making investment on behalf of banks, mutual funds, pension funds, gratuity or provident funds and FIIs registered by the SEBI.
- Transfer the acquired assets from the originators to the trust.
- Hold and administer the financial assets for the benefits of the QIBs.

The Securitisation and Reconstruction of Financial Assets and Enforcement of Security Interest Act, 2002 is an important landmark in Indian banking scenario. With the passage of the Act, the banks and the financial institutions (FIs) have been quick to initiate action against the defaulters on loans. About 9000 notices have been issued for the recovery of the loan amounting to Rs 70 billion as on March, 2003.Furthermore, the banks and the FIs are empowered to take over the assets of the defaulting borrowers. In this respect, Section 17 (2) of the Act holds that the defaulting corporates were required to deposit 75 per cent of liability before filling an application against the order of attachment of its assets.

The Act was snarled into litigation. The apex court, however, disposed of writ petitions challenging legality and constitutional validity of the Act by declaring section 17(2) as unconstitutional and suggested the guidelines regarding attachment of assets include: the banks and financial institutions should approach the DRTs to press recovery of dues, they will serve the notice to the concerned defaulting corporates before attachment of such assets and, no creation of third party interest in the attached assets till final verdict in the case.

Thus it is evident from the discussion that, the SRFAESI Act, has given the much strong weapon to the bankers, to fight the menace of NPAs and redress a historic imbalance between lenders and borrowers. However the success rate hinges on proper utilization of power vested on the banks under the act. In this respect some loopholes still need to be plugged;

(a) Can assets seized from the defaulters be sold? Without sale of assets the idea of setting up ARCs and creating market for securitised assets won't work. On the other hand assets should be disposed-off fast as delay in that process would erode the value of assets.

(b) What happens when there is a conflict of interest among lenders? Sec. 13 (9) of SRFAESI, Act states that, secured creditors can not exercise rights unless those who are three-fourths (3/4th) of the amount outstanding agree.

(c) Proper valuation of assets and finding out suitable market for selling the assets at reasonable prices to be ensured by the banks while assets without having ready market should be avoided.

(d) Where the banks decided to take over a running unit

With a view to recover the dues the bank had to recourse to the long winding legal route against the defaulting borrowers. Beginning from filling of claims in the courts a lot of time was spent in getting decree and execution thereof before the banks could make some recoveries. In the meantime promoters could seek the protection from BIFR and could also dilute the securities available to banks. The DRTs set up by the government also did not prove to be much help as huge volume of cases referred to them gradually over burdened this.

The banks were handicapped in the absence of any powers for seizure of assets charged to them and, therefore, there had been persistent demand from banks to empower them in their war against NPAs.

This apart, the Asset Reconstruction Companies (ARCs) established by the banks and the FIs for speedier resolution of the default cases. The ARCs are the centralized agencies for resolving bad loans. They are further expected to help the promoting institutions to spruce up the balance sheet by taking bad loans off their books. The ARCs are not peculiar in India. Several countries; Czech Republic (1995), Sweden (1992), Thailand (1998) have tried variants of ARCs rescue the troubled banks. The United States (1889), Korea (1997) and Malaysia (1998) during their savings and loan crisis has established single asset Management Corporation to purchase NPAs of number of banks.

Thus, it is apparent from the discussion that there are certain issues of process, accounting and fiscal aspect relating to transfer of NPAs portfolios and their subsequent recoveries. An attempt, therefore, has been made hereunder to float up the issue particularly the accounting aspect to reveal how the ARCs and transferring banks are affected with the transfer of the bad loan portfolios in their balance sheet.

Accounting Aspect

The accounting aspect relating to transfer of loan portfolio to ARCs should follow relevant Accounting Standard and GAAP. However, recoveries should be recorded only on cash basis. Furthermore, when the ARCs manage to generate enough surpluses through the sale of bad and doubtful loans transferred to them, it will be shared among the sponsors. However, the accounting entries in this respect may be proposed in the books of the originators and the ARCs / Trust if created as under.

In the books Banks / FIs :

1. On transfer of the NPAs portfolios :

Debit	ARCs A/C (negotiated value of loan portfolio)
Debit	P/L A/C (difference between book value of the loan portfolio, i.e., less provision if any and agreed value)
Credit	Borrowers (loan Portfolio) A/C (net book value)
Credit	P/L A/C (excess of negotiated value over net book value)

2. When the part of consideration is paid by the ARCs :

Debit	Security Receipts A/C
Credit	ARCs A/C (with value of instruments received)

3. On recovery of NPAs portfolio by ARCs and settlement of transaction :

Debit	Bank A/C
Debit	P/L A/C* (portion of lower side of the recovery)
Credit	ARCs A/C
Credit	*P/L A/C* (portion of upper side of the recovery).*

4. On substitution of security receipts issued earlier if any

Debit	Bank A/C
Credit	Security Receipts A/C

In the Books of the ARCs/Trust if created :

1. On receipt of Loan portfolio from the Banks :

Debit	Borrowers (Loan Portfolio) A/C (at negotiated/ agreed value)
Credit	Banks / FIs A/C (originators)

2. On payment of the portion of consideration through Security Receipts :

Debit	Banks / FIs A/C (originators)
Credit	Security Receipts A/c (if any)

3. On the issue of Security receipts to the QIBs :

Debit	Bank A/C
Credit	Security Receipts A/C

4. On the recovery of loan portfolio from the borrowers :

Debit	Bank A/C
Debit	P/L A/C (loss on recovery)
Credit	Borrowers (Loan portfolio) A/C
Credit	P/L A/C (excess recovered over negotiated value)

5. On payment to the QIBs and substitution of security receipts issued to originator

Debit	Security Receipts A/C
Debit	P/L A/C (on redemption and interest if any paid)
Credit	Bank A/C

Tax Implications

In the Income Tax Act, 1961, there are no specific provisions governing income of different entities involved in secutrisation of transactions. However, when the NPAs portfolios of the banks/FIs are transferred to the ARCs and subsequently to the trust created by the ARCs, then such transfer would conform to the principles of 'true sale'. The question therefore crops up about tax liability. Who, QIBs, or ARCs, will pay tax? When the trust pays tax then it will restrict the QIBs' to adjust any loss brought forward against the income from security receipts representing the NPAs pool.

To avoid confusion it may be argued that trust fund may be treated as pass through entity in the same manner as the law allows for MFs and Venture capital funds. As a result the investor would undertake risk of realization of NPAs portfolios and directly taxed when they realize the income or offset losses in case of under recoveries.

It is evident that, the Securitisation Act 2002 has facilitated the investors to deploy their funds in the NPAs portfolios of banks and financial institutions. With a view to create a vibrant secondary market ARCs were formed as independent body corporate to expedite the process of resolving the bad loan portfolios. However, an appropriate set of substantial financial sector regulation clarity including changes in tax laws is imperative for the banking system to get rid off NPAs as well as for the QIBs to look forward to the investment opportunity. Thus apart, ARCs should have clear distinct 'financial acquisition policy' and guidelines relating to proper diligence and valuation of NPA portfolio. The Act however is silent in this respect. The Section 3 (1) (viii) of the Act emphasizes only that ARCs should apply the principles of valuation consistently across all the schemes. This has warranted the need to create some kind of standard to make the process transparent and consistent. Moreover, some tax incentives including capital gain tax exemption, carry forward the losses to set off the same with other income, tax exemption on interest income and the like may be allowed to the QIBs as their active participation by way of investing sizeable amount in distressed assets of the banks and FIs only pave the way of success of the entire asset restructuring scheme. The retail marketing on the other hand, has been excluded in this respect as it was felt that retail investors may not be in a position to make a sound value judgment about the risk component of such investment. However, with the robust credit rating mechanisms, securitization of NPAs portfolio could be opened for retail investment.

References

1. Bhole, L.M. 1996. *Financial Institutions and Markets; Structure, Growth and Innovation*. Tata Mc Graw Hill Publishing Company Limited. New Delhi.

1. Government of India : 1991. *Report of the Committee on Financial System*, p. 54.

2. Sikidar, Sujit. 1997. *Computation of NPA, Income Recognition and Impact on Reporting of Bank Account* The Management Accountant, (November) pp. 811.

3. Report of the Committee on Financial System 1991, *Ibid*, p. 54.
4. Shajahan, K. M. 1998. *Non-Performing Assets of Banks ; Have They Really Declined ? And on Whose Account*, Economic and Political Weekly, (March 21). pp. 671.
5. RBI, *Tightens NPA Recognition Norms*, The Economic Times, Kolkata. (November 27). 2001.
6. Shrivastava, M.P., Kumari, N., Shrivastava, K. P. and Shrivastava, V. P. 2000. *Second phase of Banking and Financial Sector Reforms and Non-Performing Assets : Relevance, Mechanism, Management and Cost Structure of Assets Restructuring Companies*. Banerjee and Singh (eds), in Banking and Financial Sector Reforms in India, Deep and Deep Publications Private Ltd., New Delhi, pp. 181.
7. Government of India. 1998. *Report of the Committee on Financial System, op.cit.*
8. Government of India, Economic Survey, 2000-2001.
9. D'Souza, E. 2000. *Prudential Regulation in Indian Banking*. Economic and Political Weekly, (January 29).
10. *RBI Tightens NPA Recognition Norm*, The Economic Times, November 2001.
11. Reserve Bank of India, Trend and Progress of Banking in India, 1992-93.
12. Willful defaulters :-

A willful defaulter is one :

(a) Where either the unit has defaulted in meeting its loan obligations despite having the capacity to honour the obligations, or

(b) The units have defaulted in its obligations and has not used funds for the purpose for when finance was availed of, but has diverted funds, or

(c) The unit has defaulted in obligations and has siphoned off funds and the funds are not available with the units in the form of other assets.

8

Asset Liability Management in the Banks : An Overview

Introduction

The reform measures heralded several epoch making changes in the financial sector to make them more competitive. It includes deregulation of interest rates, reduction of reserve requirements (CRR and SLR), integration of various segment of financial markets, allowing banks to access capital market for augmenting capital base to meet their capital adequacy, freedom in operational matters, greater emphasis on the use of information technology, moving towards capital account convertibility and so on. These measures emphasize on internal consolidation of banks and covers organisational restructuring to match with competitive environment. Among the important aspects of such re-engineering are Asset Liability Management (ALM), Risk Management and greater penetration to technology and strategies management. The aim of these strategies is to improve efficiency by managing risk properly so as to improve profitability of banks. The present chapter is devoted to focus on ALM in the bank. It is divided into **three sections**. The **first section** deals with conceptual framework of ALM. It covers, need, types, guidelines; Basel Accord and RBI guidelines and techniques of risk management. **Section two** is devoted to identify the necessity of ALM in the domestic banking system and the **final section, three**, analyses structural changes of variables of banking sector during post reform period and changes of average ranking of PSBs over the years using CRAMEL approach.

I

Intricacies of ALM

ALM envisages the process of managing net interest margin (NIM) within the overall risk. The key objective of ALM is that of sustaining profitability in such a manner as to augment capital resources. It calls for an integrated approach towards simultaneous decision-making with regard to type and size of financial assets and liabilities (Baker, 1983). The success of banks hinges on its ability to match its assets with its liabilities in terms of rate and maturity to optimise the yield. This can be illustrated by the following example :

Suppose, a bank that borrows USD 100 MM at 3.00 per cent for a year and lends the same money at 3.20 per cent to a highly rated borrower for 5 years. For simplicity, we may assume interest rates are annually compounded and all interest accumulates to the maturity of the respective obligations. The net transaction appears profitable – the bank is earning a 20 basis point spread – but it entails considerable risk. At the end of a year, the bank will have to find new financing for the loan, which will have 4 more years before it matures. If interest rates have risen, the bank may have to pay a higher rate of interest on the new financing than the fixed 3.20 it is earning on its loan.

Suppose, at the end of a year, an applicable 4-years interest rate is 6.00 per cent. The bank is in serious trouble. It is going to be earning 3.20 per cent on its loan and paying 6.00 per cent on its financing. Accrual accounting does not recognise the problem.

The book value of the loan (the bank's asset) is:

$$100 \text{ MM } (1.032) = 103.2 \text{ MM}$$

The book value of the financing (the bank's liability) is :

$$100 \text{ MM } (1.030) = 103.0 \text{ M}$$

Based upon accrual accounting, the bank earned USD 2,00,000 in the first year.

Market value accounting recognises the bank's predicament. The respective market values of the bank's asset and liability are :

$$\frac{100 \text{ MM } (1.032)^5}{(1.060)^4} = 92.72 \text{ MM}$$

$$100 \text{ MM } (1.030) = 103.0 \text{ MM}$$

From a market-value accounting standpoint, the bank has lost USD 10.28 MM.

So which result offers a better portrayal of the bank' situation, the accrual accounting profit or the market-value accounting loss? The bank is in trouble, and the market-value loss reflects this.

Ultimately, accrual accounting will recognise a similar loss. It will accrue the as-yet unrecognised loss over the 4 remaining years of the position.

The problem in this example was caused by a mismatch between assets and liabilities. Prior to the 1970's such mismatches tended not to be a significant problem.

Thus ALM in practical terms involves :

(a) **Conscious decisions** – making with regard to assets-liability structure in order to maximise interest earnings within the framework of perceived risk and,

(b) **Quantification of risk** and evolving of suitable risk management techniques to minimise probable loss.

It is therefore evident that Asset/Liability Management (ALM) is a tool that enables bank management to take business decisions in a more informed framework. The ALM function informs the manager what is the current market risk profile of the bank, and the impact that various alternate business decisions would have on the future risk profile. The manager can then choose the best course of action, depending on his Board's risk appetite (Vasisbth, 1997)[2].

Objective of ALM

A Sound ALM system for the bank should encompasses:

- Review of interest rate outlooks.
- Fixation of interest product pricing of both assets and liabilities.
- Review of credit portfolio and credit risk management.
- Review of investment portfolio and risk management.
- Risk management of forex operations.
- Management of liquidity risk.

Need of Risk Management by Banks

Banks across the world are considered as financial risk takers as they live with money. They assume risk because risk is pre-requisite for survival (Sabnani, 2002)[3]. However, taking higher risks entails a loss and some times become catastrophic for the organisation. 'Eddie Cade'[4] has aptly documented these fact illustrated as under.

- Merrill Lynch lost $377 million trading mortgage-backed securities in an innovative form in 1987.
- Midland Bank lost a reported pound sterling 116 million by guessing wrong on interest rate movements in 1989.
- Bank of New England made massive bad debt provisions, suffered a run on deposits and had to be supported by Government to the tune of some $2 billion in 1991.
- Barclays Bank provided pound sterling 2.5 billion for bad and doubtful debts and declared the first loss in its history in 1992. Credit Lyonnais succumbed to similar troubles and registered a net loss of Fr. 6.9 billion in 1993.
- Barings, London's oldest merchant bank, was brought down by losses of pound sterling 830 million on a speculative proprietary position in Nikkei 22.5 stock index futures.
- In their financial year to March 1996, the major Japanese banks wrote off a total of some Japanese Yen 6000 billion of bad debts accumulated from the preceding boom years.

Risks and its Nature

Risk in general term is defined as possibility of suffering a loss. It is potential for realisation of unwanted negative consequences of an event. Thus, by defining risk one can measure the probability and severity of adverse effects (David, 1992)[5].

Categories of Risks

In the simplest words, risk may be defined as possibility of loss. It may be financial loss or loss to the reputation/image. It is difficult to think of a commercial organisation, which does not undertake any risk. Banking is also one of such commercial organizations. The concept of risk-return trade-off is applicable to all the business. However, higher risk may also result into higher losses (Salin, 1999)[6].

Various risks, to which the banks are exposed (Sehgal, 1999)[7], may broadly be categorized in the following categories: -

A. Credit Risk

B. Interest Rate Risk

C. Liquidity Risk

D. Foreign Exchange Risk

E. Operational Risk

(A) **Credit Risk:** Banks' pool assets and loans, which have a possibility of default, provide the depositors an assurance of redemption at full face value. Credit risk, in terms of possibilities of loss to the bank, due to failure of borrowers/ counter parties in meeting their commitments, is likely to hamper the capability of the bank to meet its commitment to the depositors.

Credit risk is the most significant risk, more so in Indian scenario where the NPA level of the banking system is significantly high. Its importance may be understood from the fact that during **Asian financial crisis, non-performing loans in Indonesia, Malaysia, South Korea and Thailand soared** to over 30 per cent of total assets of the financial system. The management of credit risk is thus a prerequisite, for long term sustainability/ profitability of a bank.

Credit risk depends on both internal and external factors. Some of the important external factors are state of economy, swings in commodity prices, foreign exchange rates and interest rates, etc. The internal factors may be deficiencies in loan policies and administration of loan portfolio covering areas like prudential exposure limits to various category, appraisal of borrower's financial position, excessive dependence on collateral, mechanism of review and post sanction surveillance, etc.

Risk is inherent in any business. As such it can't be avoided but has to be managed by adopting various risk mitigating methods. In banking business, funds are lent to the borrowers after due appraisal. However, the appraisal is based on certain assumptions, variation from which may affect the profitability of borrowing unit and this may ultimately culminate in the default. In most of the cases, default will not take place suddenly. An alert banker may smell the warning signals and by his pro-activeness he may take suitable steps in time either to remedy the situation or to exit from the account.

Key issue in managing credit risk is to apply a consistent evaluation and rating system of all investment opportunities. Prudential limits need to be laid down on various aspect of credit. Rating may be single point indicator of diverse risk factors of counter party. Management of credit delivery and monitoring process :-

(a) **Appraisal stage :** In addition to following the prescribed guidelines of the bank, the important point is the appraisal of the man behind the project. For this no rules can be given. However, the managers may use their own innovativeness and experience to judge the man. Some of the points that the manager may consider are as under :-

- Whether the branch has its own network for obtaining reliable information about present and prospective borrowers through some well known sources like local organizations, lead bank offices, other customers etc.
- Whether the credit officers keep an eye on local newspapers for keeping track on some developments in some units / industries etc.
- Whether marketability of the product is assured beyond reasonable doubt.
- Whether while processing the proposals a list of all the important references made by the borrowers is kept on record.
- Whether a small map of the location of the location of the unit / residence of borrowers / guarantors is kept on record.

Disbursement Stage

- Whether the branch ensures creation of assets and whether the disbursement is made in stages and checked at every stage, wherever possible.
- Whether the payments are directly made to the dealers.
- Whether the branch ensures long term availability of the business premises are on rent.

Review / Renewal

- Whether the branch considers review as a ritual or uses the opportunity to review its credit decision.

- Whether proper follow-up for obtaining financial information is stated in time and borrowers are properly educated in this regard.

(d) **Asset Verification/Inspection/Visits :** This is most important aspect of monitoring of a borrowed account. If done regularly, it gives an opportunity to interact with the borrowers and must be used to ascertain the problems that the unit is facing / likely to face. Remedial steps should be initiated at the earliest. If an eye is kept on the activities of the borrower, there is no reason as to why the account can't be kept healthy.

(e) **Credit Rating :** Credit rating is the main tool, which helps in measuring the credit risk and facilitate pricing the account. It gives vital indications of weaknesses in the account whenever rating of a particular account has slipped. It also gives triggers for portfolio management at corporate level.

(B) **Interest rate risk:** Banks fix and change interest rates on deposits and advances from time to time. Generally, changes in interest rates on advance affect the interest rates of all the advances account. However, in case of deposits, the change affects rate of interest of new/renewed accounts only. Hence, changes in interest rates can significantly impact the Net Interest Income (NII). The risk of an adverse impact on NII due to variations of interest rate may be called interest rate risk.

For measuring interest rate risk in case of trading activity – Value at Risk (VaR) is presently the standard approach. It attempts to assess the potential loss that could crystalise on trading portfolio due to variations in market interest rates and prices. In case of other balance sheet exposure, banks rely on "gap reporting system" for identifying asymmetry in re-pricing of assets and liabilities – commonly known as gap – and putting in place a gap reporting system. Supplemented with balance sheet simulation models to investigate the effect of interest rate variation on reported earnings over a medium – term horizon.

(C) **Foreign exchange risk :** Foreign exchange market is volatile. The exchange rates change from moment to moment. Every bank, which is active in international market, keeps certain open position in foreign currencies. However, there is inherent risk in running such open position due to wide variations in exchange rates. Such risks may be called as foreign exchange risks.

Various limits are key elements of risk management in FOREX trading, as they are all trading business. Banks with active trading positions are adopting VaR approach to measure the risk associated with exposure. For the banks that could not develop VaR, some stress testing is required to evaluate the potential loss associated with changes in exchange rate. This can be done with small movements as well as for historical maximum movements.

(D) **Liquidity risk :** This may arise due to funding of long-term assets (advances) by short term sources (deposits). If fresh short-term deposits are not available or existing deposits are not renewed, the bank will be put in liquidity problem.

Several traditional ratios are used for measuring liquidity risks, loan to total assets, loans to core deposits, large liabilities to earning assets, loan losses to net loans etc. Additionally prudential limits are placed on various liquidity measures like inter-bank borrowings and core deposits vis-à-vis core assets.

(E) **Operational risk :** Basel Committee for Banking Supervision has defined the operational risk as "the risk of loss, resulting from inadequate or failed internal processes, people and systems or from external events."

The operational loss has mainly three exposure classes viz. People, processes and systems. The importance of managing operational risk has increased mainly because of two reasons :-

- Higher level of automation and
- Increase in global financial inter-linkages.

Internal control mechanism has to be strengthened for mitigating the operational risk. For unexpected losses, capital has to be provided for.

In the Indian context, banks should start with an external and independent assessment of operational risk management in the bank. Based on such assessment they may identify high-risk areas and draw a phased roadmap towards attaining targeted standards.

Basel Accord Regarding Risk

Basel accord, by suggesting separate capital charges for operational risk has sensitised the financial world to this area and thereby created a valuable opportunity for banks to get into a major clean up act (Sharma, 2003)[8]. The highlights of Basel Capital Accord are briefly as under :-

Basel II Capital Accord : First Capital Accord proposed by Basel Committee is known as 1988 Basel Capital Accord. Now the accord is under review and new proposal is under consideration and the same is likely to be implemented in 2005-06. Original accord provided for only a capital risk charge. A market risk charge was implemented in 1996. The new accord has proposed operational charge at 12 per cent of Minimum Regulatory Capital.

The new accord will function on a three pillar approach :-

- Maintaining minimum capital requirement
- Undertaking supervisory renew of bank capital, and
- Effective use of market discipline

Capital charge is proposed to be maintained against credit risk, market risk and operational risk through economic capital allocation. Therefore, to enable the banks to comply with the requirements of the accord, capabilities for better risk management are to be built up.

The proposed Basel norms suggest that the risk weightage assigned by banks to each assets should depend on the underlying risk of the counter-party.

Presently, as per Basel Committee, Minimum Regulatory Capital is 8 per cent while RBI has stipulated 9 per cent for Indian Bank. There are three approaches to calculate capital adequacy ratio as per Basel Accord. Out of these three, bank may adopt any method as suits their portfolio. The approaches are as under :-

- The revised standardized approach
- The foundation Internal Rating Based (IRB) approach
- The Advanced IRB Approach

(i) **The revised standardized approach :** It is based on the external credit assessment institutions (ECAI) ratings for sovereigns, banks and corporate and is more risk sensitive as compared to existing standardized approach.

(ii) **The foundation internal rating based (IRB) approach:** It is based on banks' internal assessment of counter parties and exposures. Three main elements of this approach are:-

- Risk components / drivers of potential credit loss,
- The risk weight function, by which the risk components are converted to risk weights and
- Minimum requirements.

(iii) **The advanced IRB approach:** In IRB foundation approach, estimates of default risk of the borrowers are provided by the bank using internal estimates whereas other risk drivers are applied as per supervisory norms. However, in the case of IRB advanced approach, all the drivers would be based on banks' internal methodologies except for granularity of portfolio (which is determined by the concentration of bank's exposure to a single borrower or to a group of closely related borrowers).

The highlights of the revised accord arc that additional operational risk capital of 20 per cent (subsequently revised to 12 per cent) of minimum regulatory capital (MRC) is provided, i.e., MRC will be 8 per cent + 12 per cent of 8 per cent, i.e., 8.96 per cent.

However, the accord is yet in consultative stage and is likely to be finalized shortly.

Under the proposed accord, better risk management will lead to lower capital requirement. But banks will also have to incur expenditure for acquiring and maintaining necessary technology and equipment as also training and recruiting specialist staff.

Initiatives of Reserve Bank of India (RBI)

RBI has recognized the need of a proper risk management system in the banks. In the year 1999, it has issued guidelines regarding assets liability management, management of credit risk, market risks and operational risks. In October 2002, the RBI has issued guidance notes on credit risk and market risk management.

Risk Based Supervision : Main concern of regulators is the stability of the financial system. The ramifications of weaknesses of financial system, of which banking is a part, are manifold. Recent failures of a few co-operative banks in the country is an example as to how the public can lose hard-earned money and how the system can lose trust of the public. Bank regulators are also devising new strategies wherein they can identify potentially weak banks and focus more on their supervisory efforts on them.

RBI has proposed to switch over to risk based supervision (RBI) of banks by 2003. The focus of RBI will be on efficacy and soundness of systems and procedures for risk management in individual banks instead of individual banks will be prepared which will be the basis of prepared which will be the basis of RBS. A high-risk bank will be subjected to more intensive supervision by way of shorter supervisory cycle and greater use of supervisory tools like targeted on site inspections, additional offsite surveillance, ad-hoc information requests, structured meetings etc. A low risk bank will be subjected to a lesser degree of supervisory intervention.

The Asset – Liability Management Committee

Once the strategic plan is developed and is in place, the responsibility for day to day administration of the components that affect the financial performance passes to the asset liability management committee (ALCO). On the other hand, the planning committee has a long range perspective and meets frequently. ALCOs are primarily made of staff members headed usually by the chief executive officer. The ALCO is responsible for developing, implementing and managing the bank's annual budget or profit plan and its risk management programme (Rajwade, 2002)[9].

In managing performances, the committee reviews a variety of reports assessing the banks' performance relative to its profit plans and risk management objectives. To serve effectively all members of the ALCO should be knowledgeable about the various facets of asset – liability management. Members should understand the role and use of financial measures in evaluating the bank's performance.

Timely and accurate data for analysis and reporting, is a must for the ALCO. The ALCO should consider acquiring a software programme to enable them in carrying out their functions in an efficient manner. In choosing the software for supporting the bank's process the ALCO should clearly define the kinds of information it wants the software to produce and the amount of time available to work with the software.

The Budget or Profit Plan

A bank's annual budget or profit plan is the tool that keeps the bank on track towards achieving its strategic financial goals. The ALCO oversees the development of the budget, recommends its implementation to the board of directors and monitors the banks performance under the plan. The ALCO also makes recommendations for modifying the budget when necessary. In developing the annual budget the committee considers the time covered by the plan, the plan's level of detail, contingencies that might cause the plan to change, and the action plans, goals and timetables necessary to see that the plan is effectively implemented.

The Review System

An established system of reviewing the plan and modifying it where necessary contributes significantly to the plan's success. When the plan is written, the bank determines the frequency of its review, the types of performance reporting and the method to use in modifying the plan. Banks depend on effective plans with realistic targets. These plans enable the managers to take action consistent with the bank's short and long-range goals.

A Framework for Asset-Liability Function

Broadly essential elements in the framework for the asset/liability function are detailed as under :

Strategic Framework : The ALM function should be proactive and not reactive. The ALM function should assist the line management in product planning and pricing and help sensitise the operating people to the ALM implications of their decisions. The ALM function should not be mere analytical function, but a catalyst for the formulation of business strategies.

Organisational Framework : All elements of the organisation, namely the ALM committee, sub-committees, and the analytical support group should have clearly defined roles and responsibilities.

The analytical group should be located in the right place of the organisation to promote effective functioning. The membership and size of each organisational element should reflect business requirements. The ALM function should have full support of the top management. This includes proper resource allocation and personal commitment.

Analytical Framework : The various analytical concepts (gap analysis, simulation, duration, value at risk, etc.) should be used to obtain appropriate insights. In general heavy emphasis on cash flows, market values, risk adjusted returns and duration.

Technological Framework : This deals with utilisation of top class software, either purchased or developed in house. The software package should enable one to perform extensive analysis, planning and measurement of all the facets of the ALM function.

Operational Framework : There should be a well documented policy statement (approved by the Board of Directors) and a detailed ALM proceeds.

Performance Management Framework : The profitability of the bank comes from three sources, Assets, Liabilities and ALM. First the bank makes profits on the asset side making loans at a rate higher than economic cost of return on matched funds. This reflects the credit spread. A second source of profits arises from the liability side. The bank accesses funds at a rate lower than economic cost of risk matched funds. This reflects the franchise spread. Third, the bank makes profits through market risk transformation. For example, SBI borrows for three months and lends for six months. The performance measurement framework should enable the banks to measure profitability of these three business activities. A system of structured education and training is necessary so that the top management is sensitised to the developments in Asset/Liability Management. In a field so volatile and fast changing as ALM, ongoing training and updating is critical.

Information Reporting Framework : ALM information should be reported. In such a manner that each level of management should get information that is relevant to them. The over riding objective is that the decision-maker is neither burdened with information overload nor starved of needed information. The information should be concise and easily understandable. The information should allow the recipient to make or evaluate decisions.

Regulatory Compliance Framework : The objective is to ensure compliance with the applicable regulatory requirements such as those containing to risk based capital ratios, liquidity ratios, capital adequacy directive and the quality of risk management infrastructure.

Control Framework : The emphasis should on setting up of a system of checks and balance to ensure the integrity of data, analysis, reporting and adherence to internal policies. This should be ensured through regular external/internal reviews of the function.

(a) Management of Risks

Once the risk has been identified, the next question is – what to do about the Risks? The suitable answer to this question would be to manage the risks in an efficient and effective manner so that the organization incurs minimum loss. The recourse available to banks could be –

- If the risk is at the prospective stage, then it may be avoided.
- If the risk is likely to occur, and it is unavoidable then it has to be accepted and retained on it on an economically justified basis.
- Some effective actions to be executed as to reduce or eliminate the loss likely to be incurred due to happening of the particular risky incident.
- Diversification is required within a portfolio of risk with a view to shortening the loss.
- For risky business areas, introduction of prudent exposure norms, in advances, may help in minimizing the loss.
- Sound risks measurement procedures and information systems, if put in place in the right perspective, will help in taking timely decisions for avoidance of risk.
- Hedging the risk artificially, i.e., counter-balance and neutralize the risk to a certain degree is required by use of derivative instruments.
- Monitor various categories of risks on continuous basis and report to appropriate authority so that risks can be overcome in future.
- The risk may be liquidated by transferring without recourses to other party.
- Application of comprehensive internal control and audit systems with a view to controlling risks in appropriate places is necessary.

The effective Risk Management process in Banks, which does not result in getting rid of risks, will help in minimizing the losses.

(b) Risk Management and RBI Guidelines

The history of banking is full of major and minor failures. It is now argued that many of these failures were due to the fact that the risks were not identified and managed properly. The Reserve Bank of India has issued elaborate guidelines on Asset Liability Management and Risk Management to Banks in India. Banks have been making vigorous efforts in following these guidelines. Some of the important actions taken by Banks in India based on the RBI guidelines are discussed below –

Risk Management Structure

Banks have formulated road maps for implementation of guidelines issued by the Reserve Bank of India Systems. Investment Policy, Loan Policy, Terms Loan Policy have been articulated and the progress in implementation of these guidelines is being reviewed by the Board of Banks, Risk Management Committee has been constituted in several banks to evaluate the overall risks assumed by the Bank. Risk Management Committees are verifying adherence to various risk parameters and prudential limits by the operating departments.

Risk Management – Uncharted Areas

Risk Management is not a destination, but a journey. It is not a one-time exercise but a lifetime exercise, which needs to be undertaken repeatedly. Over the time, with identification of new risks, there is need to identify new Risk Management practices also. Although banks, in India, are generally following the guidelines of the Reserve Bank of India, the following areas need closer attention. Also, some other suggestions, if put into effect in time, may yield rich dividends for banking industry in India.

Liquidity Risk

- Estimating the cash flow profile realistically by tracking the impact of prepayment of loans and premature closure of deposits.
- Estimating the liquidity profile on a dynamic basis by giving due importance to seasonality, future growth, etc.
- Estimating properly the liquidity under Bank's specific and market crisis scenarios.

Interest Rate Risk

- Segmenting the balance sheet into trading and banking books.
- Laying down policies with regard to volume, maximum maturity, holding period, duration, stop loss, defeasance period, rating standards, etc. for classifying securities in the trading book.
- Conducting stress tests to estimate future volatility in values due to outlier events in the market.
- Assessing the magnitude of basis and embedded option risks.
- Setting up definite timeframe for moving over to Duration Gap Analysis (defined at the end of the paper).
- Adopting Balance Sheet Simulation models (defined at the end of the paper) for quantifying the market dynamics on asset-liability mixes, future earnings/economic values, subject to availability of quality data, information technology and technical expertise.

Market Risk

Middle Office functioning independent of the Treasury Department to be set up for tracking the magnitude of market risk on a real time basis.

Credit Risk

- Setting up prudential limits on (a) various financial parameters (b) single/group borrowers limits (within the limits prescribed by RBI), (c) substantial exposure limits, (d) exposures to industries, sectors especially sensitive sectors, regions, etc.
- Adoption of Risk Adjusted Return on Capital (RAROC) framework for pricing of loans.
- Stipulating – (a) quantitative ceiling on aggregate exposure in specified rating categories, (b) rating-wise distribution of borrowers in various industries, business segments, etc. (c) exposure to industries, sectors, regions, etc. (d) target rating-wise volume of loans, probable defaults and provisioning requirements.
- Undertaking rapid portfolio reviews, stress tests and scenario analysis (defined at the end of the paper) when external environment is undergoing rapid changes.

- Building adequate data and historical loan loss rates and model variables, spanning multiple credit cycles, for switching over to credit risk modeling after a specified period of time.
- Estimation the total potential exposure in respect of off-balance sheet items on a static or dynamic basis.
- Internal process and expertise in risk aggregation and capital allocation to be developed.
- Suitable methodologies to be developed for estimating and maintaining economic capital by bank operating in international market. The principle of economic capital exists to absorb unexpected loss – to the extent that current profits fall short of that capacity – and thus to minimize the probability of insolvency.
- Capital to risk to be adjusted to the risk and equity capital to be maintained according to assessed size of the risk.
- Loss of risks to be loaded on cost, as expected loss is a cost to the organization. Concept of Risk adjusted returns to be implemented.
- The risky assets (derivatives etc.) to be marked to the market.
- International best practices to be followed in developing the risk management framework particularly the organizational structure.

Techniques of Risk Measurement

Universally there are four principal approaches used to quantify the risk :

Gap Method

The gap approach addresses the rate sensitivity of assess and liabilities. The gap is the difference between the existing Rate Sensitive Assets (RSA) and Rate Sensitive Liabilities (RSL) in a particular time period. It ignores the time when in the chosen period, the assets and liabilities would need to be re-priced and, hence, shorter the period more sensitive is the model. Interest rate is minimised if the gap is managed to near zero in each period.

(i) Liquidity Gaps : Liquidity gaps are usually derived from the outstanding balance of assets and liabilities and from their changes over a period of time.

Marginal gaps are calculated as the differences between the changes in assets and liabilities during a given period.

(ii) *Interest Rate Gap (IRG) :* Interest rate gap may be defined as the difference between fixed rate assets and fixed rate liabilities or as the difference between interest sensitive assets and interest sensitive liabilities. Fixed rate gap is exactly opposite of variable rate gap when assets are equal to liabilities. Gaps are calculated as the difference between outstanding balance on a given date across maturity structure.

Simulation

Simulation involves a series of 'what' analyses of the impact of interest rate changes on the income. It requires forecasting the asset-liability picture under different scenarios, ascribing probabilities to them and choosing the most optimum model. The method being more dynamic its utility depends upon the accuracy of forecasts.

Duration

Method evaluates the impact of interest rate changes on the market value of assets and liabilities. The duration of an asset or liability is calculated as the weighted average maturity of the resultant cash flows, the weights being the present value of the cash flows. Duration expressed in the time period is less than the maturity of coupon bond. Greater the value of duration gap, higher the interest rate risk exposure of the assets/ liabilities. The method, being too complex, is, however, far more flexible. How much interest rate risk a bank should assume? However, it depends upon how risk savvy or risk averse the banks is.

Value at Risk Method (VaR)

The method enables one to work out depreciation/appreciation in the value of assets/liabilities due to change in interest rate so as to indicate the trend in economic value of portfolio. Impact of interest rate changes on the value of 'off-market' items of balance-sheet such as; loans deposits etc, need to be calculated under different interest rate scenarios for evaluating the opportunity cost/benefits of carrying such assets/liabilities in a longer time frame. Although this is a new approach for quantification of risks this is emerging as a very useful tool for calculating the new worth of the organisation at a particular time so as to focus on the long term risk implications that have already been taken.

Techniques for assessing asset-liability risk came to include gap analysis and duration analysis. These facilitated techniques of gap management and duration matching of assets and liabilities. Both approaches worked well if assets and liabilities comprised fixed cash flows. Options, such as those imbedded in mortgages or callable debt, posed problems, which gap analysis, could not address. Duration analysis could address in theory, but implementing sufficiently sophisticated duration measures was problematic. Accordingly, banks and insurance companies also performed scenario analysis (Chris, 2002)[10].

With scenario analysis, several interest rate scenarios would be specified for the next 5 or 10 years. These might specify declining rates, rising rate's, gradual decrease in rates followed by a sudden rise, etc scenarios might specify the behavior of the entire yield curve, so there could be specified in all. Next assumptions would be made about the performance of assets and liabilities under each scenario. Assumptions might repayment rates on mortgages or surrender rates on insurance products. Assumptions might also be made about firm's performance the rates at which new business would be acquired for various products. Based upon these assumptions, the performance of the firm's balance sheet could be projected under each scenario. If projected performance was poor under specific scenarios, the ALM committee might adjust assets or liabilities to address the indicated exposure shortcoming of scenario analysis in the fact that it is highly dependent on the choice of scenarios. It also requires that many assumptions be made about how specific assets or liabilities will perform under specific scenarios.

In a sense, ALM was a substitute for market value accounting in a context of accrual accounting. It was a necessary substitute because many of the assets and liabilities of financial institutions could not and yet to be marked to market. This spirit of market value accounting was not a complete solution. A firm can earn significant mark to market profits but go bankrupt due to inadequate cash flow. Some techniques of ALM such as duration analysis do not address liquidity issues at all. Others are highly compatible with cash-flow analysis. With minimal modification, a gap analysis can be used for cash flow analysis. Scenario analysis can easily be used to assess liquidity risk.

Firms recognized a potential for liquidity risks to be overlooked in ALM analyses. They also recognized that many of the tools used by ALM departments could easily be applied to assess liquidity risk. Accordingly, the assessment and management of liquidity risk became a second function of ALM departments and ALM committees. Today, liquidity risk management is generally considered a part of ALM.

ALM has evolved since the early 1980's. Today, financial firms are increasingly using market-value accounting for certain business lines. This is true of universal banks that have trading operations. For trading books, techniques of market risk management value at-risk (VaR), market risk limits, etc. are more appropriate than techniques of ALM. In financial firms. ALM is associated was those assets and liabilities those business lines that are accounted for on an accrual basis. This includes bank lending and deposit taking. It includes essentially all traditional insurance activities (Srinivasulu, 1996)[11].

Techniques of ALM have also evolved. The growth of OTC derivatives markets has facilitated a variety of hedging strategies. A significant development has been securitisation, which allows firms to directly address asset-liability risk by removing assets or liabilities from their balance sheets. This not only eliminates asset-liability risk; it also frees up the balance sheet for new business.

The scope of ALM activities has widened. Today, ALM departments are addressing (non-trading) foreign exchange risk. They are using related techniques to address commodity risks. For example, airlines' hedging of fuel prices or manufacturer's hedging of steel prices generally fall within the domain of ALM.

II

Emergence of ALM Process in India

In India, the need for ALM is a recent phenomenon. ALM is needed in the domestic banking as part of the system Memorandum of Understanding (MoU) by which banks are required to submit a policy statement on their individual liability management system. In 1995, while relaxing the interest rate structure of term deposits, the RBI emphasised on proper use of offering interest rates in various maturities of term deposits. Further it should be ensured that they do not get locked in excessively long deposit maturities. A careful review should be undertaken to ensure against overall asset-liability mismatches. Besides, in the busy season credit policy of October 1997, RBI highlighted the importance of asset-liability management of banks stating, that the need for monitoring the maturity and liquidity mismatches, interest rate risks and maintaining them at acceptable levels could not be over-emphasised and banks should put in place adequate asset liability management system (Trivedi, 1999)[12].

Need for ALM in India

In India the movement towards greater use of variable rate pending indicated an important shift in banking environment. It is no longer the case that banks will be largely asset-driven and primarily concerned with just adhere to find resources to finance lending. Banks are improving progressively to the stage of not only adjusting capabilities in accordance with potential liabilities. More generally there is a growing realisation of how an increasingly variegated balance sheet at a time of volatile economic conditions adds to the risks facing banks and takes necessary new techniques of risk management. This has led to a broad re-assessment of the nature of credit risks and credit standards, and also reduced banks previous emphasis on balance sheet growth at any cost. The concept of ALM has become important in India because of the following :

- In order to maximise income with acceptable risk, there is need to emphasises on interest margin/spread, liquidity and capital which are having desired maneuverability.
- Since sources of liquidity are distributed across both the assets and liability sides, as a prudent banker there is imperative need to manage both the sided and integrate liquidity management with the overall asset liability management.
- In the aftermath of financial sector reforms, interest rates on both deposits and advances are changing more frequently thereby exposing both assets and liabilities to volatility risk of interest rate of changes.
- Gradual dismantling of restrictions with regard to foreign exchange transactions has exposed Indian banks to the vagaries of fluctuations in Forex market.
- With the gradual increase in the ratio of current investment to permanent investment by RBI, banks are showing greater willingness to value major portion of their investment as "marked to market". While this will expose the investment portfolio to potential market risks, steps for countering the adverse impact of interest rate changes or other market risk variables can be initiated through proper ALM only.

Overall, the ALM exercise at this introductory stage, would involve the following :

- Prudential management of funds with respect to size and duration.
- Minimising undesirable maturity mismatches so as to avoid liquidity problem.
- Reducing the gap between rate sensitive assets and rate sensitive liabilities within the given risk taking capacity.

III

Structural Changes of Variables in the Post Reform Period

In November 1991, Narasimham Committee presented its report on financial sector reforms. The report suggested a number of measures to rehabilitate the weak banks, a majority of which was accepted by the Government. Besides, with the globalisation of the Indian economy, banking sector has undergone a perceptible change. As a result, the imperatives of banking have been changing towards the objectives of profitability, efficiency and competitiveness (Das, 1996)[13]. It is expected that with greater degree of transparency in balance sheet in accordance with competitive environment, the banking sector should witness some significant changes in their balance sheet. While a dramatic change was not possible, a 'slow and solid was expected to take place with the gradual progress of the reform (Tarapore, 1996)[14]. This section reviews the progress of banking sector with regard to their balance sheet indicators and presents the major trends observed in recent years. The purpose of this study is to identify empirically and explore the relationship between asset and liability of PSBs. In this respect we have selected five assets and liability items expressed as a proportion of total assets to eliminate the trend components and make them comparable across the years. The accompanying table summarises the fact.

POSITION OF VARIABLES (AS ON MARCH)

(Proportion to total assets)

Liabilities	*1991*	*1995*	*2000*	*2001*	*2002*
1. Capital (Capital + Reserve) [CAP]	2.50	6.10	5.17	4.84	4.97
2. Deposits [DEP]	76.00	78.00	82.78	83.45	83.82
3. Borrowing [BORR]	2.65	2.40	2.18	1.95	1.78

(Contd.)

(Contd. Table)

(Proportion to total assets)

Liabilities	*1991*	*1995*	*2000*	*2001*	*2002*
4. Long Term Deposit. [LT.DEP]	49.70	51.30	52.07	53.53	53.18
5. Short Term deposit. [ST.DEP]	26.30	26.70	30.71	29.92	30.04
6. Other Liabilities. [OTH. LIA]	10.23	9.80	9.86	9.76	9.43
Assets					
1. Cash & Bank [CB]	19.13	17.41	15.23	14.83	13.06
2. Investment in government securities [G.SEC]	29.60	33.60	26.63	28.35	29.82
3. Other Securities [OTH.SEC].	12.60	13.40	11.08	9.92	9.46
4. Term Loans [T. LOAN]	16.00	10.00	14.15	14.38	15.25
5. Other Assets [OTH. AST.]	6.35	7.64	6.48	5.60	5.17

In 1991, only 2.5 per cent of total assets constituted total capital that significantly increased to 6.1 per cent in 1995, declined to 5.17 per cent in 2000 and further to 4.97 per cent in 2002. The variation in the year-wise proportion of capital may be explained by the fact that, during initial years of reform achieving the target of 8 per cent of capital adequacy norms was emphasised. In the subsequent years government of India recapitalised the PSBs to the tune of Rs. 25,000 crores to achieve the capital adequacy norms at 8 per cent and higher.

The deposits on the other hand have picked its momentum in the latter part of reform period. In 2002, deposits contributed 83.82 per cent of total assets, which was about 8 percentage point higher than that in 1991. As a result a significant differences observed in both long-term and short-term deposits particularly during 2000-2002. However, borrowing portfolio (short-term borrowings and long-term borrowings) of PSBs showed a significant contraction during post reform period. It came down from its peak 2.65 per cent of total assets in 1991 to 2.18 per cent in 2000 further to 1.78 per cent in 2002. Similarly, other liabilities settled on at 9.43 per cent of total assets declining from 9.86 per cent in 2000.

On the assets side, the cash and bank items show a decline of more than 2 percentage point in 2002 over 2000. Investment in government securities has increased from 26.63 per cent of total assets in 2000 to 29.82 per cent in 2002. This has clearly revealed that the PSBs have adopted a changed investment pattern during post reform period. In contrast to this proportion of term loan recorded a significant decline from its peak of 16 per cent of total assets in 1991 to 10 per cent in 1995 thereafter, it increased to 14.15 per cent in 2000 further to 15.25 per cent in 2002.

Interrelationship of Variables

The cash and bank items of PSBs are negatively associated with the total deposits (-.96).

CORRELATIONS

MARKED CORRELATION IS SIGNIFICANT AT P < 0.05.

N = 5 (Case-wise deletion of missing data)

Variables	*CB*	*GSEC*	*Oth. Sec.*	*T. Loan*	*Oth. Ast*
CAP	-0.49	0.14	-0.08	0.02	0.29
DEP	-0.96*	0.94*	-0.90*	0.89*	-0.66
BORR	0.98*	-0.91*	0.93*	-0.87	0.75
LT. DEP	-0.96*	0.84	-0.87	0.78	-0.65
ST. DEP	-0.88*	0.94*	-0.85	0.90*	-0.61
OTH. LIA	0.66	-0.26	0.30	-0.18	0.05

Source : Self-computed on the basis of earlier table.

The negative 'r' is statistically significant. This is the fact that the cash items in particular that include statutory reserve with bank should have little correlation with these variables. The capital on the liability side was associated negatively with cash and banks and other securities. Further very little correlation was found in other variables. In case of investment in government securities it has been observed that, the deposit particularly short-term deposit was significantly associated. It indicates that during the liberalisation period there is a tendency to invest more short-term deposit with government securities. Hence, investment pattern in PSBs has undergone a significant change over the years. Interestingly total borrowings are negatively and significantly associated with government securities. It shows that PSBs have experienced borrowing contraction over the years and changes in the pattern of investment. On the other hand term loan is highly positive with deposit particularly with short-term deposit. This reveals that some sort of mismatches between assets (investment) and deposit (liabilities).

On the whole, the balance sheet items of PSBs show almost proper matching behaviour in terms of management of maturity structure of assets and liabilities and hedging activities in the management of risk portfolio. Thus the reform process has made a significant dent on this aspect. Sizeable part of the capital was invested in the government securities over the years by the PSBs due to the increase in capital base after the introduction of the capital adequacy norms.

REGRESSION SUMMARY

Dependent variables	*Intercept*	*β value 'Independent Variables'* Deposit	*Borrowing*	*Other liabilities*	R^2	*F (3, 2 df)*	*P-level*
Cash and Bank Other Assets		8.059	1.43	2.41	– 1.4**	0.930	8.88
Government		267.516	0.42	1.13	– 0.13	0.952	6.57
Securities		24.148	0.28	1.67**	0.63**	0.996	29.47
Other Securities		– 42.201	0.78	0.37	0.31	0.924	3.91
Term Loans		294.982	– 1.6	– 1.5	– 0.72	0.877	2.22

*** Significant at 1 per cent*

** Significant at 5 per cent.*

Further, to analyse how are the liabilities particularly deposits, borrowings and other liabilities hedged, we have obtained linear regression equation taking asset side variables as dependent and aforesaid liability side variables individually as independent variables. The summary of regression results is displayed in table (previous page).

It is found that, R^2 is high in each set of regression though 'F' ratio is not statistically significant except for other securities at 5 per cent level of significance. The analysis reveals the presence of multi collinearity among the variables. Though it cannot be avoided from this type of time series data, but we can draw the inferences about the trend of matching of assets and liabilities.

The cash and bank balance found to be negatively and statistically significant with other liabilities. This implies that during the post liberalisation period the PSBs have emphasised on sufficient liquidity and became cautious against other liabilities. On the other hand, the borrowing and other liabilities have positive and significant effect on other securities. This explains that in the changed environment pattern, the PSBs have emphasised on the interest sensitive securities over the years to strengthen their bottom lines for achieving competitiveness. Thus it may be argued that, the long-term assets have adequately covered the long-term liabilities during the post reform periods.

CRAMEL Analysis

In order to examine how far banks have adhered to standard norms of disclosure a ranking of PSBs have been made by using the **CRAMEL** analysis. **CRAMEL** stands for Capital Adequacy, Resource Deployed, Asset Quality, Management, Earnings Quality and Liquidity. An elaborate analysis of balance sheet of individual PSBs, in this respect, has been made during 1998 and 1999. The nuances of the aforesaid variables are summarized below :

Capital Adequacy

Capital adequacy indicates each bank's leverage calculated after assigning different risks to assets as announced by the Reserve Bank of India (RBI). In October 1998 the RBI directed banks to raise the minimum CAR from 8 per cent to 10 per cent in two phases ; 1 per cent by March 2000 and another 1 per cent by March 2002 to take the Indian CAR closer to the international standard of more than 12 per cent.

CAPITAL ADEQUACY

Bank	*CAR*	*D/E*	*ADV/AST (%)*	*G-SEC/INV (%)*	*G-SEC/AST (%)*	*Rank 1999*	*Rank 1998*
State Bank of Saurashtra	14.35	12.13	42.67	69.78	22.28	1	1
Oriental Bank of Commerce	14.10	13.73	41.03	51.91	21.66	2	3
Bank of Baroda	13.30	15.56	40.38	63.27	19.27	3	6
Corporation Bank	13.20	13.13	41.96	53.45	19.66	4	2
State Bank of India	12.51	17.12	37.01	72.60	23.26	5	4
State Bank of Patiala	12.47	13.70	44.35	72.47	23.97	6	5
State Bank of Indore	12.35	21.05	42.75	80.62	30.58	7	16
State Bank of Bikaner & Jaipur	12.26	18.70	37.55	77.11	28.66	8	13
Central Bank of India	11.88	11.87	36.23	73.44	31.73	9	14
Dena Bank	11.14	17.77	43.09	60.38	22.97	10	7
Andhra Bank	11.02	21.57	39.15	66.60	28.51	11	17
Canara Bank	10.96	17.96	40.59	57.55	20.18	12	10
Punjab and Sind Bank	10.94	25.81	38.62	60.07	24.19	13	18
Punjab National Bank	10.79	21.23	41.12	66.41	26.63	14	12
State Bank of Hyderabad	10.65	21.67	40.43	79.28	35.54	15	19
Bank of India	10.55	19.70	45.11	69.14	19.60	16	8
Allahabad Bank	10.38	18.35	40.09	68.09	27.99	17	9
State Bank of Travancore	10.27	23.07	38.96	87.23	35.04	18	8
State Bank of Mysore	10.23	24.82	43.43	70.76	23.49	19	18
Indian Overseas Bank	10.15	31.11	41.36	77.29	26.27	20	11
Union Bank of India	10.09	16.77	36.21	70.03	27.22	21	15
Vijaya Bank	10.00	13.97	33.95	64.75	25.92	22	11
Bank of Maharashtra	9.76	13.14	33.33	73.10	34.12	23	19
UCO Bank	9.63	6.29	29.98	62.43	26.20	24	7
United Bank of India	9.60	7.41	22.33	72.87	37.63	25	7
Syndicate Bank	9.57	28.66	42.53	68.14	24.63	26	1
Indian Bank	Neg	0.04	34.95	77.74	28.10	27	11

Neg-negative

Source : www.indiainfoline.com.

Other ratios which have a bearing on the CAR have been calculated as below :

- **Debt-equity ratio (D/E) :** calculated as the proportion of total outside liability to net worth.
- **Advances-to-assets (ADV/AST) :** shows a bank's aggressiveness in improving its credit-deposit ratio by higher advances, which determine profitability.
- **G-Sec's-to-investment (G-SEC/INV) :** relevant in view of the nil risk for government securities earlier and the risk weightage that is now being introduced in a phased manner.
- **G-sec's-to-assets (G-SEC/AST) :** also indicates a bank's aggressiveness in improving its credit-deposit ratio keeping investments lower.

The banks position on the basis of aforesaid ratios can be summarised in the table.

The table exhibited that the position of three weak banks as identified by the Verma Committee has declined considerably during 1999 in comparison to their position in the previous year. The Syndicate Bank has also downgraded to 26th rank from its top position in the previous year, while Indian Bank ranked at the bottom in respect of CAR. During 1999, the investment, of almost all subsidiaries of SBI, in the government security constitutes more than 70 per cent. The State Bank of Travancore topped the list.

Resources Deployed

In banking the size of the balance sheet is very significant. The ranking on this parameter is based on total assets. The other factors that have a bearing on resources and, in turn, on efficient deployment have been computed as below :

- **Liquid assets (LQD/AST) :** total proportion of resources deployed in liquid assets, which generate relatively low yields.
- **Investments (INV) :** proportion of resources deployed in investments, indicating the aggressiveness of banks.
- **Advances (ADV) :** proportion of resources deployed as advances.

RESOURCE DEPLOYED

Bank	Asset (Rs. crores)	LQD AST (%)	INV (%)	ADV (%)	FXD AST (%)	OTH AST (%)	Rank 1999	Rank 1998
State Bank of India	222509.0	23.91	32.04	37.01	0.99	6.05	1	1
Bank of India	53923.5	20.11	28.34	45.11	1.32	5.12	2	2
Bank of Baroda	52232.4	23.01	30.45	40.38	1.14	5.01	3	3
Canara Bank	48119.6	17.00	36.07	40.59	1.14	5.20	4	4
Punjab National Bank	46323.5	12.61	40.09	41.12	1.33	4.85	5	5
Central Bank of India	35328.8	12.01	43.20	36.23	2.25	6.31	6	6
Union Bank of India	31230.9	18.52	38.87	36.21	2.41	32.99	7	7
Indian Overseas Bank	24462.0	20.68	34.00	41.36	1.14	2.82	8	8
Syndicate Bank	21894.6	14.05	36.20	42.53	1.04	6.18	9	9
Indian Bank	21448.3	8.93	36.02	34.95	2.09	18.88	10	10
UCO Bank	20752.5	12.66	42.11	29.98	1.93	13.31	11	11
Oriental Bank of Commerce	18784.2	12.74	41.73	41.03	0.74	3.75	12	13
Allahabad Bank	17422.7	13.23	41.10	40.09	1.84	3.74	13	12
United Bank of India	17215.2	10.29	51.65	22.33	1.02	14.71	14	14
Corporation Bank	14983.1	1634	36.78	41.96	0.78	4.15	15	16
Dena Bank	14843.5	12.14	38.04	43.01	1.95	4.8	16	15
State Bank of Hyderabad	13186.9	10.81	44.82	40.43	0.63	3.30	17	17
Bank of Maharashtra	12185.0	14.96	46.67	33.33	0.76	4.28	18	16
Andhra Bank	11556.7	14.43	42.85	39.15	0.45	3.12	19	20
Vijaya Bank	11095.7	14.06	40.03	33.95	1.53	10.42	20	19
State Bank of Travancore	10914.2	16.15	40.17	38.96	0.42	4.31	21	21
State Bank of Patiala	10853.5	13.10	33.07	44.35	0.46	9.02	22	18
Punjab & Sind Bank	10614.9	14.69	40.26	38.62	0.78	5.64	23	22
State Bank of Bikaner & Jaipur	10228.5	16.04	37.17	37.55	0.93	8.31	24	23
State Bank of Mysore	6876.1	16.54	33.20	43.43	0.47	6.36	25	24
State Bank Saurashtra	6375.8	20.47	31.92	42.67	0.45	4.49	26	25
State Bank of Indore	4959.7	14.45	37.93	42.75	1.22	3.64	27	26

Source :*www.indiainfoline.com.*

- **Fixed assets (FXD AST) :** proportion of resources deployed in fixed assets, thus contributing indirectly to profitability.
- **Other assets (OTH AST) :** proportion of resources deployed in other assets which generate relatively low yields.

The following table presents the position of PSBs in respect of resource deployed. Banks were ranked on the basis of their total assets.

It has been observed that the Indian Bank has invested less in liquid assets, about 9 per cent , while United Bank of India adopted aggressiveness in their investment pattern as its total investment accounts 51.65 per cent of total resources. The reasons may be attributed to, in the competitive environment banks are trying hard to repair their bottom lines for achieving competitiveness amongst others.

Asset Quality

Asset quality determines a bank ability to manage its NPA level. Ranking is done on the basis of NNPAs.

- **Net Non-performing Assets (NNPA) :** calculated as (Total advances) × (Net NPA to Net advances) × 100.
- **Contingent liabilities (CONT LIAB) :** mostly off-balance-sheet items comprising fee-based income assets like bank guarantees. The ratio used in total contingent liabilities to total assets.
- **Advances to assets (ADV/AST) :** used to gauge credit disintermediation of a bank – a higher ratio indicates that the bank is aggressive in its lending operations.
- **Advances growth (ADV GWT) :** a bank's ambition to grow faster has an impact on asset quality.
- **Investments-to-assets (INV AST) :** indicates how a bank is leveraging its resources to credit and investment.

It is revealed that except Corporation Bank, others have witnessed a higher volume of NPA in their accounts during 1999. The worst sufferer is the State Bank of India, which accounted NNPA to tune of Rs. 5913 crores in 1999. However, the higher ratio of advances to assets in case of State Bank Mysore (43.4), Syndicate Bank (42.53), State Bank of Patiala (44.35), Dena Bank (43.09) and Bank of India (45.11) and so on indicates their aggressiveness in their lending operation. Similarly, on the basis of

ASSETS QUALITY

Bank	*NNPA (Rs. crores)*	*CONT LIAB*	*ADV/AST (%)*	*ADV/GWT (%)*	*INV/AST (%)*	*Rank 1999*	*Rank 1998*
Corporation Bank	124.47	19.15	41.96	46.10	36.78	1	1
Andhra Bank	192.72	14.72	39.15	34.57	42.86	2	1
State Bank of Saurashtra	209.48	18.40	42.67	20.51	31.92	3	6
State Bank of Indore	214.15	14.90	42.75	11.50	37.93	4	16
Vijaya Bank	253.16	16.09	33.95	25.61	40.03	5	11
State Bank of Mysore	315.03	22.29	43.43	13.45	33.20	6	15
Oriental Bank of Commerce	346.84	10.45	41.03	21.98	41.73	7	2
Bank of Maharashtra	354.19	35.36	33.33	13.06	46.67	8	14
Syndicate Bank	365.99	29.59	42.53	33.81	36.20	9	3
State Bank of Patiala	396.16	13.27	44.35	17.25	33.07	10	7
State Bank of Bikaner & Jaipur	401.37	8.32	37.55	4.93	37.17	11	8
Punjab & Sind Bank	429.67	12.40	38.62	28.67	40.14	12	15
State Bank of Travancore	459.20	16.01	38.96	6.28	40.17	13	17
State Bank of Hyderabad	468.15	22.06	40.43	15.16	44.82	14	16
Dena Bank	490.55	16.85	43.09	24.25	38.04	15	13
United Bank of India	565.12	4.50	22.33	12.86	51.65	16	9
UCO Bank	673.87	19.40	29.98	10.90	42.11	17	17
Indian Overseas Bank	738.58	15.13	41.36	16.68	34.00	18	5
Allahabad Bank	875.89	21.16	40.09	22.03	41.10	19	19
Union Bank of India	983.86	17.44	36.21	10.05	38.87	20	12
Central Bank of India	1253.10	21.82	36.23	19.47	43.20	21	18
Canara Bank	1384.68	30.80	40.59	16.08	36.07	22	10
Bank of Baroda	1624.05	25.30	40.38	6.50	30.45	23	6
Indian Bank	1624.50	28.09	34.95	3.25	36.03	24	20
Punjab National Bank	1706.60	18.25	41.12	18.73	40.49	25	15
Bank of India	1771.01	40.28	45.11	10.47	28.34	26	9
State Bank of India	5913.44	29.85	37.01	10.94	32.04	27	4

Source : www.indiainfoline.com.

MANAGEMENT QUALITY

Bank	Final Score	C/D (%)	RONW	EMP EFF	AST GWT	NPA/NW	Rank 1999	Rank 1998
State Bank of Hyderabad	5.0	50.2	25.19	1.09	24.2	94.4	1	11
Dena Bank	7.2	54.2	17.72	1.26	21.0	70.4	2	8
Corporation Bank	7.8	49.9	21.06	1.85	33.6	12.7	3	1
Oriental Bank of Commerce	9.6	45.9	19.89	1.70	27.1	28.2	4	2
State Bank of Travancore	9.7	49.2	11.81	1.00	19.5	120.5	5	10
State Bank of Mysore	10.1	53.6	14.59	0.71	17.3	125.9	6	11
State Bank Bikaner & Jaipur	10.2	49.6	24.07	0.74	20.0	95.7	7	9
Punjab National Bank	11.0	46.7	20.77	0.90	16.4	88.4	8	12
State Bank of Patiala	11.2	54.4	16.53	1.07	11.5	60.2	9	7
Bank of India	11.6	54.7	8.52	0.96	16.4	73.6	10	6
Punjab & Sind Bank	11.6	43.2	10.40	1.11	17.5	114.9	10	18
State Bank of Saurashtra	12.2	56.9	6.32	0.93	22.5	50.8	11	7
Allahabad Bank	12.8	40.0	16.87	0.90	14.6	103.2	12	19
State Bank of Indore	13.0	52.6	17.17	0.81	21.2	10.4	13	14
Union Bank of India	13.2	40.2	9.83	1.13	21.3	58.5	14	13
Bank of Baroda	13.2	47.3	15.15	1.35	13.9	56.0	14	5
State Bank of India	13.4	48.7	10.27	0.94	23.8	56.8	15	4
Indian Overseas Bank	13.4	46.2	7.97	1.04	14.1	102.8	15	16
Canara Bank	14.0	46.6	9.54	1.17	11.6	57.4	16	17
Syndicate Bank	15.8	46.7	12.90	0.89	12.5	52.4	17	21
Andhra Bank	16.2	43.3	15.57	0.81	25.2	39.2	18	15
State Bank of Mysore	17.0	53.6	14.59	0.71	17.3	125.9	19	3
Indian Bank	19.2	43.7	(27.31)	0.98	10.3	56.0	20	22
Vijaya Bank	19.4	38.9	4.24	0.90	17.5	35.9	20	20
Central Bank of India	19.4	41.8	5.59	0.80	15.7	48.3	21	23
United Bank of India	20.2	26.5	0.76	0.81	18.5	28.6	22	22
UCO Bank	23.0	38.3	(2.66)	0.73	11.7	25.6	23	21

Source :*www.indiainfoline.com.*

advance to growth ratio, it is observed that Punjab & Sind Bank (28.67), Dena Bank (24.25), Vijaya Bank (25.61) and Allahabad Bank (22.03) are expecting faster growth in the year 1999. While State Bank of Bikaner and Jaipur (4.93), Indian Bank (3.25) and Bank of Baroda (6.50) are yet to catch up the growth momentum and indicating thereby a declined in the asset quality over the years.

Management : To evaluate management quality, various parameters have been considered and finally ranked on final score based on average of all ranking of individual parameters.

- **Credit deposit ratio (C/D) :** total advances as proportion to total deposit, indicates the management's aggressiveness to improve income.
- **Return on average net worth (RONW) :** prime indicator of a management's capability to provide adequate returns. Net profit as percentage of average network.
- **Employee efficiency (EMP EFF) :** percentage net profit per employee. A high ratio suggests that the man power is efficiently utilised by the bank.
- **Asset growth (AST GWT) :** total balance sheet growth, indicating management's aggressiveness.
- **NPAs-to-net-worth (NPA/NW) :** NNPAs as proportion of net worth on balance sheet date. It shows the management attitude to provisioning and effective risk-taking.
- **Final score :** calculated at the average of all rankings of individual parameters.

The following table depicted the ratios relating to the aforesaid management quality.

The table exhibited that, the banks like; the State Bank of Bikaner and Jaipur (0.74), Punjab National Bank (0.90), Allahabad Bank (0.90) United Bank of India (0.81), Central Bank of India (0.80), UCO Bank (0.73), Bank of Maharashtra (0.91), Andhra Bank (0.81) are lagging behind in respect of employees efficiencies. This indicates that these banks are yet to improve their bottom lines per employee and hence failed to utilize their manpower. However, asset growth, a widely used parameter, reflects the management's aggressiveness for improving the efficiency of the banks. In this respect corporation bank (33.6), Oriental Bank of Commerce (27.1),

State Bank of Hyderabad (24.2), State Bank of India (23.8) are performing comparatively well in improving their efficiency during 1999. While Indian Bank (11.3), UCO Bank (11.7), Syndicate Bank (12.5), and Canara Bank (11.6) witnessed least performance in regard to the asset growth.

Earnings Quality

Profitability is one of the important aspects for any bank. Banks are ranked on the basis of profit after tax and provisions. The earning quality of the banks may be expressed by the following parameters:

- **Profit after tax (PAT) :** net profit after tax and provisions.
- **EPS growth (EPS GWT) :** to factor in equity dilution, if any.
- **Spread :** spreads are the operating margin of a bank, the difference between average yield on advances less average yield on deposits. Higher the spreads indicates greater earning capacity.
- **Net profit to total average assets (NP/TAA) :** this ratio reflects asset productivity.

The banks are ranked on the basis of the volume of the PAT. The other ratios indicating the strength of the earning quality of the banks have been depicted in the table.

It is observed that earning per share of most of the PSBs is negative during 1999. The EPS of Bank of Maharashtra (–108.8), Indian Bank (–147.9), State Bank of India (44.8), Punjab National Bank (22.1), Bank of India (–44.8) and so on. This indicates the performance in respect to the equity dilution of these banks is not satisfactory. However, low level of spread (yield on advances minus yield on deposits) indicated the poor operating margin of banks. Further, the ratio of net profit to total average assets in case of United Bank of India (0.9), United Commercial Bank (0.34), Vijaya Bank (0.29) indicated their poor asset productivity.

Liquidity

The banks have been ranked on the basis of proportion of liquid assets to total assets. The liquidity position of banks may be expressed by the ratio; cash to total asset, investment in government security to total assets, per cent of investment to total assets and percentage of liquid liability.

EARNINGS QUALITY

Bank	*PAT (Rs. Crores)*	*EPS Gwt*	*SPREAD (%)*	*NP/TAA (%)*	*Rank*	
					1999	*1998*
State Bank of India	1027.8	(44.8)	5.11	0.51	1	1
Bank of Baroda	421.4	8.6	5.83	0.86	2	3
Punjab National Bank	372.1	(22.1)	5.00	0.86	3	2
Oriental Bank of Commerce	230.1	9.6	4.42	1.37	4	5
Canara Bank	225.1	10.8	5.49	0.49	5	6
Bank of India	201.1	(44.8)	4.88	0.40	6	4
Corportion Bank	192.0	15.1	3.85	1.47	7	8
Union Bank of India	160.2	(35.9)	5.01	0.56	8	24
Central Bank of India	146.4	(16.3)	4.44	0.44	9	7
Syndicate Bank	142.6	541.1	4.98	0.69	10	14
Allahabad Bank	135.0	4.5	4.19	0.83	11	10
State Bank of Hyderabad	111.5	14.8	3.83	0.94	12	12
Dena Bank	110.1	(29.2)	3.90	0.81	13	9
State Bank of Patiala	101.2	4.80	5.07	0.98	14	12
State Bank of Bikaner & Jaipur	91.8	1.5	4.53	0.98	15	16
Andhra Bank	90.0	103.3	4.35	0.87	16	17
Punjab & Sind Bank	60.4	169.5	4.18	0.62	17	13
Indian Overseas Bank	55.3	(51.1)	4.72	0.24	18	19
Bank of Maharashtra	51.8	(108.8)	5.00	0.45	19	18
State Bank of Travancore	43.2	(31.6)	2.93	0.43	20	20
State Bank of Mysore	33.5	(33.6)	5.58	0.53	21	22
State Bank of Indore	31.0	12.0	5.01	0.69	22	23
Vijaya Bank	30.2	29.7	5.24	0.29	23	15
State Bank of Saurashtra	25.3	(67.5)	5.07	0.44	24	25
United Bank of India	14.7	44.3	3.83	0.09	25	21
UCO Bank	(67.77)	35.7	3.79	0.34	26	26
Indian Bank	(778.50)	(147.9)	2.52	3.81	27	27

Source : www.indiainfoline.com.

LIQUIDITY POSITION

Bank	*LIQ AST (%)*	*CASH TO AST(%)*	*GESC/AST (%)*	*INV/AST (%)*	*LIQ/LIAB (%)*	*Rank 1999*	*Rank 1998*
United Bank of India	61.9	10.29	37.63	51.65	34.66	1	1
Bank of Maharashtra	61.6	14.96	34.12	46.67	42.80	2	2
Andhra Bank	57.4	18.52	27.22	38.87	35.58	3	11
Union Bank of India	57.3	14.43	28.53	42.85	31.49	4	16
State Bank of Travancore	56.3	161.15	35.04	40.17	42.77	5	19
State Bank of India	55.9	23.91	23.06	32.04	44.49	6	15
State Bank of Hyderabad	55.6	10.81	35.54	44.82	46.77	7	6
Central Bank of India	55.2	12.01	31.73	43.20	41.57	8	11
Punjab and Sind Bank	54.9	14.69	24.19	40.26	32.85	9	9
UCO Bank	54.7	12.66	26.29	42.11	38.35	10	5
Indian Overseas Bank	54.7	20.68	26.27	34.00	34.93	11	13
Oriental Bank of Commerce	54.5	12.74	21.66	41.73	27.46	12	3
Allahabad Bank	54.3	13.23	27.99	41.10	42.85	13	9
Vijaya Bank	54.0	14.06	25.92	40.03	37.91	14	17
Bank of Baroda	53.5	23.01	19.27	30.45	35.59	15	10
State Bank of Bikaner & Jaipur	52.2	16.04	28.66	37.17	52.30	16	4
Corporation Bank	53.1	16.34	19.66	36.78	29.74	17	7
Canara Bank	53.1	17.00	20.76	36.07	37.00	18	13
Punjab National Bank	52.7	12.61	26.63	40.09	47.37	19	18
State Bank of Saurashtra	52.4	20.41	22.28	31.92	41.78	20	20
State Bank of Indore	52.4	14.45	30.58	37.93	49.31	21	8
Syndicate Bank	50.3	14.05	24.67	36.20	37.24	22	15
Dena Bank	50.2	12.14	22.97	38.04	39.71	23	21
State Bank of Mysore	49.0	16.54	23.49	33.20	40.52	24	9
Bank of India	48.5	20.11	16.60	28.34	34.49	25	22
State Bank of Patiala	46.02	13.10	23.97	33.07	48.46	26	23
Indian Bank	44.9	8.93	28.01	36.03	30.41	27	24

Source : www.indiainfoline.com.

The table exhibited State Bank of India (44.8), Punjab National Bank (22.1), Bank of India (44.8), United Bank of India (35.9), Central Bank of India (16.3), State Bank of Patiala (29.2), Indian Overseas Bank (51.1) Bank of Maharashtra (108.8), Indian Bank (147.9) witnessed a negative growth in their earning per share resulting in a downward rank in the liquidity position during 1999 in comparison to its previous year.

Final ranking

The final ranking of the banks has been made on the basis of arithmetic mean of the individual rank of banks for each of the six criteria mentioned above and calculated as follows –

$$X = \frac{\sum x_i}{n}$$

where, X_I = ranks of individual banks on the basis of the parameters viz, capital adequacy, resource deployed, asset quality, management, earning quality and liquidity.

n = the number of variables,

The result of CRAMEL analysis on the basis of the aforesaid criteria is in table -

The table discerns that Oriental Bank of Commerce appeared to the 1st rank in 1999 from its 2nd rank in the previous year 1998. Indian Overseas Bank graded as 17th rank from its 7th position in 1998. This downgrading of Indian Overseas Bank is attributed to the degradation of asset quality and lack of aggressiveness in its operation. It is further evident that, the banks viz. the State Bank of Hyderabad (5th), Union Bank of India (8th), Central Bank of India (8th) have improved their overall ranking in 1999 from their position 13th, 17th and 14th respectively in the previous year. On the other hand, three banks at the bottom of the table viz. United Bank of India, UCO Bank and Indian Bank have not improved their position in 1999 in respect of parameters used for final ranking. Thus, the **CRAMEL** technique is an indicative of future strategies for improving bank's position. In this respect the position of the Allahabad Bank may be referred as it was ranked 14th in 1999 downgraded from its peak of 6th in the previous year. The bank has consequently decided to review its assets at frequent

FINAL RANKING IN THE CRAMEL ANALYSIS

Bank	*AVG*	*C*	*R*	*A*	*M*	*E*	*L*	*Rank*	
								1999	*1998*
Oriental Bank of Commerce	6.8	2	12	7	4	4	12	1	2
State Bank of India	7.3	5	1	16	15	1	6	2	3
Corporation Bank	7.8	4	15	1	3	7	17	3	1
Bank of Baroda	10.0	3	3	23	14	2	15	4	4
State Bank of Hyderabad	11.0	15	17	14	1	12	7	5	13
Andhra Bank	11.5	11	19	2	18	16	3	6	5
Punjab National Bank	12.3	14	5	25	8	3	19	7	11
Union Bank of India	12.3	21	7	20	14	8	4	8	17
Central Bank of India	12.3	9	6	21	21	9	8	8	14
Canara Bank	12.8	12	4	22	16	5	18	9	12
Dena Bank	13.2	10	16	15	2	13	23	10	8
State Bank of Bikaner and Jaipur	13.5	8	24	11	7	15	16	11	15
State Bank of Mysore	13.5	19	5	6	6	21	24	11	19
State Bank of Travancore	13.7	18	21	13	5	20	5	12	15
Punjab and Sind Bank	14.0	13	23	12	10	17	9	13	15
State Bank Saurashtra	14.2	1	26	3	11	24	20	14	10
Allahabad Bank	14.2	17	13	19	12	11	13	14	6
Bank of India	14.2	16	2	26	10	6	25	14	18
State Bank of Patiala	14.5	6	22	10	9	14	26	15	16
Bank of Maharashtra	14.8	23	18	8	19	19	2	16	21
Indian Overseas Bank	15.0	20	8	18	15	18	11	17	7
Syndicate Bank	15.5	26	9	9	17	10	22	18	9
State Bank of Indore	15.7	7	27	4	13	22	21	19	10
United Bank of India	16.2	25	14	10	22	25	1	20	20
Vijaya Bank	17.5	22	20	5	21	23	14	21	19
UCO Bank	18.0	24	11	17	23	26	10	22	22
Indian Bank	22.5	27	10	24	20	27	27	23	23

Source : www.indiainfoline.com.

intervals and emphasised on compromise settlements and execution of decrees apart from tight fencing of fresh addition of NPAs. As a result, CAR has been improved to 11.5 per cent in 2000-01 and the bank achieved compound growth rate in deposits and advances 13.75 per cent and 18 per cent respectively during 1999-2001. (*The Economic Times*, Oct. 8, 2002).

References

1. Baker, J. V. R. 1983. *Asset Liability Management.* American Bankers Association. Washington.
2. Vasishth, D. 1997. *Asset Liability Management.* IBA Bulletin, February. 1997. pp. 14-17.
3. Sabnani, P. 2002. *Risk Management by Banks in India.* IBA Bulletin (July) pp. 8-9.
4. Eddie, Cade. Managing Banking Risks, Glenlake Publishing Company Ltd. Chicago. pp. 1, 2.
5. David, S. 1992. *Asset Liability Management.* In Diana Mcnaushton (ed.). Banking Institutions in Developing Markets; Building Strong Management and Responding to Change. Washington D. C. The World Bank. I : 138-142.
6. Salin, I. 1999. *Risk Management of Financial Sector.* Banking Finance. (August) pp. 13, 14.
7. Sehgal, M. 1999. *Asset Liability Management in Indian Banks.* Banking Finance (November). pp. 12-13.
8. Sharma, H. S. 2003. *Risk Management in Banks – Emerging Issues.* Banking Finance. (May). pp. 5-6.
9. Rajwade, A.V. 2002. *Issues in Asset Liability Management–1.* Economic and Political Weekly. (February, 2). XXXVII(5); 378-379.
10. Chris, M. 2002. Fundamentals of Risk Management. *op.cit.*
11. Srinivasulu, L.S. 1996. Practical Introduction to Asset Liability Management. London. Euro money Publications.
12. Trivedi, A.K. 1999. *Asset Liability Management.* Banking Finance (August). pp. 25, 26.

13. Das, A., 1996. *Structural Changes and Asset Liability Mismatch of Scheduled Commercial Banks in India.* RBI Occasional Paper (December). 17 (4) : 312-313.

14. Tarapore, S. S. 1996. *Conduct of Monetary Policy : The Indian Experience.* RBI Newsletter (February, 15). 22 (3).

9

Customer Services of Public Sector Banks: An Empirical Investigation

Introduction

The wind of rapid change is blowing in the banking arena over the last few years. Indian Banking scenario, therefore, in the changing environment is set for a spectacular transformation. There has been a radical shift in the market power from banks to their customers. Effectiveness and efficiency became the buzzword of the success of banking operation particularly in respect of providing services to the customers. Service is an invisible thing that is indispensable from the person who extends it. An efficient or effective service is one which is extended appropriately by identifying and understanding the needs of the individual customer from time to time (Reddy, et. al., 2000)[1]. Customer service is a dynamic interactive process, which needs continuous improvement. With the advancement of information technology and communication system, the whole world has been reduced to global village. The customers at the present juncture are well exposed to Internet and satellite, TV and so on. He is aware of the fact of service level available around the world and thus expects the best from his bank (Rao, S. 2002)[2].

Customer service is not only a critical function but also becoming key posture for the business. It is the next most business strategy. The improved customer service will definitely increase the profitability. A bank can be said as customer oriented if its various organisational activities like organisational restructuring, staffing, and coordination are geared up to fulfill customers needs (Ambashta, 2000)[3].

Various earlier studies Gronroos (1982)[4] lewis and Booms (1983)[5] suggested that service quality should stem from the point of sellers' actual service performance to meeting customers' expectations. A broad-based study conducted by Parasuraman et.al. (1985)[6] reinforced the idea of service quality is a function of customers' expectations and performance gap. Several authors have also articulated different attributes that the customers use as criteria in evaluating quality of services. Lehtinen (1982)[7]. They include three kinds of quality: *physical quality*, i.e., physical aspects associated with the service such as equipment and building; *corporate quality*, i.e., firm's image or reputation in rendering services; and *interactive quality*, which indicates interaction between service personnel and customers. Berry et.al. (1997)[8] suggested four essential approaches of quality of services. It includes:

- Transaction surveys.
- Customers' complain, comments and inquiry.
- Total market survey.
- Employee survey.

Global competition continues to heat up in markets around the world and emerging technologies continue to empower customer with more market knowledge and wider choices. As such, quality of service will increasingly become the pivotal determinants on a sustained basis. Moreover, conventional marketing will increasingly appear as a ticket to enter the competitive arena. In this context Parasuraman (2000)[9] opined that superior customer service and marketing excellence are the two sides of the same coin.

In the era of globalisation and liberalisation, economic reform has become an imperative to remain in the mainstream of global economy. The banking sector being the backbone of the economy cannot maintain the *status quo*. It is legitimately feared that the privileged status, which PSBs enjoyed for more than last three decades, has already been changed with the entry of new players in the form of private and foreign banks. Under these circumstances, the banks will have to face two pronged challenges like,

- to retain the existing customers and,
- to create new customers.

However, success rate hinges on the innovative strategies adopted by the banks include better customer services and adequate fulfillment of customers' expectations. (Joshi, Awasthi and Jinnah, 2000)[10].

Competition for customers' services is reflected in increase use of computer and telecommunication technology by PSBs to provide improved and faster banking services with greater emphasis on value added services. The improved technology has led to the low cost, instantaneous communications and electronic fund transfers (Zenoff, 1989)[11]. This has led to the integration of domestic financial market with inter-national financial markets. Moreover, due to increase in awareness and literacy ratio the customer of today has become more aware of inherent risks, costs, and returns, associated with various financial services. As consequences, banks one of the pioneer and premier financial institutions have had to face the brunt of intense competition both from their counterparts and several other privately owned financial institutions. To combat with the volatility and risks associated with these financial markets; a specialized marketing function has to be developed in the banking sector (Watkins et.al. 1989)[12]. Today, the concept of banking is not merely the function of accepting deposits, lending and money transmissions. They have now diversified into insurance, brooking, advisory services, merchant banking, factoring and almost other legitimate financial activity. In order to survive present day world of competition, the banks will have to formulate marketing strategies in a way to woo the customers towards them. Level of customer satisfaction is becoming one of the major targets in the hands of banks to increase their market share (Aurora. et. al, 1997)[13].

Realising the role played by public sector bank in regard to the service quality, Saraiya Committee (1972)[14] suggested seventy seven recommendations for improvement of customer services. Talwar Committee (1975)[15] viewed that customer service is a dynamic concept and recommended that the bank should assess and reassess the customers' perceptions about bank services. Goiporia Committee (1991)[16] emphasised, in this respect, on amicable banker customer relationship. Many of the recommendations of this committee were implemented which include introduction of attractive term deposit schemes, fixation of customer services indices and so on.

Besides, the credit cards schemes, mutual funds, merchant banking, lease financing etc were included in the banking area of operation to attract more customers. They also did a lot of marketing of their services to persuade the customers (Mohamed, 1995)[17]. The Narasimham Committee (1991)[18], in this respect, stressed on continuous evaluation and improvement of the level of customer satisfaction. Further, it suggested as a part of the banking reform that an independent outside agency may be involved to assess customers' satisfaction level, preferably, from March 1994 with signing the memorandum of understanding (MOU) by individual banks with Reserve Bank of India. The Ministry of Finance proposed in December 1993 that banks should draw up a comprehensive code of banking practices, outlining standards for disclosure of information about the bank's services and rights and obligations for its customers. The banking Ombudsman scheme* was initiated in 1995 for expeditious and inexpensive resolutions of deficiencies in banking services.

With this backdrop an analysis has been made to examine whether the banks have acquired efficiency over the period of time from the competitive environment. An empirical study has, therefore, been undertaken to assess the nature of services rendered by the banks in the area under study.

Objective

The objectives of the present chapter are: -

1. To analyse the factors affecting the level of customers' satisfaction.
2. To compare satisfaction level regarding banking services between rural and urban customers.
3. To evolve strategies for increasing the level of customer satisfaction from the banking services as well as market share.
4. To ascertain whether profession-wise groups of customers differ in their level of satisfaction from the banking services.

Sample design

A sample of 100 customers who are directly associated with the banks, i.e., at least having accounts with the banks and operating the same on a regular basis, were selected for the purpose of the study. An equal, 50

---

* The banking ombudsman was established to create a forum for the speedy redressal of customers' complaints and also to receive unresolved complaints about the provision of banking services, and to facilitate the settlement or withdrawal of such complaints.

each, number of respondents, i.e., persons who are directly associated with banks both from rural and urban areas were considered. The information has been collected through structured questionnaire. Since the banks refused to provide the list of customer, we have collected information based on questionnaire from the customer personally visiting to the bank premises. In this respect, we have visited the bank during the month of March-April 2000. We have contacted very 10 customers who come out of the banks on the very day. The purposes of the study were explained and then the customer was requested to provide his/ her responses with regard to the items of the questionnaire. The following tables demonstrate details of sample selected for this purpose.

SAMPLE DISTRIBUTION

Fig. – I

Name of the banks	*Rural respondents*	*Urban respondents*	*Total*
State Bank of India	6	6	12
United Bank of India	6	6	12
Punjab National Bank	5	5	10
Punjab & Sind Bank	5	5	10
United Commercial Bank	5	5	10
Union Bank of India	5	5	10
Central Bank of India	5	5	10
Allahabad Bank	5	5	10
Bank of Baroda	4	4	8
Canara Bank	4	4	8
Total	**50**	**50**	**100**

Note : Figures against each bank indicate number of the bank customer.

DISTRICTWISE SAMPLE DISTRIBUTION

Fig. – II

District	*Branches covered*	*No of respondents*						
		Rural Urban-wise			*Profession-wise*			
		Rural	*Urban*	*Total*	*Service-men*	*Business-men*	*General customer*	*Total*
Cachar	8	20	20	40	14	13	13	40
Karimganj	6	18	18	36	12	12	12	36
Hailakandi	6	12	12	24	8	8	8	24
Total	**20**	**50**	**50**	**100**	**34**	**33**	**33**	**100**

Source: Our Sample

40 bank customers from 8 branches in Cachar district, 36 in Karimganj district and 24 from Hailakandi district are finally taken into consideration for the study. The opinion of respondents on 25 variables indicating satisfaction/dissatisfaction level were measured on a five point sale (Likert scale) ranging from 5 to 1 depending on the importance (fig. – III). For example, 'Highly satisfied' was ranked 5 followed by 'satisfied' with 4, 'Neither satisfied non dissatisfied' with 3, 'Dissatisfied' with 2 and 'Highly dissatisfied' with 1.

Fig. – III

Code	Variables
C1.	Service charges.
C2.	Time taken for opening an account.
C3.	Speed of withdrawal.
C4.	Speed of depositing money.
C5.	Décor of bank.
C6.	Interest on savings/loans.
C7.	Computerisation of bank.
C8.	Bank's innovativeness in introducing new services.
C9.	Bank's parking place.
C10.	Atmosphere in the bank.
C11.	Bank's publication regarding services and performance.
C12.	Banker – customer meet.
C13.	Attitude of staffs towards customers.
C14.	Location of the bank.
C15.	Knowledge of bank employees regarding bank services.
C16.	Efficiency of the staffs.
C17.	Availability of staffs in the respective counter.
C18.	Layout of the bank.
C19.	Sitting facility.
C20.	Bank's advertising regarding services.
C21.	Cash credit facility.
C22.	Management of banks.
C23.	Genuineness of overdraft facility.
C24.	Reputation of banks.
C25.	Quality and quantity of services.

These variables have been selected on the basis of studies conducted, by Rao (1987)[19], Kaptan and Sagane (1995)[20], Gavini and Athma (1997)[21], David and Bro (1989)[22], Aurora and Malhotra (1997)[23], Terninko (1997)[24], Reddy, et. al. (2000)[25], Bhattacharyy et.al. (2002)[26], Reinartz. et al. (2002)[27].

Methodology

Factor Analysis technique has been employed to determine factors representing satisfaction/dissatisfactions level customers. It identifies common dimensions of factors from observed variables that link together the unrelated data and provides insight into the underlying structure of the data (Dillion and Goldstein, 1984).

The first step involves calculation of correlation matrix which shows the interrelationship among the observed variables. The next step in factor analysis is the choice of factor model depending upon the objective of the analysis. Since the objective in this study is to summarize most of the original information (variance) in a minimum number of factors, Principal component analysis (PCA) with *varimax rotation* has been used. A *Principal component analysis* is a factor model in which the factors are based upon the total variance. In addition to selecting the factor model, we have specified how the factors are to be extracted. In the present study we have used orthogonal factors. Here the factors are extracted in such a way that each factor is independent of all other factors. Therefore, the correlation between the factors is arbitrarily determined to be zero.

An important concept in factor analysis is the rotation of factors. Since the *unrotated factor* solution may or may not provide a meaningful patterning of variables, the factors have to be rotated using unorthogonal or an oblique method. *Varimax rotation* is one of the most popular algorithms for orthogonal rotation. In this study, we have used *varimax rotation* to simplify the factor structure by maximizing the variance of a column of the pattern matrix. Next step in the process is to decide the number of factors to be extracted. The most commonly used technique is referred as the latent root (*eigen values*) representing the extent of variance in data. Now we have to interpret the factors, i.e., which factor loading is worth considering, from the rotated factor matrix? We select those factor loading which were greater than 0.45 (ignoring the signs) and loaded them on the extracted factors. A factor loading is the correlation between is the original variables and the factors squared factor loadings indicate what percentage of the variance in an original variable is explained by a factor.

The final step in factor analysis is naming the factors based on appropriateness for representing the underlying dimensions of a particular factor. Variables with higher loadings are considered more important in this type of factor interpretation. They strongly influence the name or level selected to represent a factor.

To find out how the customers ranked the various factors in terms of satisfaction, we have used *factor-wise average scores* with a view to interpret the results. These average scores have been used to find out the level of satisfaction/dissatisfaction of the customers in relations to each variable.

The Analysis

The 25 variables used for the factor analysis were coded using a five point scale stated earlier. The results of factor analysis of public sector banks customers are shown as under. Initially the inter correlation among the variables were calculated and presented in the Table-1.

Principal Factors

The inter correlation analysis suggests that out of 25 variables 7 are closely related as the values of correlation co-efficient are relatively high in their case. This indicates that all these variables can be reduced to 7 factors. These variables, stated below, showed higher correlation coefficients, which are statistically significant at 5 per cent level of significance.

(1) Décor of banks with sitting facility (C_5 vs C_{19}).

(2) Service charges with atmosphere in the banks (C_1 vs C_{10})

(3) Bank's innovativeness in introducing new services with the efficiency of staff (C_8 vs C_{16}).

(4) Bank's Parking place with atmosphere in banks (C_9 vs C_{10}).

(5) Bank's publication regarding services with reputation of banks (C_{11} vs C_{24}).

(6) Knowledge of bank employees regarding bank services with sitting facilities (C_{15} vs C_{19}).

(7) Location of the banks with availability of staff in the respective counter (C_{14} vs C_{17}).

However, correlation coefficient of variables viz., interest on savings/ loans (C_6) and Bank's parking place (C_9) also availability of staff in the

TABLE - 1

INTERCORRELATION OF VARIABLES

Marked Correlations are Significant at P< 0.05000 N = 100 (casewise deletion of missing data)

Variables	*C1*	*C2*	*C3*	*C4*	*C5*	*C6*	*C7*	*C8*	*C9*	*C10*	*C11*	*C12*
C1	1.00											
C2	–.07	1.00										
C3	.06	–.04	1.00									
C4	–.05	–.04	.11	1.00								
C5	–.02	–.01	–.13	.03	1.00							
C6	–.01	.04	.03	–.07	.08	1.00						
C7	.11	–.16	–.05	–.11	–.06	–.09	1.00					
C8	–.02	–.19	–.09	–.02	–.12	–.05	.10	1.00				
C9	.01	.07	.03	.04	–.09	**–.23***	–.06	–.08	1.00			
C10	**.23***	–.10	.03	.03	.09	.04	–.05	–.11	**.21***	1.00		
C11	–.03	–.02	–.11	–.06	.03	.09	.12	.11	.04	–.06	1.00	
C12	–.08	.04	.04	–.15	–.11	.08	.11	–.07	–.03	–.15	**.20***	1.00
C13	–.02	.18	–.19	.06	.13	.06	.08	–.03	–.08	.02	–.01	.15
C14	–.16	.02	.17	.08	–.16	–.05	.02	–.09	–.03	–.01	–.11	–.03
C15	–.17	–.07	.01	–.01	.00	.11	–.12	–.03	–.08	–.07	–.10	–.03
C16	–.03	–.05	–.04	–.09	.02	–.15	.06	**.23***	–.06	.03	–.06	.03
C17	.06	–.01	–.15	.04	.10	.13	–.07	–.11	.04	–.09	–.16	–.16
C18	–.23*	–.04	.05	.14	.05	.18	–.19	.10	–.07	–.10	.03	–.01
C19	–.12	–.10	–.02	.01	**.25***	.07	.05	–.03	–.15	.09	–.06	.05
C20	–.01	.03	–.12	.02	–.03	–.09	–.10	.09	.04	.14	–.15	–.12
C21	–.15	.01	–.13	.04	–.15	–.04	.03	.09	–.08	–.02	.13	.09
C22	–.12	.14	–.11	–.02	.08	.03	–.07	.04	–.05	.15	.04	.16
C23	–.04	.03	–.04	.05	.11	.08	.01	.04	–.02	.03	.09	–.07
C24	.03	–.01	.02	.01	–.13	–.11	.07	.03	.09	.14	**.21***	.03
C25	–.18	.03	–.10	–.15	.08	–.05	.04	–.16	.06	.05	.10	.09

(Contd.)

(Contd. Table-1)

Variables	*C13*	*C14*	*C15*	*C16*	*C17*	*C18*	*C19*	*C20*	*C21*	*C22*	*C23*	*C24*	*C25*
C1													
C2													
C3													
C4													
C5													
C6													
C7													
C8													
C9													
C10													
C11													
C12													
C13	1.00												
C14	–.08	1.00											
C15	–.02	–.01	1.00										
C16	.02	.15	–.15	1.00									
C17	.03	**.20***	.02	–.16	1.00								
C18	–.08	–.07	.01	.04	–.01	1.00							
C19	–.01	–.08	**.21***	.10	–.03	–.05	1.00						
C20	.07	.04	–.02	–.19	–.03	–.01	–.19	1.00					
C21	–.05	–.07	.15	.14	.08	.03	–.05	–.08	1.00				
C22	–.08	–.06	–.02	–.08	**–.23***	–.01	.05	.03	–.05	1.00			
C23	–.08	.05	–.10	.12	–.01	.17	–.08	–.03	–.00	.03	1.00		
C24	.04	.05	.11	.09	.03	–.08	–.06	.06	–.07	–.00	–.19	1.00	
C25	.10	–.20*	–.06	–.10	**–.20***	.16	–.02	.01	.07	–.04	–.05	.00	1.00

C6 vs C9 = '–' ve
C17 vs C22 = '–' ve

TABLE – 2

FACTOR LOADINGS (VARIMAX RAW) ALONGWITH EIGEN VALUE (Extraction : Principal Components)

Variables	*Factor 1*	*Factor 2*	*Factor 3*	*Factor 4*	*Factor 5*	*Factor 6*	*Factor 7*
C1	0.272512	**–0.490827**	–0.125312	–0.333123	0.86096	0.257036	–0.084771
C2	**0.523481**	0.133640	–0.224282	0.357712	0.313991	–0.059517	–0.140297
C3	**–0.500754**	0.038019	–0.098998	–0.318511	0.305629	0.057250	0.159382
C4	**–0.549598**	0.307669	0.066742	–0.203560	0.089354	0.307774	0.114642
C5	0.276659	0.068012	**0.513262**	0.215479	0.056898	0.265807	–0.274695
C6	0.185215	**0.640544**	0.359162	–0.071872	0.241106	–0.260461	–0.226651
C7	–0.030896	–0.181397	0.169221	0.009648	**0.550941**	–0.206462	0.176696
C8	0.120841	0.03905	0.032179	–0.195415	**–0.700973***	–0.081388	0.196534
C9	0.062834	–0.072831	**–0.542829**	0.099162	0.208690	0.299421	0.095262
C10	0.170235	–0.068555	–0.065890	0.069854	0.075735	**0.622958**	0.119952
C11	0.293443	–0.099788	0.059008	0.215125	–0.047912	**–0.538110**	0.360449
C12	0.128368	–0.000846	–0.209014	0.087395	0.191229	**–0.656170**	0.090125
C13	0.146613	–0.038843	0.304534	0.253055	0.025911	**0.568896**	–0.014386
C14	–0.177327	–0.000189	–0.004386	**0.693257**	–0.080383	0.002997	–0.098162
C15	–0.153533	0.158905	0.031723	**–0.484244**	–0.075253	–0.203230	–0.220084
C16	–0.195244	0.009943	–0.148054	0.213524	**–0.675498**	0.163425	–0.189024
C17	0.202691	–0.006339	–0.083163	–0.004819	0.103577	0.003816	**–0.630423**
C18	0.074491	**0.667399**	0.083841	0.026795	–0.099115	–0.040228	**0.728120***
C19	–0.037645	0.000020	**0.669732**	–0.085291	0.119521	0.171269	0.106119
C20	0.292748	0.271876	–0.353094	–0.231131	–0.281509	0.089594	**–0.507526**
C21	0.057172	0.087318	0.012431	0.043067	–0.115306	–0.284195	**0.483362**
C22	–0.009919	0.240551	–0.034583	**0.582951**	–0.162508	0.209017	0.030913
C23	0.027298	–0.016988	0.044245	0.017558	–0.182146	–0.110671	**–0.472334**
C24	0.308877	0.079055	–0.135016	–0.018528	0.087204	0.076968	**0.637386**
C25	–0.039439	–0.089227	–0.012772	**0.724570***	0.091541	–0.110487	0.016740
Eigen value	1.890183	1.784558	1.688277	1.568620	1.526090	1.499830	1.401386
Total Variance (%)	7.560751	7.138234	6.753108	6.274481	6.104360	5.999321	5.605543
Cumulative Eigen value	1.89019	3.67475	5.36302	6.93164	8.45773	9.95756	11.35895
Cumulative (%)	7.56075	14.69898	21.45209	27.72657	33.83093	39.83026	45.43580

respective counter (C_{17}) and management of banks (C_{22}) are found to be negatively significant, hence excluded as the major factor influencing the level of satisfaction.

The Results of Factor Analysis : The Table 2 represents the results of factor analysis performed to this set of data by *principal component analysis* with varimax rotation – a method which is very frequently used in factor analysis.

Determinants of Customer's Satisfaction Level and Their Ranking : The table discerns the factor loadings along with the eigen values. It shows close relationship of all variables with seven underlined factors of the analysis. These are clustered in next page 279.

It can be extracted from the above table that 25 different variables based upon their appropriateness for representing the underlying dimensions of a particular factor have been summarised into seven factors. The factors are :-

Factor 1. Routine Operation Factor

Factor 2. Price Factor

Factor 3. Environmental Factor

Factor 4. Management Factor

Factor 5. Technology Factor

Factor 6. Interactive Factor

Factor 7. Service Factor.

(It may be noted that the factor loading in some cases is negative but while interpreting the data the negative sign has been ignored.) The last row in bottom of the table shows the ***eigen value*** of the factors. Each value indicates relative importance of each factor in accounting for the particular set of variables. The cumulative total of eigen value is 11.35895. Hence, the index, i.e., 11.35895 ÷ 25 = 0.446 shows how well factors account for all variables taken together. A low value of index shows that the variables are unrelated with each other and vice-versa. Thus it indicates that factor ***routine operation*** ranked first followed by price, environmental, management, technology, and interactive and service factors respectively. It may be inferred from the analysis that the respondents are emphasising more on *routine operations* of banks operating in the area under study.

The *eigen value* of routine operation factor ranks first (eigen value = 1.890188) indicating the satisfactions level of the customers in regard

INFLUENCING FACTORS OF PUBLIC SECTOR BANK CUSTOMERS

Factor - 1	*Factor – 2*	*Factor - 3*	*Factor - 4*	*Factor - 5*	*Factor – 6*	*Factor - 7*
Routine Operation Factors	*Price Factors*	*Environmental Factors*	*Management Factors*	*Technology Factors*	*Interactive Factors*	*Service Factors*
C2. Time taken for opening an account	C1. Service charges	C5. Décor of banks	C14. Location of the bank	C8. Bank's innovativeness in introducing new services	C10. Atmosphere in the bank	C17. Availability of staff in the respective counter
C.3 Speed of withdrawal	C6. Interest on loans/ savings	C9. Bank's Parking Place	C15. Knowledge of the bank employees regarding bank services	C7. Computeriz-ation of banks	C11. Bank's publications regarding services & performance	C20. Bank's advertising regarding services
C4. Speed of depositing money	C18. Layout of the banks	C19. Sitting facility	C 22. Management of banks	C16. Efficiency of the staffs	C12. Banker customer meet	C21. Cash credit facility
			C.25. Quality & Quantity of Services		C13. Attitude of banks towards customer	C.23 Genuiness of overdraft facility
						C24. Reputation of the bank

to the procedural process relating to the time taken for opening an account, speed of withdrawing and depositing money is not appreciable. The price factor which is second on the list (eigen value = 1.784558) generates slight satisfaction because the customers feel that they are not getting enough for the price they are paying to avail bank services relating to service charges, interest on loans/savings and layout of the banks. They are quite willing to pay more only if the quality of services is enhanced. More over the PSBs in the area under study are not making an extra effort to improve the banks condition with regard to the environmental factors (eigen value = 1.688277) viz, bank's parking place, sitting facility, decor of banks which are well within the control of the banks. The other factors that yield poor satisfaction are management factor and technology factor, (eigen value = 1.568620 and 1.526090 respectively). Though much can not be done about the management factor viz. quality and quantity of services, knowledge of bank employee regarding bank services, location of banks etc., PSBs in the area under study are yet to step in technology up-gradation in the bank branches like computerisation, innovativeness of new services etc to survive in the present day world of competition. Further the banks have a lot to do in regard to the decors of banks. Innovativeness and mechanisation is the need of the hour but PSBs in the districts under study is showing a dismal service performance in this respect. Very few PSBs have fully computerised their operations and are stuck on to manual computations and calculations, which increase the work load and reduce the efficiency of the staff. As a result, *interactive factor*, i.e., communication gap between banker and customer, bank's publication regarding services, banks atmosphere etc stands sixth position on the hierarchy of satisfaction list (eigen value = 1.49830). The services factor pertaining to the availability of staff in the respective counter, banks advertisement relating to services, genuineness of overdraft facility etc indicating lowest level of satisfaction which appeared at the bottom (eigen value = 1.401386) of the satisfaction list.

The variable-wise satisfaction level : The satisfaction level of customers with regard to each variables may be measured. In this respect we have followed the following average score to measure the extent of level of satisfaction. This satisfaction level of the factors on the basis of factor-wise average scores has been categorised as under.

Average score	*Satisfaction level*
4.00 – 5.00	Highest
4.00 – 3.99	Moderate
2.00 – 2.99	Slight
1.00 – 1.99	Lowest

The satisfaction level of the respondents with regard to each variable has been calculated and presented in the following Table – 3. It is worth mentioning that, the average score has been calculated by using weighted arithmetic mean i.e.,

$$X = \Sigma f_i x_i / N$$

where, x_i = level of satisfaction measured in 5 points scale (Likert)

f_i = number of respondents in each category of satisfaction level, i.e., HS, S, N, DS, and HDS

N = total number of respondents, i.e., 100.

TABLE – 3
SATISFACTION LEVEL OF PUBLIC SECTOR BANK CUSTOMERS

	Variables	*Average score*
A.	**Moderate satisfaction level :**	
	C8. Bank's innovativeness in introducing new services	3.28
	C4. Speed of depositing money	3.20
	C7. Computerisation of banks	3.24
	C1. Service charges	3.08
	C3. Speed of withdrawal	3.04
	C5. Décor of banks	3.02
B.	**Slight satisfaction level :**	
	C2. Time taken for opening an account	2.94
	C10. Atmosphere of the banks	2.90
	C6. Interest on savings/loans	2.85
	C16. Efficiency of staffs	2.74
	C15. Knowledge of the bank employee regarding services	2.73
	C14. Location of the banks	2.66
	C13. Attitude of staff towards customers.	2.40
	C18. Layout of the banks	2.37

(Contd.)

(Contd. Table-3)

	Variables	Average score
	C17. Availability of staff at the respective counters.	2.37
	C19. Sitting facility in the bank	2.23
	C9. Bank's parking place	2.20
	C11. Banks publication regarding service	2.13
C.	**Lowest satisfaction level:**	
	C21. Cash credit facility	1.96
	C23. Genuiness of overdraft facilities	1.96
	C20. Bank's advertising regarding services	1.93
	C12. Banker customer meets	1.92
	C24. Reputation of the banks	1.82
	C22. Management of banks	1.80
	C25. Quality and quantity of services	1.70

The factors-wise average score revealed that the bank customers in the area under study appear to be dissatisfied lot. It has been observed that none of the variables found to be ranked 4.00 or above. Out of a total of 25 variables customers are moderately satisfied in only 6 variables, while, 12 variables come under slight and 7 are in the least satisfied group. This signifies that the respondents are more or less dissatisfied with the workings of their bank in respect of these factors. Many of the PSBs have old, dark worn out interiors, which makes working an unpleasant task for the staff. The customers have to wait for a long time to get their work done. The computerisation and mechanization thus, need to be emphasised on the banks operation in the districts under study. There it may be argued that, efficiency, diligence and gracefulness of the staff in carrying out the work assigned to them are the pre-requisite for rendering better customer services.

Respondents Perception : Urban vs. Rural

The foregoing discussion discerned the overall impression of the respondents about the services rendered by the banks operating in the Valley. Now, it is imperative to identify whether opinion of respondents from urban and rural areas differs each other. This will indicate the banks' attitude in serving the society as a whole. Irrespective of areas, it is expected that the banks would provide qualitative services to all segment of customers and make the people aware about the services available with

VARIABLES AMOUNTING TO DISSATISFACTION
(BASED ON NEGATIVE SKEWNESS AND HIGHER IQR)

Urban		*Rural*	
Code	*Variable*	*Code*	*Variable*
C_3	Speed of withdrawal	C_4	Speed of depositing money
C_7	Computerisation of banks	C_5	Décor of bank
C_{13}	Attitude of staff towards customers	C_6	Interest on savings/loan
C_{16}	Efficiency of the staffs	C_8	Banks innovativeness in introducing new services
C_{19}	Sitting facility	C_{11}	Banks publications regarding services
C_{20}	Bank's advertising regarding services	C_{12}	Banker customer meet
C_{21}	Cash credit facility	C_{13}	Attitude of staff towards customers
		C_{18}	Layout of the bank
		C_{19}	Sitting facility
		C_{20}	Bank advertising regarding services
		C_{22}	Management of banks
		C_{24}	Reputation of banks

them. In this respect we have calculated Inter Quartile Range (IQR), Standard Deviation and Skewness of each of 25 variables pertaining to the opinion as expressed by the respondents (50 from urban and same number from rural areas). The Table - 4 summarises the results.

The negatively skewed distribution suggests that maximum number of respondents is either dissatisfied or highly dissatisfied about particular service rendered by the bank branch. On the other hand, higher IQR indicates lack of consistency among the respondents regarding their perception of services provided by the banks. Further, lack of consistency in the opinion of respondents is revealed by higher degree of standard deviation. On the basis of these parameters, dissatisfaction level of bank customer both in the urban and rural areas is summarised in previous page.

The aforesaid table discerns that, there is some commonality in the opinion of the respondents both in rural and urban segment. In respect of variables viz., C_{13}, C_{19}, and C_{20} all respondents expressed their dissatisfaction. On the other hand, out of 25 structure variables, the respondents from the rural area expressed their dissatisfaction in as many as in 12 variables while urban customers of the sample are dissatisfied with 7 variables. This has indicated that a wide gap persists in rendering services by the banks. In other words rural areas in the districts under study are still left uncared for by the banks and rural masses are yet to enjoy modern banking facilities. Further, the banks have failed to meet the aspirations of customers irrespective of areas in the districts as a whole. Thus, in the competitive environment the PSBs should reassess their strength and weaknesses and accordingly redefine their business focus.

Overall Observations : The foregoing discussions revealed that the factors affecting the customers' satisfaction level in the districts under study are grouped in the routine operation factor, price factor, environmental factor, management factor, technological factor, interactive factor and service factor. It is observed that the PSBs are yet to make full efforts to improve the environmental factors like décor of bank, sitting facilities etc. The management and technology factor attributed comparatively lower satisfaction than routine operations as well as price factor. The technology upgradation, innovation of newer services etc is essential in the present global competition but PSBs in the districts has rarely stepped in this respect. This is due to the management factor viz, dismal service quality, inadequate knowledge of employee regarding bank services and locational inconveniences. The communication gap is one of

TABLE - 4
MEDIAN, FIRST AND THIRD QUARTILE, INTER-QUARTILE RANGE, STANDARD DEVIATION AND SKEWNESS OF BANK SERVICES – URBAN VS RURAL CUSTOMERS.

N = 100 (Urban 50 & Rural 50 respondents)

Variables	*Median*	*Lower Quartile*	*Upper Quartile*	*Quartile Range*	*Standard Deviation*	*Skewness*
Urban (N = 50)						
C1	10.00	10.00	10.00	0.00	1.41	0.00
C2	10.00	8.00	12.00	4.00	3.16	0.00
C3	10.00	8.00	14.00	6.00	4.24	-0.52
C4	8.00	6.00	14.00	8.00	4.69	0.58
C5	10.00	8.00	12.00	4.00	2.00	0.00
C6	8.00	6.00	10.00	4.00	5.83	1.81
C7	12.00	8.00	12.00	4.00	2.19	-0.60
C8	8.00	6.00	12.00	6.00	6.32	1.18
C9	10.00	6.00	14.00	8.00	5.09	0.00
C10	10.00	8.00	12.00	4.00	3.16	0.00
C11	10.00	8.00	10.00	2.00	2.45	1.36
C12	10.00	10.00	10.00	0.00	1.41	0.00
C13	10.00	10.00	12.00	2.00	3.75	- 1.15
C14	10.00	6.00	12.00	6.00	5.98	1.08
C15	10.00	8.00	10.00	2.00	4.41	1.01
C16	12.00	6.00	14.00	8.00	4.69	-0.58
C17	10.00	8.00	10.00	2.00	5.40	1.70
C18	10.00	8.00	10.00	2.00	3.74	1.14
C19	10.00	8.00	14.00	6.00	4.77	-0.21
C20	10.00	10.00	12.00	2.00	3.74	-1.15
C21	12.00	6.00	12.00	6.00	3.74	-0.38
C22	10.00	6.00	10.00	4.00	3.96	0.59
C23	10.00	10.00	10.00	0.00	2.83	0.00
C24	8.00	8.00	10.00	2.00	3.84	1.51
C25	8.00	6.00	14.00	8.00	5.83	0.60

Contd.

(Contd. Table-4)

N = 100 (Urban 50 & Rural 50 respondents)

Variables	*Median*	*Lower Quartile*	*Upper Quartile*	*Quartile Range*	*Standard Deviation*	*Skewness*
Rural (N = 50)						
C1	10.00	8.00	12.00	4.00	3.16	0.00
C2	10.00	6.00	14.00	8.00	4.00	0.00
C3	10.00	8.00	12.00	4.00	3.16	0.00
C4	12.00	6.00	14.00	8.00	4.69	-0.58
C5	10.00	10.00	12.00	2.00	2.45	-1.36
C6	14.00	8.00	14.00	6.00	4.34	-0.55
C7	10.00	8.00	12.00	4.00	3.16	0.00
C8	12.00	8.00	12.00	4.00	4.00	-0.93
C9	10.00	6.00	10.00	4.00	5.36	0.99
C10	10.00	8.00	10.00	2.00	3.28	1.73
C11	10.00	6.00	12.00	6.00	3.03	-0.32
C12	10.00	8.00	10.00	2.00	2.28	-0.40
C13	10.00	8.00	11.00	3.00	3.36	-0.15
C14	10.00	8.00	10.00	2.00	4.56	1.49
C15	12.00	8.00	14.00	6.00	5.41	0.22
C16	6.00	4.00	10.00	6.00	4.33	0.91
C17	10.00	10.00	14.00	4.00	4.00	0.93
C18	10.00	10.00	10.00	0.00	2.19	-1.29
C19	10.00	10.00	10.00	0.00	4.97	-0.59
C20	12.00	12.00	12.00	0.00	3.89	-1.94
C21	6.00	6.00	14.00	8.00	4.87	0.59
C22	10.00	8.00	10.00	2.00	2.28	-0.40
C23	10.00	10.00	12.00	2.00	1.10	0.60
C24	12.00	8.00	14.00	6.00	3.63	-0.56
C25	8.00	6.00	10.00	4.00	5.40	1.34

the root causes of all ills of the banking services. The regular and frequent meetings between the banker and customers would help the banks in receiving proper feed-back as to the requirements of the customer. It would also help the customer to be loyal and co-operative with bank. The factor-wise average score revealed that none of the variables rank 4.00 and above which indicates that the customers of PSBs are dissatisfied with the workings of the banks.

Thus, condition of PSBs in regard to the service rendered is quite dismal. Even the routine operations factors indicating daily procedural processes like depositing and withdrawing money, the banks fail to serve the customers fully. The factor wise average scores in respect of management factors, technology factor and interactive factors revealed that the customers are turned to be dissatisfied lot. The main reasons' lower level of customers' satisfaction may be attributed to low service charge demanded by the banks from their customers. As a result, they are unable to improve the quality, standards. More over, the negatively skewed opinion of the respondents of rural and urban areas suggests that maximum numbers of respondents are either dissatisfied or highly dissatisfied about a particular service rendered by the banks. A wide gap persists in rendering the services by the banks in rural and urban areas. Out of 25 variables, respondents from rural areas expressed their dissatisfaction in as many as 12 variables while urban customers are dissatisfied in 7 variables. The rural areas of the districts under study are still left un-cared for by the banks and rural masses are yet to enjoy modern banking facilities. From the above analysis it is evident that PSBs in the districts need to adopt certain specific marketing strategies in order to survive in the present globalised environment and in the world of competition.

The areas need immediate intervention : On the basis of the above analysis and observations the following suggestions are offered for further action :

1. The management must understand that with a view to satisfy the customers, they first have to educate, train, motivate and satisfy their own staff because an organisation can only meet its customers expectations and needs only if the staff are efficient.Thus, PSBs in this regard should inculcate marketing orientation in their work culture. There should be separate marketing cell which will specially deal with proper training and development of the bank staffs.

2. The banker customers' meet should be made an important practice in the banks agenda. The PSBs in the districts under study should be geared up still move to promote their activities in order to lure and attract their customers. Customer service committee may help in establishing better banker-customer relationship.
3. Continuous up-gradation of technology, innovative services, beautiful bank decors may be provided to the customers as the customers do not mind spending more for the quality services if provided.
4. Efforts should be made to avoid long queues in the banks since these convey an impression of its efficiency. This task can be accomplished by mechanising the bank services. The PSBs in the study area should work in this direction of providing properly furnished waiting lounge.
5. The well-lighted, ventilated and clear surroundings increase the overall efficiency of the staff. Efforts should be made to provide amenities like proper lighting, heaters, coolers etc. according to the seasonal need because the staff can satisfy the customer only if they fell comfort both physically and mentally.
6. The PSBs in the districts should conduct regular market surveys to monitor their performances and to understand what the customers requirements. This would require frequent organising interactive programme with the customers.
7. Another strategy of enhancing service quality is the use of personalised service. The banks in the area under study must make it sure that once a customer enters into the bank premises to open an account, he should feel that he has entered in to a strong, life long relationship with the bank.

References

1. Reddy, B.R., Reddy, S.V. and Sakunthala, B. 2000. *Customer Service In Banks*. Banking Finance. (Feb.) pp. 8, 9.
2. Sankara Rao, C. 2002. *The Dynamics of Customer Service.* IBA Bulletins. (March). p. 116.
3. Ambashta, M. K. 2000. *Customer Oriented – A Pre-Requisite for Banks Success*. The Journal of Indian Institute of Bankers.

4. Gronroos, C. 1982. *Strategic Management and Marketing in the Service Sector*, Helsinki, Finland : Swedish School of Economics and Business Administration.
5. Lewis, R. C. and Booms, B. H. 1983. *The Marketing Aspects of Service Quality.* in Berry, L. L; Shostack, G. L. and Upah, G (eds.), Emerging Perspectives in Services Marketing, Chicago : American Marketing Association, pp. 99-107.
6. Parasuraman, A; Zeithaml, V. A and Berrym L.L. 1985. *A Conceptual Model of Service Quality and its Implications for Future Research.* Journal of Marketing, Fall. 49 : 42-50.
7. Lehtinen, U. and Lehtinen, J.R. 1982. *Service Quality : A Study of Quality Dimensions.* Unpublished Research Report, Service Management Group, OY, Finland.
8. Berry, L. L. and Parasuraman, A. 1997. *Listening to the Customer : The Concept of Service Quality Information System.* Sloan Management Review, Spring. 38 : 65-67.
9. Parasuraman, A. 2000. Superior Customer Service and Marketing Excellence : Two Sides of the Same Success Coin. Vikalpa. (July-September) 25 (3) : 3-12.
10. Joshi, J. K. ; Awasthi B. D. and Jinnah-M. M. 2000. Customers Expectations and level of Satisfaction From the Banking Services : An Empirical Investigation. Report of the UGC sponsored seminar on Liberalisation and Role of Nationalised Banks, 6-7 January, 2000, Kumaun University, Nainital, U.P.
11. Zenoff, David. B. 1989. *Marketing Financial Services, Massachusetts* : Balimger Publishing Company.
12. Watkins, T. and Wright, M. 1989. *Marketing Financial Services.* Oxford : Butter Worth, Heinemann.
13. Aurora, S and Malhotra, M. 1997. *Customer Satisfaction; A Comparative Analysis of Public and Private Sector Banks.* Decision. (January – December) 24 (1.4) : 109-112.
14. *Report of the banking commission* (Chairman; R.G. Sarayia) Government of India. 1972.
15. Report of Talwar Committee. 1975.
16. Rao. N. 1987. Customer Service in Banks Must Improve. Yojana. (July) 31 (31) ; 2022.

17. Kaptan, S and Sagane, N. V. 1995. *Customer Service in Banks : Some Points to Ponders*. Business Analyst. 15 (1).
18. Gavini, A.L. and Athma P. 1997. *Customer Service in Commercial Banks – Expectations & Reality*. Indian Journal of Marketing. (May-June-July) XXVII (5,6,7).
19. Davido, W.H. and Bro, U, 1989. *Total Customer Service : The Ultimate Weapon*. New York : Harper and Row. 30.
20. Aurora, S. and Malhotra, M. 1997. Ibid.
21. Terninko, J. 1997. *Step by Step QFD, Customer Driven product Design*. Boca Raton, Florida. St. Lucie Press. P. 68-69.
22. Reddy, B.R., Reddy, S.V. and Sakunthala, B. 2000. Ibid.
23. Bhattacharyya, S.K. and Rahman, Z. 2002. *Capturing the Customer's Voice : A Case Study in Banking*. Productivity (July-September) 43 (2) : 237.
24. Reinartz, W and Kumar, V. 2002. *The Mismanagement of Customer Loyalty*. Harvard Business Review. (July) p – 86.
25. Dillion, W.R. and Golstein, M.1984. *Multivariate Analysis; Methods and Applications*. London. John Wiley and sons.

10

Epilogue

Banks play a positive role in the process of economic development of a country as repositories of the community's savings and as purveyor of credit. Indian banking has boosted the economic development during last more than 50 years in an effective way. The banking sector has shown remarkable responsiveness to the needs of planned economy. It has brought about a considerable progress in its efforts in respect of deposit mobilisation and has taken a number of measures in the recent past for accelerating the pace of growth of deposits. Under the lead banks scheme, in each district, a lead bank undertakes the responsibility of ensuring the geographical spread of bank branches all over the country. The underlying rationale was to see no part of the country remain under banked and everybody should have access to banking facilities. The commercial viability of the branch was never an issue. The commercial banks have opened a number of branches in urban, semi-urban and rural areas and introduced a number of attractive schemes and free services to the customers to attract more deposits.

The country however faced macro economic crisis in 1991. The foreign exchange reserve had plummeted to US $1.2 billion, barely sufficient to pay for two weeks of imports. The fiscal deficit of the country in 1990-91 accounted 8.5 per cent of GDP. The industrial production was falling and inflation was rising and touched all time high to an uncomfortable level of 17 per cent by mid 1991. The current account deficit also accounted 3.5 per cent of GDP in 1990-91. The country was on the verge of defaulting on its external debts.

The Government of India pursued economic reform process to overcome the macro economic imbalance. A number of reforms programmes as a part of the economic reform have been introduced in the financial sector. Despite, widening of banking activities, there was general consensus that it had not actually become sound and vibrant, as it needed to be. There was serious concern about the poor performance of PSBs most of which become unprofitable, under capitalised and burdened with unsustainable level of NPAs on their books.

In view of the above volatility, Government of India appointed committee on financial system under the chairmanship of M. Narasimham, popularly known as Narasimham Committee I & II to address the problems and suggest remedial measures. On the basis of the recommendations of the committee the reform measures were undertaken in the banking sector. Consequently the banks come under severc pressure to improve their bottom line and faced global competition through judicious blending with their efficiency and profitability consideration.

The analysis relating to the issue on various facets of reform packages on banking sector revealed that the first phase of reform packages have not made a lasting impression on the performance and soundness of banks. The government of India pumped about Rs. 25000 crores to the weak banks to repair their bottom line and to attain international standard in their activities. Moreover, there had been significant deregulation of interest rate, reduction of SLR and CRR. Besides, technological upgradation was considered as sine-qua-non for improving the quality of services. It is discerned from the fact that despite the entry of both private and foreign sector banks, oligopolistic dominance of PSBs still continued. However, the performance of PSBs, of late, was under severe criticism. The PSBs failed to attain the level of profitability and productivity at par with international standard. The NPAs continued to the drug down the bank profitability and bank's portfolio has been shifted from credit to risk-less government securities. During 1952-58, investment in Government securities to-deposits (I-D) ratio was 27.7 per cent, which peaked at 35.0 per cent during 1952-60 and ratio then declined steadily to 27.5 per cent in 1960-70 and hovered around 24.0 per cent during 1970's and 1980's and finally increased to 29.6 per cent during 1990-98.

It is in this context Narashimham committee-II recommended a package of measures in October 1998 which includes increase in minimum capital adequacy ratio, recognition of market risks, income recognition and provisioning norms, introduction of ALM system for further enhancing transparency and disclosure practices etc. However, the banking sector is yet to show remarkable progress in attaining competitiveness. The profitability and efficiency are still to be achieved at par with international standard.

The analysis of the growth of development of PSBs exhibited that the number of banks remained same after 1991 while there was a quantum jump in the number of bank branches over the years. It increased from 7015 on June 1969 to 40933 on March 1991 and further to 46318 in March 2001. The number of population per branch on the other hand was 64,000 in June 1969 that declined dramatically to 14000 in March 1991. However it has increased to 15000 populations per branch in March 1997 and thereafter it remained unmoved till 2001. The amount of deposits of PSBs rose to Rs. 210811 crores in 1991 from Rs. 40222 crores in 1969 and further increased significantly by about four times to Rs. 830314 crores in March 2001. The amount of deposit per office also increased significantly during the post reform period. It rose from Rs. 5.05 crores in 1991 to Rs. 19.83 crores in March 2001.

This has indicated the efficiency of banking sector in mobilizing deposits from the economy as a whole. As regard to the advances per office, the PSBs had failed to catch up the overall growth rate of deposits of the banking system. The C/D ratio significant indicator of banking activity indicating bank's deployments of credit in commercial sector has dwindled from 57.06 per cent on March 1991 to 51.56 per cent on March 1998, further to 45.91 per cent on March 2001. PSBs, however, have made significant achievement in respect of attaining the objective of bank nationalisation specially diversification the pattern of lending in favour priority sector, weaker sections and backward areas during post nationalisation era. Its share to priority sector lending has significantly increased from a mere 14.6 per cent in June 1969 to 32.1 per cent in March 1991 and further to 43.6 per cent on March 2001. The investment deposit ratio, one of the most important banking indicator was 29.3 per cent in 1969. It increased significantly to 37.3 per cent in 1991 and remained constant in 1997 before it decreases to 36.1 per cent in 1998.

The profitability, an essential requirement of survival and healthy operation of banks has come under severe pressure due to increased costs and consequent decrease of earnings over the years. The operating profits increased from Rs. 8887 crores in 1996-97 to Rs. 16264 crores in 1997-98 though ratio moved down marginally from 1.6 per cent in 1996-97 to 1.58 in the next year. Nationalised banks, which account 52.3 per cent of total assets of scheduled commercial banks, showed a substantial improvement in the profitability; both operating and net profit as a ratio to total asset increased to 1.33 per cent in 1997-98 (1.26 per cent in 1996-97) from 0.62 per cent in previous year (0.41 per cent in 1996-97) respectively. In a comparative term, thc PSBs are lagging behind the foreign banks in respect of profitability performance during the pre and post reform era. The average annual growth (**agr**) of profits of PSBs in the pre reform era was 33.6 per cent while private and foreign banks attained **agr** of 39.1 per cent and 52.3 per cent respectively during pre-reform years. During the post reform years, **agr** of profits of PSBs was 18.6 per cent while 33.8 per cent for private and 10.4 per cent for foreign banks. The analysis of component wise profits of PSBs compound growth rate (**cgr**) indicated that in the pre reform era **cgr** of income (27.3) was higher than the expenditure (26.2) while in the post reform period the growth of expenditure (14.6) surpassed the growth rate of income (13.7). As a result, the **cgr** of profits of PSBs during post reform period was comparatively lower (6.5) than that of pre reform era (28.8).

However, PSBs witnessed a low percentage of profits to total assets during the post reform years due to lower interest spread (interest income – interest paid), greater priority sector lending as well as lesser involvement in the private sector lending. On the other hand, the higher percentage of manpower expenses (per cent of manpower expenses to volume of business), resulted in higher burden (manpower expenses + other establishment expenses – non-interest income) ratio. As a result, PSBs experienced low profitability than private and foreign banks. It recorded a yearly profit of Rs. 0.6 per hundred-rupee volume of business while foreign banks and private banks recorded 3.1 and 1.0 per hundred-rupee volume of business during post liberalisation period. In absolute term PSBs though have earned good quantum of profit in the post reform years but the undeniable fact remains that foreign banks have still fared comparatively better in earning profitability.

The labour productivity measured in terms of per employee deposits, advances or total business is found to be lowest in the public sector banks than that of foreign and private sector banks. The deposit per office of PSBs increased from Rs. 2.2 lakhs in 1985-86 to Rs. 104.1 lakhs in 2000-01, which was lower than that of foreign and private banks. The same for foreign banks increased steadily from Rs. 32.8 lakhs in 1985-86 to Rs. 416.7 lakhs in 2000-01. The advances and the total business per employee of PSBs also accounted a lower growth. This lower level of labour productivity may be due to the national level trade union that opposes the move of modernisation, automation and computerisation etc. The average productivity of branches of PSBs on the other hand in terms of deposits, advances and total business was better than private banks but much higher than the foreign banks in the pre-reform years. But it has significantly dwindled during post reform periods. The PSBs accounted business per branch Rs. 1874.9 lakhs in 1999-2000 in the context of private banks Rs. 3905 and Rs. 53782.1 lakhs for foreign banks. The cost responsiveness of PSBs measured in terms of percentage variation in costs to percentage variation in earnings depicted that there is a clear symptom of cost effectiveness until 1998. The PSBs lost the cost effectiveness during 1998 – 2001. It has increased from 0.14 in 1995-96 to 0.71 in 1997-98 and further to 1.06 in 2000-01.

In India 70 per cent people live in rural areas, 34 per cent are still illiterate. The banking model of the country should therefore, be driven by the slogan of uplifting the economy and helping in social development along with the present day dictum of abiding by the international norms.

With a view to enhance the quality in the bank management in respect of encouraging and pursing market discipline through transparency, consistency and accountability, the corporate governance should be implemented in the banks. Banks should be given greater autonomy, authority for laying down internal guidance and procedures for transparency, disclosure and risk management. The banking industry on the other hand bring forward required cultural transformation by continuously enriching the knowledge of its staff.

Moreover, the re-engineering and restructuring process of Indian banking industry which have already been initiated should exclusively focus on; maintaining capital adequacy norms, keeping uniformity in the accounting practices with international standard, implementing prudential norms, carrying out candid auditing practices and enhancing transparency in the balance sheet/profit and loss statement.

Bibliography

Adam Smith, The Wealth of Nations.

Agarwal, R.K., 1988. *Evaluation of the Working Regional Rural Banks*, Mittal Publications, New Delhi.

Ahluwalia, M. S. 1999. *India's Economic Reforms; An Appraisal*. India in the era of Economic Reform, Oxford University Press.

Ansari, S.A. 1998. *Financial Intermediaries and Industrial Development*, APH Publishing Corporation, New Delhi.

Banerjee, A and Singh, S. K. 2001. *Banking and Financial Reform in India*. Deep & Deep Publications Pvt. Ltd., New Delhi.

Batra, G. S. and Dangwal, R. C. 2000. *Banking and Development Finance: New Vistas*. Deep and Deep Publication Pvt. Ltd., New Delhi.

Beck, U. 1992. *Risk Society, Towards a New Modernity*, Sage, London.

Bernanke, B. and Gertler, M. and Gilchrist, S. 1999. *The Financial Accelerator in a Quantitative Business Cycle Framework*. In J B Taylor and M Woodford, North Holland Publishing Company, Amsterdam.

Bhat, N. S. 1988. *Aspects of Rural Banking*, Common Wealth Publishers, New Delhi.

Bhole, L.M. 1999. *Financial Institutions and Markets; Structure, Growth and Innovations*, Tata Mc Graw Hill Publishing Company Ltd., New Delhi.

Bilgrani, S. A. R., 1982. *Growth of Public Sector Bank*, Deep and Deep Publication, New Delhi.

Chippa, M. L. 1992. *Monetary and Banking Development in India*, Vol. I, Printwell, Jaipur.

Chris, M. 2002. *Fundamental of Risk Management.*

Culp, C. and Merton, M. 1999. *Corporate Hedging in Theory and Practice.*

Desai, V. 1997. *Indian Banking : Nature and Problems*, Himalaya Publishing House, Bombay.

Dewartipoint, M. and Tirole, J. 1994. *The Prudential Regulation of Banks*, MIT Press, Cambridge.

Dillion, W.R. and Golstein, M. 1984. *Multivariate Analysis; Methods, and Applications*. London. John Wiley and Sons.

Drucker, P.F. 1980. *Managing in Turbulent Times*, New York, Harper-Row.

Eddie Cade, *Managing Banking Risks*, Glenlake Publishing Company Ltd., Chicago.

Freixas, X. and Rochet, J. C. 1997. *Micro Economics of Banking*. MIT Press, Cambridge, M. A.

Garp, S. C. 1989. *Indian Banking; Cost and Profitability*. Anmol Publications, New Delhi.

Ghonasgi, B. D. 1991. *Financial System of India*, Vol. I and II, Himalaya Publishing House, New Delhi.

Ghosh, U. N. *Practical Banking*. Industry Publishers Limited, Calcutta.

Gill, A. 2000. *Rural Credit Markets : Financial Sector Reforms and the Informal Lenders*. Deep and Deep Publication Pvt. Ltd., New Delhi.

Gopalan, M. S. 2000. *Indian Money Market : Structure, Operation and Developments*. Deep and Deep Publication Pvt. Ltd., New Delhi.

Gupta, L. N. 1977. *"Profitability and Public Sector"*, Oxford and IBH Publishing Company, New Delhi.

Gupta, M. C., 1989 *"Profitability Analysis; An Empirical Approach"* Pointer Publisher, Jaipur.

Gupta, S. 2001. *Research Methodology and Statistical Techniques*. Deep and Deep Publication Pvt. Ltd., New Delhi.

Hajela P.D. and Goswami, P.D. 1999. *Economic Reform and Employment.* Deep & Deep publication, New Delhi.

Hanson, J. A. and Kathuria, S. 1999. *India : A Financial Sector for the 21st Century*. Oxford University Press. The World Bank.

Hartough K. J. 1994. *Entrepreneurial Banker: The Bankers' Personal Action Plan For Building a Profitable Small Business Portfolio*. Probus Publishing, Chicago.

Hasan, Z., 1975. *Theory of Profit*, Vikash Publishing House Pvt. Ltd., New Delhi.

Hodgman, D. R. *Commercial Bank Loan and Investment Policy*, Bureau of Economic and Business Research, University of Illiniois Champaign, Illiniois.

Hogenson, P. T. *The Economics of Group Banking*, Public Affairs Press, Washington, D. C.

Jagit Singh. 1993. *Indian Banking Industry*, Deep & Deep Publications. New Delhi.

Joshi, M.S. 1965. *Financial Intermediaries in India*, Makhanlal and Sons Pvt. Ltd. Bombay.

Joshi, V. and Little M.D. 1996. *India's Economic Reforms 1991-2000*, OUP, Delhi.

Joshi, V C. and Joshi V. V. 1998. *Managing Indian Banks; The Challenges Ahead*, Response Books, New Delhi.

Kohn, M. 1996. *Financial Institution and Markets*, Tata Mc Graw Hill Publishing Company Ltd. New Delhi.

Levi, M.D. 1996. *International Finance*, Mc Graw Hill, Inc., New Delhi.

Marrison, C. 2002. *The Fundamentals of Risk Management*.

Mathur, B.L. 1995. *Emerging Perspectives of Indian Banking 2 : Credit Planning and Management in Indian Banking*, Arihant Publishing House, Jaipur.

Mckinnon, R.I. 1993, *Money and Capital in Economic Development*, (Washington D.C.; Brooking Institute).

Misra, S.K. and Puri, V.K. 1989. *Indian Industrial Economy*, Himalaya Publishing House, New Delhi.

Misra, P. N. *Development of Banks and New Entrepreneurship in India*, National Publishing House, New Delhi.

Mithani, D. M. 1991. *Money Banking, International Trade and Finance*. Himalaya Publishing House, New Delhi.

Nair, C. N. P. 1994. *Recent Trend in Banking*. Discovery Publishing House, New Delhi.

Nayyar, D. 1996. *Economic Liberalisation in India ; Analytics, Experience and Lessons*. Orient Longman.

Offe, C. 1996. *Modernity and The State, Polity*, Cambridge.

Pandey, K. L. 1968. *Development of Banking in India, Since 1947*, Calcutta Scientific Book Agency.

Rajagopalan, A.V. 1993. *Productivity in Banks : An Overview; Trends and Challenges to India Banking*, Deep and Deep Publications, New Delhi.

Ramala, K. S., and Negi, K. S. 1994. *Sickness In Small Scale Industries; Problems and Prospect, New trends in Indian Industries*, Vol. 2. Chugh Publications, Allahabad.

Rangaswamy, B. 1985. *Public Sector Banks in India*. Government of India, New Delhi.

Raul, R.K. 1997. *Industrial Finance in India*, Anmol Publications Pvt. Ltd., New Delhi.

Raut, K.C. and Das, S.K. 1996. *Commercial Banks in India; Profitability, Growth and Development*, Kanishka Publishers Distributors, New Delhi.

Rose, P. S. 2001. *Commercial Bank Management*. Website.

Rosen, G. 1962. *Some Aspects of Industrial Finance*, Asia Publishing House, Bombay.

Sachs, J. D., Varshney, A. and Bajpai, N. 1999. *India in the Era of Economic Reforms*. Oxford University Press.

Sareen, S. 2001. *Financial and Investment Management*. DVS Publishers, Guwahati.

Sayers, R. S. 1964. *Modern Banking*. Oxford University Press. Oxford.

Shaw, E. S. 1973. *Financial Deepening in Economy*, Oxford University Press, New York.

Shekar K. C. and Shekar, L. 1998. *Banking Theory and Practice*, Vikash Publishing House Pvt Ltd.

Sing, S., Bansal, M. L., Singh, T. and Kumar, R. 1984. *Statistical Method for Research Workers*, USG Publishers and Distributors. Ludhiana.

Singh, A., 1985. *Rural Development and Banking in India; Theory and Practice*, Deep & Deep Publications, New Delhi.

Singh, J. 1993. *Indian Banking Industry; Growth and Trends in Productivity*; Deep & Deep Publications, New Delhi.

Srinivasulu, L. S. 1996. *Practical Introduction to Asset Liability Management*. London. Euromoney Publications.

Uyemura, D. G. and Deventer, D. R. V. 1993. *Financial Risk Management in Banking.*

Verma Saveeta, & Verma Satish, (2002) "Determinants of Profitability of SBI groups, other Nationalised Banks and foreign banks" Banking & financial sector Reforms in India, Deep & Deep Publications, pp. 321.

Vij, Madhu. 1991, *Management of Financial Institutions in India*, Anmol Publications, New Delhi.

Vinaykam, N. 1995. *Indian Banking by .2000 A. D.*, Kanishka Publishing, Distributors, New Delhi.

Zenoff. David. B. 1989. *Marketing Financial Services*, Massachusetts, Balimger Publishing Company.

2. Articles and Research Paper

Agarwal, K.P., Puhazhendi, V. and Satyasai, K.J.S. 1997. *Gearing Rural Credit for the Twenty-First Century*. Economic and Political weekly. October, 18.

Agarwal, R., Leal, R. and Hernandez, L. 1993. *The After Market Performance of Initial Public Offering*. Financial Management, 22 (1).

Ahmed, A., Takeda, C. and Thomas, S. 1999. *Bank Loan Loss Provisions : A Reexamination of Capital Management, Earnings Management and Signaling Effects*. Journal of Accounting and Economics.

Ahmed, J. U. *Foreign Direct Investment and Indian Economy*. 29th Annual Meet of All India Association for Educational Technology; 29-31 January, 1999, (Conference volume). Guwahati.

Ahuja, K. 1996. *The Banking Sector After Reform*. Presidential Address, Seventy-ninth Conference, Indian Economics Association, Gwalior, [27-29 December].

Ajit, D. 1997. *Para Banking in India, Some Issue*. Economic and Political Weekly, XXXII. (42) [October 18].

Amershi, A. H., Rajiv D. B., Srikant M. D. 1990. *Economic Sufficiency and Statistical Sufficiency in the Aggregation of Accounting Signals*. The Accounting Review, 65(1) [January].

Angadi V.B. and Devraj, V.J. (1983). *"Productivity and profitability of banks in India"* Economic and Political Weekly, Vol. 18, No. 48.

Angadi, V. B. (1987). *"Integrated Approach to Study of Banks Profitability,"* Prajyan, No. 4, Vol. XV Oct-Dec. 1987.

Angadi, V. B. 1983. *Measurement of Efficiency in Banking Industry*. RBI Occasional Paper. 4 (1). [June].

Angadi. V. B. 1984. *Some Issues Relating to Productivity of Indian Scheduled Commercials Banks*. The Journal of the Indian Institute of Bankers, 58 (4).

Aschheim, J. 1970. *Commercial Bank Uniqueness*. Journal of Political Economy, 78 (2) [March-April].

Asil, D.K. and Enrica D. 1999. *Financial Liberalisation and Financial Fragility*. In Boris P. and Joseph E. S. (eds.) : Annual World Bank Conference on Development Economics. Washington. DC, World Bank.

Athma, P. and Srinivas P. 1997. *Productivity in Commercial Banks*. Productivity, (Oct. Nov.) 38 (3).

Aurora, S. and Malhotra, M. 1997. *Customer Satisfaction; A Comparative Analysis of Public and Private Sector Banks*. Decision. (January-December) 24 (1.4).

Baker, J. V. R. 1983. *Asset Liability Management*. Washington. American Bankers Association.

Bandi, R. P. and Jayashri, M. 1997. *Banking Group-wise Banking Data*. In Proceedings of the Bank Economists Conference.

Banmali, O. P. 2001. *Life line of Banking; New RBI formula for NPA Recovery*. IBA Bulletin (January).

Bashki, S. K. 1997. *Interest Rates Risk Identification; Measurement and Control*. The Management Accountant. [November] 32 (11).

Bedingfied, J. P., Reckers, P.M.J. and Stagliano, A.J. 1985. *Distributions of Financial Ratios in the Commercial Banking Industry*. Journal of Financial Research, 8 (Spring).

Berger A. N. and Loretta J. M. 1997. *Inside the Black Box : What Explains Differences in the Efficiencies of Financial Institutions?*, Journal of Banking and Finance, 21 (7) [July].

Berger, A. N. and Robert, D. 1997. *Problem of Loans and Cost Efficiency in Commercial Banks*. Journal of Banking and Finance, 21 (6) [June].

Berger, A. N. Herring, R. and, Szego, G. 1995. *The Role of Capital in Financial Institutions*. Journal of Banking and Finance. 19.

Bernanke, B. and Gertler, M. M. 1989. *Agency Costs, Net Worth and Economic Fluctuations*. American Economic Review, 79.

Berry, L. L and Parasuraman, A. 1997. *Listening to the Customer : The Concept of Service Quality Information System*. Sloan Management Review, Spring. 38.

Bhagawati, J. N. and Srinivasan, T. N. 1999. *Indias Economic Reforms*, New Delhi.

Bhagawati, S K. (1999) *"Credit Deposit Ratio of Commercial Banks; A Case Study of North Eastern Region"* Journal of North Eastern Council Vol. 19, No. 2 April, June.

Bhat, N. S. 1986. *The Banking System as the Financial Infrastructure of the Economy*. The Indian Economic Journal. 34 (1). [July-Sept.]

Bhatt, V. V. 1974. *A Decade of Performance of Industrial Development Bank of India*. Commerce. 151.

Bhattacharya, K.M. 2001. *Management of Non Performing Advances in Banks*. Journal of Accounting and Finance, (October 2001-March 2002).

Bhattacharya, A., Boot, W.A. and Thakur, A. V. 1998. *The Economics of Banking Regulation*. Journal of Money, Credit Societies. Vikalpa, 24 (1) [Jan-March].

Bhattacharyya, A., Lovell, CAK and Pankaj, S, 1997. *The Impact of Liberalisation on the Productive Efficiency of Indian Commercial Banks*. European Journal of Operational Research, 98.

Bhattacharyya, S.K. and Rahman, Z. 2002. *Capturing the Customer's Voice : A Case Study, in Banking*. Productivity (July-September) 43 [2].

Bhukta, A. 2002. *Banking Sector Reform in India. A study*, Yojana, (July).

Bhulla, V. K. 1997. *Restructuring the Indian Financial System*. Chartered Secretary, (November).

Boardman, A. and Launin, C. 1996. *The Long Run Financial Performance of Privatised Firms : An Empirical Investigation*. University of British, Columbia. Working Paper [October].

Cavallo, M. and Majnoni, G. 2001, *Do Banks Provisions for Bad Loans in Good Times? Empirical Evidence and Policy, Implications*. The IFCAI Journal of Applied Finance, 7.

Chandha, B. L. 1994. *Changing Phase of Indian Banking since 1969; Emergence Scenario*. Pigmy Economic Review (Nov. January).

Chandrasekhar, K. 1989. *History of Indian Banking in Subrahmanya* (ed) Trend and Progress of Banking in India.

Chopra, R.N. 1990. *RRBs have come to stay*. Kurushetra, New Delhi. [July] XXXVIII (10).

Choudhury, S. 1984. *Growth of Commercial Banking in Cachar and Its Impact of the District with Special Reference to Nationalised Banks*. Ph.D. dissertations, Guwahati University.

Cross, R., Majikes, M. and Kelleher, J. 1997. *Activity Based Costing in Commercial Lending : The Case of Signet Bank*. Commercial Lending Review. Fall.

D'Souza, E. 2000. *Predential Regulation in Indian Banking*. Economic and Political Weekly. XXXV (5). [January 29].

Das, A. 2002. *Risk & Productivity change of Public Sector Banks*, Economic & Political Weekly, (February 2).

Das, A. 1996. *Structural Changes and Asset Liability Mismatch of Scheduled Commercial Banks in India*. RBI Occasional Paper (December). 17 (4).

David, S. 1992. *Asset Liability Management*. In Diana Mcnaushton (ed.). Banking Institutions in Developing Markets; Building Strong Management and Responding to Change. Washington D. C. The World Bank

Dhanasekran, K.B. 2002. *Banking Sector Reforms In India; An Assessment*. In Banerjee A. and Singh, S.K., (ed.). Banking and Financial Sector Reform in India, Deep and Deep Publications Pvt. Ltd.

Dholakia, H.R. and Kapur, D. 2001. *Economic Reforms and Trade Performance Private Corporate Sector in India*. Economic & Political Weekly, (December 8).

Diwan, P. 1997. *Productivity and Technology Management*. A Pentagon Press Publication, Hari Nagar, New Delhi.

Easterly, W. Loayza, N. and Montiel, P. 1997. *Has Latin-America's Post Reform Growth Been Disappointing?* Journal of International Economics, 43.

Editorial. 1997. *Bank's Recovery Position Extremely Grim*. The Banker, (Oct.) 7.

Edwards, S. and Khan, M. S. 1985. *Interest Rate Determination in Developing Countries*. IMF staff papers. 32.

EPW Research Foundation-1999. *High Cost of Funds Forces Industrial Slowdown*, Economic & Political Weekly, (August 10).

Fernandez, L. S., Paues, J. M. and Saunina, J. 2002. *Credit Growth, Problem Loans and Credit Risk Provisioning in Spain*. BIS Paper No. 1, BIS : Basel.

Gadkari, 2000. *Corporate Governance; An Agenda for Public Sector Banks*. Banking Finance-(January).

Ghosh, D.N. 2000. *Weak Banks; A Strategy for Self-Renewal*. Economic & Political Weekly, XXXV (5) [January 29].

Godse, V. T. and Padwal, S.M. 1987. *Profit Planning, Budgeting and Control*. Seminar on Bank Profitability (Ed.) Kangasabathy. K. Bankers Training College. RBI, Bombay.

Goiporia, M.N. 1992. *Bank's Profitability-Some Issues*. Pigmy Economic Review. 37(9). [April].

Gokarn, S. 1997. *The East Asian Crisis of 1997 ; Some Implications for India*, India Development Report. Indira Gandhi Institute of Development Research. Oxford University Press.

Goldstein, M. 1996. *The case for an International Banking Standard*. Washington, D.C. Institute for International Economics.

Gosh, A. K., Banerjee, B. B. and Mitter, B. 1979. *Cost Accounting in Commercial Banking Industry*. The Institute of Cost and Works Accountants of India. Calcutta.

Gronroos, C. 1982. *Strategic Management and Marketing in the Service Sector*, Helsinki Finland-Swedish School of Economics and Business Administration.

Gurley, J., and Shaw, E. S. 1995. *Financial Aspects of Economic Development*. American Economic Review (Sept, 1995).

Hagemann, M. 1999. *The Structural Budget Balance-The IMF's Methodology*. IMF Working Paper No 95. International Monetary Fund, Washington. DC.

Handa, R. 1998. *Debt Vs. Equity—India Vs. Rest. Investor Guide*. The Economic Times. 4-6, 1998.

Hellmann, T. K., Murdock and Joseph E. Stiglitz. 1998. *Liberalisation, Moral Hazard in Banking and Prudential Regulation : Are Capital Requirements Enough?* Research Paper, 1466, Standford Calif : Standford University.

Hugar, R.S. 1998. *Challenges to the Banking Industry*. The Indian Institute of Bankers, [Oct-Dec].

Islam, M. and Ahmed, J. U. *Infrastructure Development in Barak valley of Assam*. Paper presented in the National Seminar (UGC sponsored) on History of Assam since 1947 organised by Lala Rural College, Hailakandi, Assam. 9-10 January, 2003.

Jagirdar, B. 1996. *Capital Adequacy; Some Issue*. Economic and Political Weekly, (March 23).

Jain, S.C. 1971. *Institutional Finance of Small Scale Industries in UP since 1956, With Particular Reference to Meerut*. Agra University, Agra.

Jaiswal, G. C. R., 1997. *Emergence of Euro-Issues as a Source of International Financial Flow*. The Management Accountant, (Nov.).

Jalan, B. 2002. *Indian Banking and Finance : Managing New Challenges*. Inaugural address at the Bank Economists Conference. [January, 14] Kolkata.

Johnson, A. S. 1997. *The Effects of Bank Debt on Optimum Capital Structure*. Financial Management. 27 (1).

Joshi, J. K., Awasthi B. D. and Jinnah, M. M. 2000. *Customers Expectations and level of Satisfaction From the Banking Services : An Empirical Investigation*. Report of the UGC sponsored seminar on Liberalisation and Role of Nationalised Banks, [6-7 January] 2000, Kumaun University, Nainital, U.P.

Joshi, N. C. 1995. *Capital Market Reforms Brook No Delay*. Journal of Indian Institute of Bankers. [April-June] 66 (2).

Joshi, P.L. and Ramani, S. 1991. *Using Discriminate Analysis to Determine a set of Financial Ratios to Control the Company Level Performance : An Empirical Study of the Paint Industry in India*, Finance India, 5 (3). [September].

Joshi, P.N. 1986. *Profitability and Profit Planning in Banks*. The Journal of Indian Institute of Bankers. 57 (2). [April-June].

Joshi, P.N. 1999. *Banking Sector Reforms; The Other Side of Coin*. Economic and Political Weekly, (April 3) XXXIV (14).

Kaladhar, K. 1997. *Micro finance in India : Design, Structure and Governance*. Economic and Political Weekly. [Oct. 18].

Kamesam, V. 2001. *Developments in the Indian banking Industry and the Emerging Challenges*. IBA Bulletin, (March).

Kanthale, A. K. 1984. *The Impact of Monetary and Credit Policies on The Working Result of Commercial Banks and Suggestions for off-setting the Effects on Their Profitability*. Paper presented at Bank Economists Meet, hosted by Indian Banks. Madras.

Kapila, R. and Kapila, U. 1997. *Banking and Financial Sector Reforms in India*. Academic Foundation, Delhi.

Kaplan, R. S. 1987. *American Bank (Case 9-187-194)*. Harvard Business School Cases.

Kaveri, V. S. 2000. *Banking in the North-East : An Overview*. Vinimaya. XX (4).

Khanna, S. 1999. *Financial Reforms and Industrial Sector in India*. Economic and Political Weekly. [November 6]

Khuntia, N. 1995. *Merchant Banking Approach to Rural Lending*. Kurukshetra, New Delhi. XLIII. (10). [July].

King, R. G. and Ross, L. 1993. *Financial and Growth : Schumpeter may be Right*. Quarterly Journal of Economics, Vol. 108.

Kohli, R. 1997. *Directed Credit and Financial Reforms*. Economic and Political Weekly. [Oct 18].

Kolari, J. M., Thomas, H. and Saniga, E. M. 1989. *A Note on the Distribution Types of Financial Ratios in the Commercial Banking Industry*. Journal of Banking and Finance, Vol. 1-3, July.

Lehtinen, U. and Lehtinen, J.R. 1982. *Service Quality : A Study of Quality Dimensions*. Unpublished Research Report, Service Management Group, OY, Finland.

Levine, R. 1997. *Financial Development and Growth : Views and Agenda*. Journal of Economic Literature, Vol. 35.

Levine, R. and Zervos, S. 1998. *Stock Markets, Banks and Economic Growth*. The American Economic Review, Vol. 88, No. 3, June.

Levis, M. 1993. *The Long-Run Performance of Initial Public Offerings : The UK Experience 1980-88*. Financial Management. 22(1).

Lewis, R. C. and Booms, B. H. 1983. *The Marketing Aspects of Service Quality*. in Berry, L. L. Shostack, G. L. and Upah, G. (eds.),

Emerging Perspectives in Services Marketing, Chicago : American Marketing Association.

Mathur, H. P. 2001. *Indian Banking; Challenges Ahead.* Yojana. [February] 45 (2).

Mathur, KBL. 2002. *Public Sector Banks in India : Should They be Privatised?* EPW, [June 8].

May, J. W. and Sweeney, R. B. *Activity-Based Costing in Banking.* A Case Study. CMA Magazine. [May].

Mohamed, M.S. 1995. *Bank Reforms : An Overview.* In Vinayakam, N. et al. Indian Banking by 2000 A.D., Kanishka Publisher's Distributors. Delhi.

Monga, R. C. 1992. *Dynamics of Productivity Management*, Productivity 33 (1).

Moorthy, V. 1998. *How Efficient are Third District Banks?* Business Review.

Mujumder, N. A. 1996. *Financial Sector Reforms; An Exercise in Introspection.* Economic and Political Weekly. XXXII (12) [March 23].

Naidu, V. N. and Nair, M.S. 2002. *Technical Efficiency of Scheduled Commercial Bank Groups.* Productivity, (July-September) 43 (2).

Pai, V. S. and Jayanna, S. 1997. *Regulating NBFIs; Limitations of the Present Status.* The Management Accountant. [November] 32 (11).

Pandey, R.K. 1997. *A study on Priority Sector Financing by Commercial Bank in India.* Ph. D. dissertation, Banaras Hindu University, Varanasi.

Parasuraman, A. 2000. *Superior Customer Service and Marketing Excellence : Two Sides of the Same Success Coin.* Vikalpa. (July September) 25 (3).

Parasuraman, A., Zeithaml, V. A and Berry, L.L. 1985. *A Conceptual Model of Service Quality and its Implications for Future Research.* Journal of Marketing, Fall. 49.

Parmar, T. 1995. *Reducing NPAs.* IBA Bulletin. [May].

Patel, U.R. 1997. *Emerging Reforms in India Banking: International Perspectives*. Economic and Political Weekly. [Oct, 18] XXXII (42).

Pati, A. P. 1999. *Non-Performing Assets — Causes, Consequences and Cures*. The Management Accountant, [November]. 34 (11).

Patibandla, M. and Prusty, R. 1998. *East Asian Crisis as a Result of Institutional Failure, Lessons for India*. Economic and Political Weekly, (February 28).

Pedgaonkar, S. L. 2002. *Competition ; The Rationale of Financial Sector Reform in Banking and Financial Sector*, Reform in India.

Rajwade, A. V. 2002. *Issues in Asset Liability Management-I*. Economic and Political Weekly. (February, 2).

Ram Mohan, T.T. 2002. *Deregulation and Performance of Public Sector Banks*. Economic and Political Weekly. XXXVII (5).

Ramaiah and Ghosh. 2002. *Understanding the Determinants of Bank Spreads in India*. An Empirical Analysis. Prajnan. (July). XXXI (1).

Ramanathan, A. and Samuel, A. 1997-98. *Financial Liberaslisation and Economic Development : The Theory, and Experience*. The Indian Economic Journal, Vol. 46, No. I (Special Number in Monetary Economics), July-September.

Rangarajan, C. 1990. *The Financial System and Economic Development : The Indian Experience*. Journal of the Indian Institute of Bankers. 61 (4). [October-December]

Rangarajan, C. 1997. *Competition in the Financial System : Issues and Implication*. [January].

Rangarajan, C. 1999. *Rationale of Reforms in the Financial Sector*. The Indian Economics Journal. [January-March] 46 (3). 1998-99.

Rao, V. L. 1993-94, *India's Financial System and Liberation and Reform*. Conference Volume, IEA.

Rao, C. S. 2001. *The Dynamic of Customer Service*. IBA Bulletins (March).

Ravi, K. 2002. *Rationalising Bank Branches; Some Issues*, IBA Bulletin, (March).

Reddy, Y.V. 1999. *Financial Sector Reform : Review and Prospects.* Reserve Bank of India Bulletin, [January].

Reddy, B.R., Reddy, S.V. and Sakunthala, B. 2000. *Customer Service in Banks*. Banking Finance. (February).

Reinartz, W. and Kumar, V. 2002. *The Mismanagement of Customer Loyalty*. Harvard Business Review. (July).

Ricketts, D. and Stover, R. 1978. *An Examination of Commercial Bank Financial Ratios*. Journal of Bank Research, Vol. 9, Summer.

Ritter, J. R. 1991. *The Long-Run Performance of Initial Public Offerings*. Journal of Finance.

Rotch, W. 1990. *Activity-Based Costing in Service Industries*. Journal of Cost Management. Summer.

Roy, D. C. 2001. *Customer Loyalty Management; Branch level Perspective*. Vinimaya, XXI. (2).

Sabnani, P. 2002. *Risk Management by Banks in India.* IBA Bulletin (July).

Salin, I. 1999. *Risk Management of Financial Sector*. Banking Finance. (August)

Sankara, Rao, C. 2002. *The Dynamics of Customer Service.* IBA Bulletins. (March).

Ambashta, M. K. 2000. *Customer Oriented-A Pre-Requisite for Banks Success*. The Journal of Indian Institute of Bankers.

Santhanaraman, V. 1999. *The Role of Cost Accountants in the Banking Services in the Changing Environment*. The Management Accountant, 18 (4) [December].

Sarkar, H. C. 1978. *Profitability of Commercial Banks*. Commerce. 137 (3507). [August 26].

Sarkar, J. and Agrawal. 1997. *Banking the Challenges of Deregulation*. In India Development Report. JGIDR, Oxford.

Sarma, R. H. 1995. *Banking Round-up*. The Journal of Indian Institute of Bankers, [April-June] 66 (2).

Sastry, J. S. R. 1996. *Recovery management.* IBA Bulletin, Special Issue, [January].

Satish, P. and Gopalakrishna, C. K. 1997. *Viability of Rural Banking.* Economic and Political Weekly. [Oct., 18].

Sehgal, M. 1999. *Asset Liability Management in Indian Banks.* Banking Finance (November).

Sengupta, A. 1995. *Financial Sector and Economic Reforms in India.* Economic and Political Weekly. [January 7].

Seshadri, J. H. (1980) *"An Economic Analysis of Profitability in Commercial Banks".* Prajnamn, July-Sept, Vol. IX.

Shah, S. G. 1979. *Bank Profitability : The Real Issues.* The Journal of the Indian Institute of Bankers. 50 (3). [July-Sept.].

Shajahan, K. M. 1998. *Non-Performing Assets of Banks; Have They Really Declined? And on Whose Account?* Economic and Political Weekly, [March 21]. XXXIII (12).

Shanbhag, N. A. 1997. *Second Banking Revolution Competing for the Future.* Pigmy Economic Review. [January].

Shanbhag, N.A. 1994. *Resource Allocation and Price Composition for Better Profitability.* Paper Presented in Bank's Economic Conference-1991 at Bangalore. [January].

Sharma, H. S. 2003. *Risk Management in Banks-Emerging Issues.* Banking Finance. [May].

Shenoy, B. S. 2001. *Indian Banking Emerging Challenges, Some Key issues.* IBA Bulletins, (March).

Shetty, N.S. 1997. *New Economic Policy, and Financial Sector Reforms.* Pigmy Economic Review. [Nov.]

Sikidar, S. 1997. *Computation of NPA, Income Recognition and Impact on Reporting of Bank Accounts.* The Management Accountant. [Nov.]

Singh, N. T. and Das, N. C. 2002. *Reforms in the Banking Sector; An overview.* Banking Finance, (July).

Singh, K. 1998. *End of the Free-Market Financial Globalisation.* Mainstream, [Nov 7], XXXVI (46).

Singh, S. 1987. *Profitability of Commercial Banks in India.* Punjab National Bank Monthly Review. 11 (II) [October].

Smith, T. R. 1998. *Banking Competition and Macro-economic Performance*. Journal of Money, Credit and Banking. Vol. 30. No. 4, November.

Srivastava, R. 2000. *Computerisation in Indian Banks*. Banking Finance. (February).

Sylla, R. 2002. *Financial Systems and Economic Modernisation*. The Journal of Economic History. 62 (2).

Talley, S. 1993. *Are Failproof Banking Systems Feasible Desirable?* Policy Research Working Paper 1095. The World Bank, Washington. DC.

Taori, K. J. 1998. *Management of NPA-Policies and Perspectives*, SBI monthly Review. [February].

Taori, K. J. 2000. *Management of NTAs in Public Sector Banks*. Banking Finance, (August).

Tarapore, S. S. 1996. *Conduct of Monetary Policy : The Indian Experience*. RBI Newsletter (February, 15).

Tarapore, S. S. 1996. *Financial Sector Reform; Retrospect and Prospect*. Chartered Secretary, [Oct].

Thingalaya, N. K. 1987. *Banking Development in India Since Independence*, Pigmy Economic Review (August).

Tobin, J. 1978. *A Proposal for International Monetary Reform*. EEJ, [July-October].

Toor, N S., 1993. *Public Sector Banks, MOU, An Agenda For Performance and Accountability*. Indian Economic Panorama. 3 (3). [October].

Trivedi, A. K. 1999. *Asset Liability Management*. Banking Finance (August).

Upadhyaya, G. 2001. *Corporate Governance in the Financial System*. Banking Finance. (December).

Varde, V.S. and Singh, S.P. 1981. *Profitability: The Inter-Banks Comparison*, Prajnan, X (2). [April-June]

Vasishth, D. 1997. *Asset Liability Management*. IBA Bulletin, February. 1997.

Venkitaramanan, S. 1998. *Non-Performing Assets-Reconstruction the Best Bet*. Business line, [February 9].

Verma, M. S. 1998. *Commercial Banking in the Next Millennium*. The Journal of the India Institute of Bankers. [October-December].

Verma, M.S. 1998. *Indian Financial Sector in the Next Millennium*. SBI Monthly Review. [July] Mumbai.

Watkins, T. and Wright, M. 1989. *Marketing Financial Services*. Oxford : Butter Worth, Heinemann.

Wheelock, D. C. and Wilson, P. W. 1999. *Technical Progress, Efficiency and Productivity Change in US Banking, 1984-93*. Journal of Money. Credit and Banking. 31 (2) [May].

3. Reports and Official Publications:

All India Rural Credit Review Committee, RBI, Bombay, 1969.

Annual Report on Trend and Progress of Banking, in India RBI. Various issues.

Annual Report, 1974, State Bank of India.

Bank for International Settlements. BIS, Basel. (1999) Basle Accord.

Basel Committee on Banking Supervision (1997); Risk Disclosure and Related matters, Bank for International Settlements. BIS, Basel.

Basel Committee on Banking Supervision (1999): Sound Policies for Loan Accounting, Credit Risk Disclosure and Related Matters, BIS : Basel.

Chore Committee Report (1979), Report of the Working Group of review the system of cash credit, RBI, Bombay.

CIER's *Industrial Data Book, 1998*. Centre for Industrial & Economic Research.

Dehejia Committee Report. (1969). *On the Extent to Which Credit needs of Industry and trade are likely to be inflated and how such trend could be eluded*, RBI Bombay.

Economic Survey 1997-1998, 1998-99, Ministry of Finance, Government of India, New Delhi.

Gedam, R. (1999) Statistical Profile of India, Deep and Deep Publications, New Delhi.

Goiporia Committee (1991). Report on Customer Service, December.

Government of India, (1972). Report of the Banking Commission, New Delhi.

Government of Assam (1997). Statistical Handbook, Assam, Directorate of Economics and Statistics, Guwahati.

Government of India (1987). Basic Statistics of North Eastern Region 1987, NEC Publications, (Ministry of Home Affairs), Shillong.

Government of India (1991a) Report of the Committee on Financial System (Narasimham Committee).

Government of India (1998), Report on Banking Sector Reforms (Narasimham Committee 11) Ministry of Finance, (April).

IBA Bulletins, *Performance Highlights of Banks*, Various Issues.

IMF, 1995. *India: Economic Reforms and Growth*. Occasional Paper. Washington. No. 134.

Marathe Committee Report (1983). Report of the Committee to review the working of credit authorisation scheme, RBI, Bombay.

RBI (2002). Report on Currency and Finance 2000-01, Reserve Bank of India, Mumbai.

RBI (2001). Expert Committee to Review the System of Administered interest Rates and other related Issues (Chairman: Dr. Y. V. Reddy). September.

RBI (2001). Standing Committee on International Financial Standards and Codes Constituted Non-official Advisory Group on Corporate Governance. March.

RBI, Banking Statistics Various Issues.

RBI (1999). Report of the Standing Committee on International Financial Standard and codes (Website-www.rbi.org.in. (December).

RBI (1999). Report on the Working Group on Restructuring of Weak Public Sector Banks. (Chairman-M.S. Verma) [Verma Committee].

Report of Committee to Review the Working of Monetary System (Chairman : Prof Sukhmay Chakrabortty) RBI, Bombay, 1985.

Report of the Committee of Productivity, Efficiency and Profitability of Banks, RBI, Bombay, 1977. (Chairman; J. C. Lathur) [PEP Committee).

Report of the Talwar Committee (1975).

Report of the Working Group to review the Functioning of DRTs (Chairman; N.B. Desh Pande). August 1998.

Report of Working Group to examine the harmonising the role and Operations of DFIs and Banks (Chairman; S.H. Khan), RBI, April 1998.

Report on Trend & Progress of Banking in India, Various Issues.

Reserve Bank of India (1985). The Committee to Review with Working of the Monetary system (Chakravorty Committee).

Reserve Bank of India (2000). Report of The Advisory Group on Transparency in Monetary and Financial Policies.

Special Credit Schemes of Banks: Guidelines, RBI, Bombay, 1972.

Tata Services Limited, Statistical Outline of India, 1996-97.

The Report of the Study Group to frame the guidelines for follow-up of Bank Credit. Tandon Committee Report (1975), RBI, Bombay.

Vaghul Committee Report (1987), Report of the Working Group on Many Market, RBI, Bombay.

World Bank (2002). 'Bank Loan Classification and Provisioning Practices in selected Developing and Emerging Countries', Finance Forum, June.

World Bank (2002) World Development Report.

—(2001): The New Basal Capital Accord: Consultative, BIS : Basel.

—(2002b) : 'Mid-Term Review of Monetary and Credit Policy for the Year 2002-2003', Reserve Bank of India Bulletin, Vol. LVI, No. 11.

—(2002b) : 'Public Sector Banks and the Governance Challenge', Reserve Bank of India Bulletin, Vol. LVI, No. 5.

Index